DATE DUE

DEC 0 1 1998			

DEMCO 38-296

Writing-Across-the-Curriculum and the Academic Library

Writing-Across-the-Curriculum and the Academic Library

A Guide for Librarians, Instructors, and Writing Program Directors

EDITED BY JEAN SHERIDAN

Foreword by Thomas G. Kirk, Jr.
Afterword by Elaine P. Maimon

GREENWOOD PRESS
WESTPORT, CONNECTICUT • LONDON

Library of Congress Cataloging-in-Publication Data

Writing-across-the-curriculum and the academic library : a guide for
   librarians, instructors, and writing program directors / edited by
   Jean Sheridan ; foreword by Thomas G. Kirk, Jr. ; afterword by
   Elaine P. Maimon.
         p.   cm.
      Includes bibliographical references (p.   ) and index.
      ISBN 0–313–29134–9
      1. Library orientation for college students—United States.
   2. Academic libraries—United States—Relations with faculty and
   curriculum.   3. Language arts (Higher)—United States.
   I.   Sheridan, Jean.
   Z675.U5W83   1995
   025.5'677'0973—dc20   95–10224

British Library Cataloguing in Publication Data is available.

Library of Congress Catalog Card Number: 95–10224
ISBN: 0–313–29134–9

First published in 1995

Greenwood Press, 88 Post Road West, Westport, CT 06881
An imprint of Greenwood Publishing Group, Inc.

Printed in the United States of America

The paper used in this book complies with the
Permanent Paper Standard issued by the National
Information Standards Organization (Z39.48–1984).

10 9 8 7 6 5 4 3 2 1

Copyright Acknowledgments

Extracts from Linda Shamoon, (1993). *URI's writing across the curriculum handbook: Writing
assignments and teaching tips from the WAC demonstration faculty*. Kingston, RI: University of
Rhode Island. Used by permission of the author.

This book is lovingly dedicated to my mother,
Eleanor Faith Caulfield Sheridan

Contents

Foreword

Thomas G. Kirk, Jr.

Jean Sheridan, the prime creator of and contributor to this volume, explains in the introduction her purposes in preparing this book. Sheridan and the contributing authors, Barbara Fister, Craig Gibson, Ross LaBaugh, and Marilyn Lutzker, experienced librarians with outstanding contributions to the bibliographic instruction (BI) literature to their credit, have realized those purposes in an admirable way. The presented ideas are important for instruction librarians and classroom faculty to consider.

I want to do more than recommend this book to you. From the vantage of thirty years as an academic librarian, there are four major points I would like to emphasize. Each is fundamental to all of the individual topics of this book. Together the four points are central to advancing the programs this book espouses. The points are drawn from Sheridan and the contributing authors' examination of writing-across-the-curriculum (WAC) activities. This examination provides useful guidance to those who are committed to the development of bibliographic instruction programs.

NETWORKING

Today networking elicits pictures of computer terminals linked by telephone wires. The connectedness of computer networks is a metaphor for another type of networking, that of personal and professional connections. We have learned that our computers, when connected to telephone lines, become more powerful tools than machines that stand alone. We also recognize an increased effectiveness on our own part if we make personal connections with other librarians and with colleagues in other professions, such as classroom teachers, computer services staff, and other college and university staff. This networking is more than just personal acknowledgment of others and a facility for carrying on personal conversation. It is the capacity to interact, to explore mutual concerns, and ultimately to make progress in achieving the respective goals of those engaged in dialogue. One party's success is not achieved at the expense of others, but by building mutual support of common educational goals.

THE CHANGING NATURE OF BIBLIOGRAPHIC INSTRUCTION

As instruction librarians reach out toward others and relate their goals to those of other educators, they must also understand their own goals and how best to achieve them. Bibliographic instruction, as a subdiscipline of librarianship, now has a well-developed history and set of traditions. However, advances on many fronts suggest that some of those traditions are obsolete while others are as vitally important now as they were ten and twenty years ago. A central theme of this book is the importance of reinterpreting bibliographic instruction. Changes in the subdiscipline's understanding of (1) the cognitive and emotive dimensions of information searching, (2) the nature of information search tools and processes, (3) learning theory, and (4) the nature of the undergraduate curriculum have forced librarians to reexamine their activities. The examination of the teaching of writing, particularly WAC programs, helps librarians understand more clearly the nature of changes in bibliographic instruction.

EDUCATIONAL CHANGE

As I read the manuscript for this book, I could not help but reflect on the fact that WAC and BI are marginal to most academic programs and are isolated from each other. The literature of librarianship often explores the reasons for the lack of development of bibliographic instruction programs. Sheridan and her colleagues have reviewed these reasons with ample reference to the extensive body of literature.

It is my contention that WAC and BI programs are marginal and isolated because the revolution in undergraduate education has not completed the process of synthesizing subject content and process content into an integrated whole. We can look upon the end of the twentieth century as a period in which educators have argued for the primacy of content or of process. However, neither viewpoint can ignore the importance of the other. We see this argument in the assertion that a specific subject content is essential to good education. This assertion is often followed by claims that process activities, such as research, critical analysis, and synthesis of information, can be done only after students reach a certain level of mastery of material. The counterargument stresses the importance of process activities as mechanisms for finding, organizing, and understanding the wealth of information. For proponents of this viewpoint, the ability to seek, analyze, and synthesize information becomes the primary goal.

For them, these process skills have a generic quality that makes them applicable to any body of knowledge.

This dichotomy is false. Subject knowledge and process skills are interrelated parts of the whole. In the best examples of WAC and BI, content and process are integrated and interrelated as one entity. The best examples of teaching the processes of research, analysis, and synthesis focus on helping students learn specific subject content. In turn, learning new information requires the processes of research, analysis, and synthesis in order to create an understanding of how the information fits together.

WAC and BI proponents should show the interrelatedness of subject and process. Therefore, the agenda of BI and WAC practitioners should not be narrowly constructed so that they focus only on mechanisms for getting into the classroom and the curriculum. Instead they should show how WAC and BI working together can improve teaching and learning. In short, practitioners should help complete the revolution that has struggled to unify the artificial separation of content and process.

LIBRARIANS AS CHANGE AGENTS

Because this revolution in higher education is not complete, librarians can play an important role beyond the development of bibliographic instruction programs. Librarians need to continue their work with colleagues, like those involved in WAC, to develop a wholistic curriculum that finds ways to use content and process in mutually supportive ways. In this volume Sheridan and her colleagues have suggested ways to accomplished these goals.

Writing-Across-the-Curriculum and the Academic Library: A Guide for Librarians, Instructors, and Writing Program Directors, is a perceptive analysis of bibliographic instruction developments of the past thirty years. This perceptive examination of past activities provides a useful guide for charting future paths.

Read this book carefully, for it has many good ideas to offer. I commend the use of the authors' ideas to create models of the integration of content and process.

Acknowledgments

A library is a wonderful place to work while researching and writing a book, and mine has been a writer's utopia, but this is the time and place to give thanks to human beings. I have always imagined having the opportunity to acknowledge the influence of Dan Bergen, a professor in the University of Rhode Island Graduate School of Library and Information Studies when I was a student there, and now that opportunity has arisen. His vision of the scholar/librarian compelled me to keep up with areas of scholarship outside librarianship. Thanks also go to David Maslyn, Chair of Public Services at the University Library, for granting me research time under trying circumstances, and to Sylvia Krausse, Head of Reference at the Library, who made possible the state-of-the-art electronic devices that have eased this effort. Thanks are also in order to Interlibrary Loan wizards Marie Rudd and Vicky Burnett, who handled dozens of requests with a smile. To my colleagues in the Reference Unit—Robin Devin, Larry Kelland, Mimi Keefe, Ken Morse, and Kathe Ellison James—for their patience and forbearance. To Judy Barnett, for her helpful advice and counsel, and her friendship. To Jan Sieburth, able in all she does, who encouraged me along the way. To Ann Crimmons Byrne and Marilyn Lutzker for setting me straight on a few things. To Michelle Bradley for her meticulous processing of the bibliographies, and Cynthia Grabke whose help with the index was invaluable. To my children, Susan Timpson, Mark Langham, Julia Langham, and Elizabeth Harrison, for their unswerving affection and support. To my mother, to whom this book is lovingly dedicated, for her affirmation and encouragement, and for keeping her promise not to brag until it was published.

Introduction

Librarians have always held a special place in the academic community—they are admired and even revered at times for their skill in managing the vast body of information housed in libraries. At other times, however, they have been berated for managing only too well and accused of creating systems too esoteric or complex for the average user. Seldom is proficiency in the use of the library deemed equal in value to other proficiencies required by the academy, and in spite of their efforts to educate, librarians have rarely been included in its deliberations, even when new educational concepts that affect their work are introduced into the curriculum.

Historically, however, this situation has not deterred librarians from informing themselves about these matters. They have made heroic efforts to read widely in all areas, to find seats on committees, and to articulate their responses to pedagogical innovations assertively and creatively. Library administrators have used their strategic positions to ensure that the library point of view is heard. Collection management officers have developed policies that support the teaching and subject area needs of the faculty. Public services librarians have taught research strategies suitable for individual disciplines and responded to the requests of instructors. Bibliographic instruction librarians have zealously imparted their wisdom to anyone willing to listen.

The literature of librarianship demonstrates that these efforts have been continuous. Librarians need not apologize for any neglect of their collegial duties. Rather they should remember the words of Miriam Dudley, who urged, "live by your faith in your profession [and] take a stand on the same ground as our fellow humanitarians" (Dudley, 1983 p. 62).

This professional reference book, written in the same spirit, seeks to educate librarians about writing-across-the-curriculum, familiarly known as WAC. It is hoped that with a full understanding of the nature and scope of writing-across-the-curriculum, as presented in this book, librarians will be better prepared to meet with their colleagues in the academic forum, their students in the classroom, and their colleagues in the profession.

WAC, a pedagogic reform that has been gathering strength since the 1970s, is an effort to shift the full burden of writing instruction away from composition classes, where it has traditionally resided, and return the charge to the disciplines or content areas.

WAC is a multifaceted pedagogy that represents a dramatic departure from certain long-held assumptions about the nature of writing. First, it is an effort, as has been said, to reverse the long-established tradition of placing responsibility for writing instruction on composition teachers. As this policy became more and more entrenched, the disciplines, relieved, eventually reserved instruction in the writing conventions of their fields for graduate students, who often had to learn in a hit-or-miss fashion. At the same time, they decried students' ignorance of these conventions and blamed composition instructors for this failure.

Second, writing-across-the-curriculum reverses the perception that student writers should be assigned to write only informative or transactional documents, those which seek to deliver information and insist on an objective relationship between writers and their material. Writing in this mode makes it difficult for students to become engaged with their writing, let alone passionately engaged with it.

To encourage closer identification between the writer and the work, a more subjective stance toward the material is recommended. Short expressive assignments are integrated into the course work, and the keeping of journals is encouraged. In these journals, students record their reactions to textbook readings, classroom lectures, laboratory experiments, writing assignments, group work, and library research—the possibilities are endless. Some professors even encourage students to keep personal journals so that they can develop the practice of being reflective about their own lives.

Process writing, an innovative way of approaching the construction of longer texts, is a third aspect central to writing-across-the-curriculum. For decades, writing has been taught as a linear process that unfolds in a clear and precise manner, in strict accordance with all grammar and editing rules. This perception is now being challenged, and writing is seen instead as a ''messy'' process that occurs in recursive stages until the finished document is produced. In writing-across-the-curriculum, these steps or stages are clearly delineated.

Along with these aspects—writing instruction in the content areas, expressive writing, the keeping of journals, and process writing—other elements have become identified with writing-across-the-curriculum. One of these is collaborative learning, an instructional classroom configuration that democratizes the relationship between instructors and students. Collaborative learning recognizes writing as a social activity and replaces individual writing experiences and papers returned with only red marks as comments with small group projects and peer review of written drafts. As we shall see in Chapter 1, it also entails implications that are clearly political and are characteristic of a new paradigm emerging throughout modern society, as well as in education. Writing-across-the-curriculum, because it has its roots in these theories and is expressed both philosophically and pedagogically, is looked upon as part of this pervasive reform. For this reason, its permanent place in education is assured.

As these new attitudes and approaches have been adopted, other long-held assumptions have been called into question, among them the value of the lecture method of instruction and of the ever-present research or term paper, which some believe to be a counterfeit form of writing. In the spirit of throwing the baby out with the bathwater, library use has also been jettisoned. Only infrequently in the literature of writing-across-the-curriculum is the library mentioned, and then usually as a disconnected afterthought with perhaps a bow to the ubiquitous library tour or "scavenger hunt." A list of library sources may be found in an appendix, but no real effort to link the library to expressive or process writing is apparent. (A countereffort to this trend is *Research Projects for College Students,* the excellent guide for instructors by librarian Marilyn Lutzker [1988].) It is the thesis of this book that the use of library resources fits quite naturally into the model of writing-across-the-curriculum and that the apparent indifference to the library, rather than an indictment, is nothing more than an omission that can easily be corrected.

The fact that library use has been largely overlooked can have serious implications for the quality of learning in higher education. Without a familiarity with scholarly materials, without an introduction to the conventions and forms of the disciplines, without the nourishment of content apart from textbook readings, students are at risk of leaving the university only partially educated, with the strengths of writing-across-the-curriculum diluted. If this situation is to be reversed and if instructors in writing-intensive courses are to be inspired to have a renewed interest in encouraging students to use the library, librarians must take the initiative, for the community will not. Thus, writing-across-the-curriculum presents librarians with both a challenge and an opportunity to reinforce the centrality of their function in the academy. To do this, however, they must take a proactive stance; the connection is a natural one, but the effort to make the connection must be extraordinary.

The purposes of this book are several. One is to inform librarians about the complexities of writing-across-the-curriculum, thus enabling them to enter more fully into dialogue with instructors in writing-intensive courses, with composition teachers, and with writing program administrators. Another is to encourage bibliographic instruction librarians to reconsider their own pedagogical methods and to incorporate some elements of writing-across-the-curriculum and collaborative learning into their classes. Third, it is to be hoped that instructors in the content areas, finding this book useful and accepting its thesis, will rediscover the usefulness of library resources.

Part I, "Writing-Across-the-Curriculum: Three Perspectives in Three Styles," describes some aspects, historical as well as pedagogical, of discourse theory and of the place of writing and writing-across-the-curriculum in it. Chapter 1 examines the movement in the context of its history and theoretical grounding, describes the model as it appears today, and considers future developments. It also places writing-across-the-curriculum in the context of the social and political revisioning of our times. In Chapter 2, Ross LaBaugh defends his belief that the link between library research and writing is implicit and that librarians need to have a grounding in the theory of rhetoric. His "irreverent history of discourse" has a refreshing style that might be one way academic writing could look in the future. (It is only to be hoped that the impetus to transform the language of academic discourse will continue to gain momentum.) Chapter 3 is written by Barbara Fister, who correlates bibliographic instruction and writing instruction and calls for a new collaborative model for both. She "reimagines" the library along the lines of WAC "as a socially constructed artifact of our culture," and calls upon librarians and composition teachers to reconsider the research process in the context of this revisioning.

Part II, "Writing-Across-the-Curriculum: Making the Library Connection," begins with a chapter by Craig Gibson, who develops the concept of "research process." He asks important questions of librarians who wish to create research skills programs to complement writing-across-the-curriculum programs. Chapter 5 provides librarians and instructors with specific recommendations for library-based assignments that harmonize with the steps in process writing. Chapter 6 describes a writing course covering the humanities, natural sciences, and social sciences. It is based on the use of primary sources and other scholarly materials and could be taught by an individual librarian or by a librarian in collaboration with an instructor.

Part III, "Writing-Across-the-Curriculum: Happy Endings," takes a look at the interdependencies and collaborations writing-across-the-curriculum makes possible. In Chapter 7, Marilyn Lutzker speaks from the perspective of the instructor who wants to develop fruitful collaborations with the library. In Chapter 8, librarians are urged to apply writing-across-the-curriculum and collaborative learning classroom practices to bibliographic instruction. Chapter 9 presents a scenario in which librarians take proactive measures to introduce writing-across-the-curriculum at their institutions or become more involved in existing programs.

Part IV, "Writing-Across-the-Curriculum: Real Life Collaborations," is a collection of case studies describing successful alliances among librarians, writing program directors, and instructors in writing-intensive/library-intensive courses. This speaks of the goodwill that exists at those institutions and certainly at others, perhaps your own. My heartfelt thanks goes to all who contributed, especially those who coordinated the gathering of material for each case study, not an easy task.

The book closes with a selected bibliography. Additional bibliographies and lists of suggested readings append each chapter. For those who wish to study writing-across-the-curriculum even further, the Anson, Schwiebert, and Williamson bibliography (1994), containing over 1,000 entries, is highly recommended, as is Russell's chapter on the history of the movement contained in *Writing in the Academic Disciplines* (1991). In Fulwiler and Young's *Programs That Work* (1990), a number of successful programs are described. In that book the case study from the University of Vermont includes a statement by librarians Nancy Crane and Maura Saule. Saule also contributed a chapter, "The New Library," to Fulwiler and Biddle's *A Community of Voices* (1992). A new program at the University of Vermont is described in Part IV.

A July 1994 exploration of the Educational Resources Information Clearinghouse (ERIC) data base for the years 1990–1994 produced the following results. A search combining the academic library and writing instruction resulted in five references, library instruction and writing instruction a slightly better fourteen. Not surprisingly, a search on writing-across-the-curriculum retrieved 410 citations, but only one when combined with academic libraries. This book will add one more; hopefully, it will inspire other librarians to contribute to this important aspect of the literature.

I am honored that Thomas G. Kirk, Jr., an outstanding leader in the library field, who speaks eloquently for our profession, and Elaine P. Maimon, one of the "guiding lights" of the writing-across-the-curriculum movement and its constant and faithful articulator, agreed to add their words. In so doing, they strengthened this effort, an effort which I hope will foster strong and fruitful collaborations, not only in this arena, but "across-the-campus" as well.

REFERENCES

Anson, C. M., Schwiebert, J. E., and Williamson, M. M. (1994). *Writing across the curriculum: An annotated bibliography.* Westport, CT: Greenwood.

Crane, N., & Saule, M. (1990). The university libraries. In T. Fulwiler & A. Young (Eds.), *Programs that work* (p. 57). Portsmouth, NH: Boynton/Cook.

Dudley, M. (1983). A philosophy of library instruction. *Research Strategies, 1*(2), pp. 58–63.

Fulwiler, T., & Biddle, A. W. (Eds.). (1992). *A community of voices: Reading and writing in the disciplines.* New York: Macmillan.

Fulwiler, T., & Young, A. (Eds.). (1990). *Programs that work.* Portsmouth, NH: Boynton/Cook.

Lutzker, M. (1988). *Research projects for college students: What to write across the curriculum.* Westport, CT: Greenwood.

Russell, D. R. (1991). *Writing in the academic disciplines, 1870–1990: A curricular history.* Carbondale: Southern Illinois University Press.

Part I

Writing-Across-the-Curriculum: Three Perspectives in Three Styles

Chapter 1

An Overview and Some Observations

Jean Sheridan

THE BEGINNINGS

In large part, the writing-across-the-curriculum movement arose in response to "the problem" Johnny (and Jane) presented to the nation in the 1970s, when it was discovered that they could neither read nor write; by inference, neither could they learn ("Why Johnny," 1975). College and university educators, along with their counterparts in the primary and secondary schools, were stunned. Studies of MIT and Harvard students corroborated that the blight had spread even to those hallowed halls (Bruffee, 1983; Russell, 1991). Today, even after heroic efforts to reverse the situation have been made, there are still negative evaluations. As recently as 1990, the National Assessment of Educational Progress (NAEP) report, studying grades 4, 8, and 12, confirmed that writing skills continue to be deficient across the board (Smit, 1991). Television is blamed, as are computers, telephones, mothers, and a variety of societal and cultural ills, but ultimately the educational system is forced to assume responsibility.

According to James Britton, a British educator who analyzed writing in British secondary schools and published the results of his study in 1975, the crisis in student writing came about because most school-sponsored writing had encouraged only information transfer, with the teacher as sole receiver and responder, the single audience. He called this type of writing transactional. In the process of focusing on transferring information, students had forgotten how to write expressively. Therefore, they remained detached from their own work and from any sense of audience other than the teacher. Furthermore, Britton observed, students, as they moved through the grades, were asked to write less and less often, but at the same time, were expected to produce longer and longer documents. Concluding that writing for the sole purpose of transferring information negated the potential of writing to encourage thinking and understanding, he condemned "the stranglehold that the expository essay has maintained over writing in American higher education" (Britton, 1984, p. vii). Others agreed that expository writing, usually scientific and informative, was the norm, and that this reliance impeded rather than encouraged skill in writing (Kinneavy, 1983).

The history of writing instruction in the United States points to the causes of these intrinsic difficulties. Since writing was firmly connected to literature, the teaching of writing came to be placed in the hands of English departments and separated from other kinds of teaching. Although no one contested that the training of new scholars was the responsibility of the disciplines, writing eventually became isolated from the curriculum, and the content-area departments deferred the training of new scholars to the graduate level.

In the 1970s, Harriet Sheridan of Carleton College made a concerted attempt to reverse that firmly entrenched practice by insisting that instructors in all departments assume responsibility for training their students to write. Her "Writing Fellows Program" became the model for a series of workshops that served to spur a national movement. Inspired by her, Elaine Maimon brought the "Carleton Plan" to Beaver College and began a program which David Russell called "the most influential of the early private, liberal arts college WAC programs" (Russell, 1991, p. 284).

In 1975, the Newsweek cover story "Why Johnny Can't Write" added impetus to an already growing momentum. In that same year, the report of the British Schools Council Project was published by James Britton and his team of researchers. They had studied the writing habits of British schoolchildren aged 11–18. Britton's conclusions soon reached Janet Emig, an eminent researcher in writing development at Rutgers. Her essay "Writing as a Mode of Learning" (1983b), delivered at a 1977 National Endowment for the Humanities summer institute, alerted the participants to Britton's study and connected his findings to the behavioral and pedagogical theories of Vygotsky, Piaget, Bruner, and Dewey, among others.

Toby Fulwiler, Art Young, and Elaine Maimon, inspired by Emig, became what Russell (1991) calls the evangelists of the movement. They based their work on the theoretical background developed by Britton and the workshop model begun at Carleton. Fulwiler and Young, then at Michigan Technological University, began a series of faculty retreats designed to educate their colleagues. It was largely through these efforts that the model for writing-across-the-curriculum evolved.

WHY WRITE?

Before we take a closer look at this model, it would be good to pause and consider the larger question of why language in its written form is valued so highly, since all use of language facilitates a process whereby thoughts can separate from immediate concerns and bring them into some order (Hays, Roth, Ramsey, & Foulke, 1983, p. xi). The act of speaking itself assists in the processing of ideas. "With the aid of language as an organizing principle," says Britton (1972, p. 31), "we construct each for himself a world representation. . . ." But writing is a higher skill; it concretizes ideas in a more systematic way and deepens their impact. During the process of writing, new knowledge emerges because new relationships are seen and new connections are made. The writer is drawn deeper into the experience because writing requires the ordering of insights, which leads to deepened understanding. Furthermore, writing is a holistic activity in which all functions are integrated and eye, hand, and both hemispheres of the brain are coordinated cyclically (Emig, 1983b).

In academic life, there is general acceptance of the belief that writing enables learning and that writers clarify their thoughts in the process of writing them down. All scholars understand that this is how competence can be judged. Students know it is an expectation in most courses and believe that it will help them get and keep a job in their chosen professions.

Fulwiler and Jones claim that writing allows thoughts to formulate by making them concrete and visible and that in the process of writing we interact with our thoughts and modify them (Fulwiler & Jones, 1982, p. 15). Because it is such a demanding process and requires the writer to stay focused, it aids students in formulating their ideas and forms a bond between the student and the material until a deeper relationship is developed (Fulwiler, 1987, p. 365). It also helps to organize and clarify the internal thought process, helps the articulation of the writer's message, and leads to "intellectual confidence" (Zinsser, 1986, p. 60).

Writing helps students decentralize. The problem of student egocentrism is pervasive in higher education, not only among traditional students but, to an even higher degree, among those who are older (Sheridan, 1989). When students arrive at college, most still view their education subjectively, but "when students write to learn," says Maimon (1991, p. 1), "they interact with subject matter in such a way that makes it their own." In other words, they become actively engaged with the material and are broadened by it. The goal is not to draw students away from familiar discourse—that of family, peer groups, and work— to the point where they are uncomfortable (Shaughnessy, 1987, p. 153), but to move them away from a self-centered stance and help them become fluent in different kinds of discourse and capable of moving among them.

WRITING AS A SOCIAL ACT

Today a new emphasis is being placed on the social and interdisciplinary nature of education, and within it, writing is newly recognized as a skill that empowers and connects the writer to larger social constructs, both local and global. Within this construct, the writer is seen as attempting to communicate with an audience and engage with a community which includes those who went before, those who will succeed, and those who are mutually and simultaneously engaged with the subject. The writer is not involved in a solitary, introverted act, but is attempting to connect with other human beings, taking part, as Kenneth Bruffee (1984) has said, in a conversation as long as the history of mankind.

This perception of writing in a social context is part of a paradigm shift in education, and indeed throughout all of Western society, which is attempting to replace old constructs and barriers with interdependent models. Some would call it a universal movement. Dewey promoted it for schoolchildren in the 1930s, Mina Shaughnessy and others for college students in the 1960s. Educational experiences with adult students (Sheridan, 1989), with women (Belenky, Clinchy, Goldberger, & Taruler, 1986), and with indigenous people (Freire, 1982, 1987, 1989) show that these issues are not exclusive to the education of children and young people.

Mina Shaughnessy, a teacher at the City University of New York in the 1960s, was influential in promoting new ways of looking at basic writing instruction and incorporated this new perspective into her writings. Because her institution had become committed to the concept of open enrollment, she found herself working with students who were limited in academic skills. Through this experience, she began to reconsider some beliefs she had previously held about the nature of education and to report on her primary research in the field (Shaughnessy, 1977, 1987, 1988). She concluded that personal, even autobiographical, writing could advance learning and the acquisition of writing skills. At the same time, Kenneth Bruffee, then at Brooklyn College, began to experiment in and write about peer tutoring in writing classes and collaborative learning in general. Both concepts—personal reflection and collaborative learning— would become incorporated into writing-across-the-curriculum.

Writing-across-the-curriculum helps to bridge the gap between understanding education as a social act and understanding it as an individual solitary experience. It invites the learner to move out of a purely subjective stance into one that provides access to the community of choice, and does this by providing the experience through an introduction to the written texts of that community. In the classroom, students are made aware that the nature of a discipline and its future development are controlled to a large extent by those who write within it. These students are invited into the community through carefully constructed learning experiences involving writing, reading, and responding (Maimon, 1986, p. 89).

Along with a perception of writing as a social act came an awareness of its potential in the political context. Among the first to demonstrate this were Mina Shaughnessy and Paulo Freire, whose work in adult literacy in Brazil (Freire, 1989) has had immense worldwide influence. These educators perceive writing as a powerful tool, not only for the intellect, but politically and spiritually as well. Their belief that as students master subject matter through writing they grow in their ability to communicate their knowledge and thoughts to others, both in the classroom and in later life, is another underlying assumption in writing-across-the-curriculum.

One who continues to articulate this belief fervently is Elaine Maimon, now at Queens College. Continuing the legacy of Shaughnessy, Maimon (most of whose students commute from and graduate into New York City neighborhoods) articulates her own philosophy of education, which is that an open classroom community will bear fruit in larger social communities. "Students who differ in gender, race, class, and ethnic background have a voice in the writing-across-the-curriculum classroom," she says (1991, p. 1), because both instructors and students are open to diverse perspectives, peer groups evaluate one another, journals promote internal and external dialogue, and an awareness of diverse audiences is pervasive. The disadvantages these students suffer in a society attempting to move away from, but still holding onto, a class structure result from their inability to transfer their experiences to new locations, a skill implanted early in the children of the privileged. This skill, which Maimon calls "intellectual mobility," results from being educated to read and listen in active, critical ways, from developing an ability to talk to strangers, and from competency in writing. She believes that these ways of knowing are learnable through such pedagogical innovations as collaborative learning and writing-across-the-curriculum, which empower students to become personally, professionally, and politically effective. (For a thorough discussion of writing as social and political power, see Cooper & Holzmann, 1989.)

THE MODEL

With these thoughts in mind, let us now look at the specific dimensions of WAC. As a pedagogy, writing-across-the-curriculum is often linked with other innovations, such as writing to learn and critical thinking (Thaiss, 1988, p. 7). heir common aim is to improve the quality of writing, while also encouraging better thinking and learning skills (Gere, 1985, p. 5). This latter approach is emphasized in the British response to the Britton study, where it is called "language for learning"—a concept which focuses as much on content as on writing skills (Herrington & Moran, 1992, p. 5).

Writing-across-the-curriculum refers to the attempt on all educational levels to encourage writing in all subject areas studied in the curriculum, not solely in composition or literature classes. It implies a concern of all faculty, not only writing instructors. In the typical classroom, students engage with the subject matter through writing; in-class discussions are preceded by short writing tasks; frequent writing is encouraged; students keep journals; long writing assignments are prepared incrementally; there is much revising and editing; and students are asked to write to different audiences. It is a student-centered pedagogy that incorporates the concept of the classroom as community, acknowledges that social reform in education is essential at this time, and recognizes approvingly the Deweyan model that focuses on students' subjective engagement with the material.

Writing-across-the-curriculum, so named by James Britton (Fulwiler & Jones,

1982, p. ix), grew and expanded through workshops that introduced faculty to its principles and practices. Incorporating concepts from the innovative work of Peter Elbow, Donald Murray, James Moffett, and others, workshop leaders encouraged participants to break open the conventional concepts of typical writing assignments—term papers, book reviews, and essay exams—and discover more innovative writing experiences, such as free writing, personal journal writing, dialogue, and letters and other correspondence where the writer is directly involved with the subject. They were asked to use prose models of student writing to stimulate the use of writing assignments and to encourage audience awareness and collaboration in the classroom. They read journals and books on composition and discussed discipline-specific writing conventions as they designed tasks specific to their fields.

Workshop facilitators also stressed what had come to be known as process writing, a recursive approach to the creation of a written document. In process writing, the emphasis is always on the process rather than the product, and multiple drafts and peer review are emphasized. With the addition of personal writing experiences, such as short expressive exercises and the keeping of journals, the writing-across-the-curriculum movement took on a shape of its own.

Process Writing

Process writing, which by the late 1970s had became a basic tenet of writing instruction, is deeply embedded in the concept of writing-across-the-curriculum. It is grounded in the theories of Jerome Bruner, whose work on the structure of the disciplines and the concept of process in learning strongly influenced James Britton while he was conducting his study of writing in British schools (Russell, 1991, p. 271). Conditioned by his reading of Bruner, Britton perceived that writing moves through various stages, becoming increasingly structured and abstract, and that this is a process that must be respected. The underlying assumption, that learning is an ongoing process during which connections are made, had also been made by George Kelly (1963). These patterns and relationships evolve cyclically, he believed, as students acquire knowledge, challenge it, and thereby discover new knowledge.

Process writing has been embraced by composition teachers at all educational levels and is part of the return to expressive/subjective forms of writing and the concept of writing in its social and community aspects. It asserts that the function of writing is procedural, that the finished product, carefully edited and conforming perfectly to the rules of grammar, does not emerge whole, but rather is developed in bits and pieces, not necessarily sequentially. At any time, any part of the process may be repeated. Composition teachers are no longer seen as stern keepers of the rules of grammar, punctuation, and spelling, but rather as collaborative guides.

During the act of composing, say Flower and Hayes (1981), writers organize by a set of thinking processes that are intertwined and can be activated and reactivated at any time during the process. Reading and writing are acknowledged as reciprocal functions that reoccur and overlap as the written document unfolds. Although writers develop and change their goals as they write, the process is goal oriented.

Mina Shaughnessy has called writing a "messy process that leads to clarity" (Maimon, 1988, p. 739). The steps within this mess, however, can now be carefully defined and include: (1) prewriting, which may include mapping, listing, outlining, journaling, information gathering, reading, reading, more reading, and being open to new directions of thought; (2) drafting, in which thoughts become sentences and paragraphs and an audience is selected; (3) sharing, when drafts are read aloud to peers and a conference with the instructor may occur; (4) revising, when the writer expands, clarifies, reads some more, and reorganizes; (5) editing, when grammar, spelling, punctuation, and other technical tasks are attended to; and (6) publishing, in such forms as newsletters, literary magazines, or e-mail documents (Maimon, 1988, p. 736). In Chapter 5, we will take a closer look at process writing and the ways in which libraries can assist both faculty who create assignments and student writers who prepare them.

Collaborative Learning

Collaborative learning, another component of the writing-across-the-curriculum model, is a pedagogy designed to close the gap between learner and teacher. The collaborative classroom is one in which the instructor stands on the same level with the student, each acknowledging a commitment to new learning through the other, student to student, instructor to student.

Collaborative learning demands that the lecture method be replaced by a configuration in which students work together in small discussion groups. Students typically work on their assignments individually and then within the group, the instructor acting as a facilitator or resource person who maintains an unobtrusive stance. They are not told what to write about, or how to write about it, by overly directive teachers or contrived textbook exercises. Writing instead for peer response, they are made to become aware of the social nature of writing and are encouraged to create community.

The primary spokesperson for collaborative learning is Kenneth Bruffee, who contends that "collaboration bridges the gap between the solitary act of writing and the conversation of which it is a part" (Bruffee, 1983, p. 23). While teaching at Brooklyn College, Bruffee began to train small groups of students to tutor each other in each phase of the writing process, working recursively through that process toward the goal of a well-crafted, finished product. Students writing for peer response, he believed, become aware of the social nature of writing and begin to create community. A further step toward that understanding is taken when students learn about the conventions of writing forms within specific disciplines. Seen from the perspective of the content courses, this becomes a further step toward inclusion in communities of discourse (p. 28).

As Shaughnessy and Bruffee saw in their classrooms, writing was increasingly seen as a social activity, and the academic or professional disciplines as communities each with its own conventions, that is, styles of diction, argument, evidence, organization, and documentation. Thus, along with collaborative learning, the concept of "communities of discourse" (Russell, 1991, p. 26) came into being and was likewise folded into the model.

Institutionalization

Since its introduction in the mid-1970s, there has been a dramatic increase in the number of institutions of higher education developing writing-across-the-curriculum programs. Each type of institution has its own unique need and application. In community colleges, for instance, there is less emphasis on learning the research forms of specific disciplines, while on the college and university level this is a high priority. Smaller four-year colleges find implementation relatively easy, while large research institutions, because of heavy administrative burdens and the resistance of research faculty who are generally more concerned with their own projects, have difficulty introducing any revolutionary new pedagogy like writing-across-the-curriculum.

Notwithstanding some resistance, however, acceptance is widespread. In a 1985 Modern Language Association (MLA) study of four-year colleges, 47 percent responded that they had instituted such programs where ten years earlier there were none (Kinneavy, 1987, p. 253). Herrington reported in 1992 that more than one-third of the institutions polled in the United States support programs named, variously, writing in the disciplines, writing-across-the-curriculum, writing in the content areas, and language for learning, and that instruction at all levels from elementary grades upward has been influenced by placing responsibility in the content-dependent courses (Herrington & Moran, 1992, p. ix).

The administration of writing-across-the-curriculum programs is usually carried out in one of two ways. In the "single-subject" approach, courses are taught by the faculty within specific departments, such as chemistry or sociology, who are encouraged to incorporate writing exercises into their course requirements under the guidance of teachers of writing. In the "centralized" approach, the writing program or English faculty teach the models of academic discourse and sometimes even develop courses in other disciplines (Braine, 1990).

THE TENSION

There was, and still is, a division between those who believe that the English departments, or the writing programs that reside within them, should be responsible for training students to write and those who believe that it is the disciplines that should be in charge. The tension that surrounds the issue is dramatically reflected in the experience of composition teachers Jeannette Harris and Christine Hult (1985). Wishing to broaden their program to include instruction in other disciplines, they polled faculty members from a diverse range of departments, asking them what types of writing assignments they preferred. They named the short research paper, the essay exam, and the theme or essay. However, in no way were these instructors willing to take responsibility for training students in these forms. They were unwilling either to instruct students in library research skills or writing skills, feeling that this was expressly the function of the English department.

Priscilla Davidson (1984), director of the composition staff at Roosevelt University, met her opposition head-on after receiving the following memo from a colleague. It said, ''I want to know why this student turned in such a lousy research paper in *my* course when he passed *your* freshman composition course last semester. Wasn't the course supposed to teach him how to write a term paper?'' (p. 241).

Davidson responded to her critic and to the entire faculty in a series of memos entitled, ''A Brief Theoretical and Practical Guide to Writing in All Disciplines at Roosevelt University.'' In the first three memos, she clarified the institution's policies regarding student writing, presented a profile of the student body, and explained the composition program. In the fourth memo, ''Assignments in Research and Research Writing,'' she suggested to faculty in the content areas a series of ten progressive writing tasks, beginning with an intensive introduction to the library and continuing, step-by-step, through the creation of a research paper (p. 251). Through these efforts, she helped to create an environment where both the writing program and the content area departments could share responsibility.

Like the young child in the Bible wanted by two mothers, the one who suffers in the tug of war is Johnny again—or is it Johnny still?—the student. The student subject of Lucille McCarthy's frequently cited article ''A Stranger in Strange Lands'' (1987) is a case in point. McCarthy tracked her subject's experience in two classes he was taking simultaneously—a freshman composition class and a biology class. It was the student's perception that the purposes of writing in each class were significantly different. In the composition class, where he was encouraged to choose his own topics and to work collaboratively with other students, he felt that he was being prepared for writing in later life. In the biology class, on the other hand, the writing assignments were designed to assist him in learning the language of the discipline, to prepare him for further academic writing, and to help him become a participant in the fieldwork of professional biologists.

His instructors, too, taught from different perspectives. His composition instructor insisted that without the development of writing skills such as coherence, presentation of clear thesis statements, development of subpoints, and unity, it was unrealistic to expect students to be able to handle content-specific writing. Moreover, she discouraged the use of critical sources held in the library. However, in his cell biology course, he was asked to use an article he found in the library as a model for a four-page review of an experiment. McCarthy concludes that writing in some way needs to be content-dependent and that composition programs should take note.

The Term Paper Debate

One of the factors in the continuing debate between the departments on the one side and the composition instructors on the other is the value of the term paper. Many instructors view this type of writing assignment as an irritating inconvenience, believing that it is an artificial and flawed simulation of "real" scholarship and that most students lack the necessary skill and sophistication to produce such a document. They believe that today's students are unable to assimilate the content of the sources they uncover after a search of the library and that there is little evidence in undergraduate papers that adequate research has been done or that students have digested the research they have undertaken. They ask if student writers should be required to do any research writing at all since what they produce is disappointing and consists of nothing more than a confusing conglomeration of opinions rather than their own original insights.

Because they have little guidance, students themselves dread the term paper assignment and quickly become confused and frustrated when they try to do research and write one. The end result is that both the students and the instructors are disappointed, the students because they are unsure of the quality of their effort and they never see their papers after handing them in, and the instructors because they despair over the poor quality of the writing and must read the papers hurriedly before posting grades.

The problem with most term paper assignments lies in the fact that term papers are researched and written in isolation from the rest of the course work. Furthermore, in those institutions where English departments still control the part of the curriculum responsible for introducing students to college-level writing, the "literary" forms of narration, description, exposition, and persuasion are still being taught, in spite of the widespread belief that the "mission" of writing instruction should be to prepare students for participation in content courses. When students are assigned research papers at a later time in other courses, they receive little or no instruction on how to design or execute them because instructors incorrectly assume that they have a mastery of the complex tasks involved. Until content-area instructors and composition instructors come to agreement about what is to be expected of student writers and, therefore, what and how they are to be taught in Comp 101 and beyond, there will be no satisfactory resolution.

Solutions

While Jane and Johnny's writing problem did not reside in the debate between content-area instructors and composition instructors—nor necessarily result from it—the ensuing dialogue has forced both camps to seek solutions. If the strength of the writing-across-the-curriculum concept is to hold, then composition teachers need to teach a variety of research processes and not only those, such as the humanities, with which they are most familiar. Conversely, content-area faculty need to understand that writing is an important learning tool.

This may, in fact, be happening. One study of composition instructors found that recently they have become more willing than they once were to instruct in library research skills, to reconfigure the argumentative paper to match more closely the needs of content-area scholars, and to redesign the teaching of research papers to conform more closely to the models students will be required to emulate in content courses (Schwegler & Shamoon, 1982, p. 822). A solution which acknowledges both points of view and also encourages collaboration is the cross-curricular writing course, or what Sills (1991) calls paired composition. In her example, College English I, a composition course, and Introduction to Sociology are taught in conjunction with one another. The content of the sociology course provides the material which the composition instructor uses as she/ he guides students through the writing process. The sociology professor does not need to know about writing instruction, nor the writing instructor about sociology. The dilemma Stanley Fish (1988) and others warn against, namely that a teacher in one discipline cannot adequately interpret the matter of another, is thus avoided.

READING AS EXPERIENCE

No discussion of writing instruction can omit reference to the content of the documents, whether they be short and expressive or long and transactional. As John Dewey said long ago, learning cannot occur in a void. It must rise out of the experience of the learner. On some level, however, experience resides not only in the personal life of the student, but in what she or he has been reading. There are few instances where someone can write intelligently without having read beforehand.

As professional writers and students read the printed word, they begin to make connections with the material and thus create an experiential association with it. They develop a feeling for proper forms, language, and nuance and create their own styles from having experienced the style of others through reading.

The relationship between reading and writing is an intimate one; one can read without having the experience of writing, but the opposite is not true. Writing of the relationship between reading and writing, Janet Emig (1983a) quoted Paulo Freire, who said that "teaching men to read and write is no longer an inconsequential matter of ba, be, bi, bo, bu, of memorizing an alienated word, but a difficult apprenticeship in naming the world" (p. 176). Both reading and writing then are opportunities to arrive at meaning, to reflect on that meaning, and to act.

Textbook Teaching

What do college students read? All too often it is lecture notes from class or pages from their textbooks. Educators often anticipate the needs of their students too well—some call this spoonfeeding—by relying on texts, on "sample" essays, on library reserve materials, and on prepared topic lists.

Reliance on textbooks has become pervasive, even in composition classes (which, ironically, present an obvious opportunity for introducing students to research skills and the reading of primary texts), and many have attempted to design a text that deals with all the conventional forms of scholarly writing. A plethora of anthologies to be used as texts for composition courses have been published, all claiming to provide the proper way to introduce and instruct in writing in the disciplines. Thaiss (1988, p. 93) calls them "static texts" containing excerpts which do nothing to promote a real understanding of discipline-specific writing. These texts are actually collections of beautifully crafted essays that may teach the student to recognize good writing, but in no way demonstrate the models they will be required to emulate when they enter their major fields of study. They are irrelevant to "real-world" writing in academic life, and they do not teach the student how to plan ahead, write outlines, observe editing rules, or engage in the recursive writing process.

If such texts do not fulfill the mission of writing-across-the-curriculum, and if, as is the growing perception of composition theorists, the role of content in writing has been neglected (Anson, 1988, p. 1), then where do the models come from, and from where is the content material derived? The obvious answer is that they come from the scholarly writings of the disciplines themselves.

Reading primary papers is a learning device, as well as a source of content material. When a student prepares an example of writing, a lab report for example, and learns by analyzing the parts marked "wrong" in red, the perception of what constitutes writing can be skewed. Teachers in the content areas would better achieve their goals by having students examine appropriate and correct models and base their writing on them. In this way, the students will discover what these conventions reveal about the field, what constitutes evidence, and how it is presented.

Texts, of course, can be all manner of things, from train schedules to job applications, but in higher education they are uniquely expressed in the writings of the discourse communities of which the disciplines are a part. These texts become the subjective experience demanded by the Deweyan model of education. Composition instructors should then instruct their students in the forms unique to the disciplines, as well as in the traditional literary forms of narration, description, exposition, and persuasion, and instructors in the content areas must learn to trust the ability of their students to read and understand the forms that define their disciplines. Stevenson (1984) was speaking of fiction when he said that "what students discovered from their reading of good writers was the delight of language freshly used—the happy phrase, the unexpected image, the balanced sentence, the care of the diction, and the true voice" (p. 62), but his words are equally well applied to academic reading, the best of which has a unique vitality. Although academic texts are difficult to read, classroom discussions of such texts and their attendant concepts, vocabulary, logic, figures of speech, and voices can demystify them and foster new competencies. Such learning can be a liberating experience for students as it encourages them to become familiar and competent in the conventions of others and thus approach the "intellectual mobility" spoken of by Elaine Maimon (1990).

THE PRESENT AND THE FUTURE

Writing-across-the-curriculum, partly because of the way it was introduced to the academic community in the workshop model, is firmly established in all types of institutions of higher education and is still considered by many to be the best response to the crisis education faced in the 1970s. At the present time, established programs are becoming institutionalized and given a place in the structure of the overall curriculum. This is an important development, as it is common for early enthusiasm to falter when the "guiding lights" move on to other institutions. In some larger institutions, teaching assistants are being trained to work with faculty who wish to integrate more writing into their courses. Team teaching is also encouraged and has proven successful. The interdisciplinary paired course (Sills, 1991) is another option, as is the course described in Chapter 6, one with special appeal to librarians.

New Criticism

Today, however, strong criticisms test the metal of WAC programs. Some come from colleagues, what Fulwiler calls the "enemies from within" (Fulwiler & Young, 1990, p. 294).

- English departments may be more committed to their "literary mission" and leave the teaching of writing to graduate students and part-time faculty.
- Academic administrative structures as they are presently defined do not easily admit programs such as writing-across-the-curriculum.
- Research efforts in many larger institutions are more highly honored than teaching excellence, which is given prominence in the movement.
- Testing and grading today are highly quantified, making it difficult to evaluate writing.
- Certain pervasive attitudes abound—a general apathy on the part of entrenched faculty, resistance from students who have been trained to learn by rote and are highly focused on grades, and the perception that writing-across-the-curriculum is a quick fix for what ails student performance.

Even writing practitioners themselves are beginning to assert that too much emphasis is being placed on the process, as opposed to the content, of the finished product and that expressive writing disregards substance (Anson, Schwiebert, & Williamson, 1994, p. xviii; Benderson, 1989, p. 19). These critics contend that students, in order to write competently and produce longer, more substantial documents, must read sufficient content material. One of them commented about a group writing project that ''[the group] writes well, but they write well about nothing'' (Odell, 1992, p. 86).

It is quite possible, then, that we will begin to see instructors returning to a reliance on content-dependent resources (books, journals, and so forth). They will be supported in this effort by the 1985 position statement of the National Council of Teachers of English, which states clearly that textbooks and other instructional materials should be of secondary importance to ''reading what others have written, speaking about one's response to their writing, and listening to the responses of others'' (Foster, 1992, p. 225).

Future Possibilities

What does the future hold? Because it is so flexible, intrinsically rational, and natural, writing-across-the-curriculum is ensured a permanent place in the academic classroom, but this will not happen without nurturance. Barr and Healy (1988) suggest that the future success of writing-across-the-curriculum requires collaboration between secondary schools and universities, an increase in faculty/ staff development, and a commitment to collaborative learning and teaching. With Kelly (1985), they agree that the key to successful writing-across-the-curriculum programs lies in the ability to garner administrative support. In-service education and program assessment should also be built into support systems, as should ongoing workshops, stipends, released time, and fully staffed writing centers. Faculty must continue to remain open to new ways of thinking about instructing and must honor the value of writing in the classroom. Graduation requirements need to include demonstration of writing competency. (For excellent overviews of the movement, past, present, and future, see Anson, Schwiebert, and Williamson, 1994; Griffin, 1985; and Russell, 1992.)

CONCLUSION

Johnny and Jane could not write because they did not know how to go about it, and because they did not have a close connection to their material. As we have seen, behavioral and cognitive theorists and educational practitioners have studied the processes through which they and all who follow them learn to write. Many of their assumptions are grounded in the work of John Dewey, who stated unequivocally that learning originates in the material students experience in subjective ways. As writing-across-the-curriculum matures, it is becoming more and more apparent to those who developed it and to those who employ it in their teaching that students need to expand their understanding of experience and to go beyond personal reflection into the realm of academic reading. They need to hear the language of the ''conversations'' of the disciplines as it is expressed in written form and thus be further initiated into its rites and rituals.

Student writers, if encouraged by their instructors to use appropriate ways (ways other than scavenger hunts), will find that the library is a ready place to provide a deepening of experience, and that librarians are willing guides. Instructors, if they are looking for new ways to incorporate content into writing assignments, will likewise find that librarians are ready allies. Libraries are as social and eclectic as the varieties of literature housed within them, process and product, interdisciplinary and diverse, and they provide the most expedient and convenient place to hear the language of the discourse communities and to find background material for original research.

Librarians, then, have a unique opportunity in writing-across-the-curriculum to make the connection between content and libraries visible and to demonstrate in a variety of ways their readiness to enter the discussion and to seek solutions. Given certain prevailing attitudes, however—about complicated library systems, and dependence on expressive writing—progress may be slow. Thus they will need to position themselves strategically, ask to be assigned to teaching teams, become the third participant in paired courses, gain administrative approval for librarian-taught writing courses, and initiate campus-wide activities intended to clarify the relationship between writing and the library. (For a fuller discussion, see Chapters 5 and 9.) Such collaborations will be fruitful for all concerned and a way to ensure that writing-across-the-curriculum remains a vital educational effort involving all segments of the academic community.

REFERENCES

Anson, C. M. (1988). Toward a multidimensional model of writing in the academic disciplines. In D. A. Jolliffe (Ed.), *Advances in writing research, Vol. 2: Writing in academic disciplines* (pp. 1–19). Norwood, NJ: Ablex.

Anson, C. M., Schwiebert, J. E., & Williamson, M. M. (1994). *Writing across the curriculum: An annotated bibliography.* Westport, CT: Greenwood Press.

Barr, M. A., & Healy, M. K. (1988). School and university articulation: Different contexts for writing across the curriculum. In S. H. McLeod (Ed.), *Strengthening programs for writing across the curriculum: New directions for teaching and learning,* pp. 43–53). San Francisco: Jossey-Bass.

Belenky, M. F., Clinchy, B. M., Goldberger, N. R., & Taruler, J. M. (1986). *Woman's ways of knowing: The development of self, voice, and mind.* New York: Basic Books.

Benderson, A. (Ed.). (1989). The student writer: An endangered species? *Focus 23.* Princeton: Educational Testing Service.

Braine, G. (1990). *Writing across the curriculum: A case study of faculty practices at a research university* (Report No. CS21-2-534). Mobile: University of Alabama, Department of English. (ERIC Document Reproduction Service No. ED 324 680)

Britton, J. N. (1972). *Language and learning.* New York: Penguin Books.

Britton, J. N. (1984). Introduction. In C. H. Klaus & N. Jones (Eds.), *Courses for change in writing* (pp. v–ix). Upper Montclair, NJ: Boynton/Cook.

Britton, J. N., Burgess, T., Martin, N., McLeod, A., & Rosen, H. (1975). *The development of writing abilities (11–18).* London: Macmillan.

Bruffee, K. A. (1983). Writing and reading as collaborative or social acts. In J. N. Hays, P. A. Roth, J. R. Ramsey, & R. D. Foulke (Eds.), *The writer's mind: Writing as a mode of thinking* (pp. 159–170). Urbana, IL: National Council of Teachers of English.

Bruffee, K. A. (1984). Collaborative learning and the "conversation of mankind." *College English, 46*(7), 635–652.

Cooper, M. M., & Holzman, M. (1989). *Writing as social action.* Portsmouth, NH: Boynton/Cook.

Davidson, P. (1984). Writing across the disciplines: A memo to colleagues. In C. H. Klaus & N. Jones (Eds.), *Courses for change in writing* (pp. 241–259). Upper Montclair, NJ: Boynton/Cook.

Emig, J. (1983a). Literature and freedom. In D. Goswami & M. Butler (Eds.), *The web of meaning* (pp. 171–178). Upper Montclair, NJ: Boynton/Cook.

Emig, J. (1983b). Writing as a mode of learning. In D. Goswami & M. Butler (Eds.), *The web of meaning* (pp. 123–131). Upper Montclair, NJ: Boynton/Cook.

Fish, S. (1988). Being interdisciplinary is so very hard to do. *Profession, 89,* 15–22.

Flower, L., & Hayes, J. R. (1981, December). A cognitive process theory of writing. *College Composition and Communication, 32,* 365–387.

Foster, D. (1992). *A primer for writing teachers: Theories, theorists, issues, problems* (2nd ed.). Portsmouth, NH: Boynton/Cook.

Freire, P. (1982). *Pedagogy of the oppressed.* New York: Continuum.

Freire, P. (1987). *Literacy: Reading the word and the world.* South Hadley, MA: Bergin and Garvey.

Freire, P. (1989). *Learning to question: A pedagogy for liberation.* New York: Continuum.

Fulwiler, T. (Ed.). (1987). *The journal book.* Portsmouth, NH: Heinemann.

Fulwiler, T., & Jones, R. (1982). Assigning and evaluating transactional writing. In T. Fulwiler & A. Young (Eds.), *Language connections: Writing and reading across the curriculum* (pp. 45–56). Urbana, IL: National Council of Teachers of English.

Fulwiler, T., & Young, A. (Eds.). (1990). *Programs that work.* Portsmouth, NH: Boynton/Cook.

Gere, A. R. (Ed.). (1985). *Roots in the sawdust: Writing to learn across the disciplines.* Urbana, IL: National Council of Teachers of English.

Griffin, C. W. (1985). Programs for writing across the curriculum: A report. *College Composition and Communication, 36*(4), 398–403.

Harris, J., & Hult, C. (1985). Using a survey of writing assignments to make informed curricular decisions. *Writing Program Administration, 8*(3), 7–14.

Hays, J. N., Roth, P. A., Ramsey, J. R., & Foulke, R. D. (Eds.). (1983). *A writer's mind: Writing as a mode of thinking.* Urbana, IL: National Council of Teachers of English.

Herrington, A., & Moran, C. (1992). Writing in the disciplines: A prospect. In A. Herrington & C. Moran (Eds.), *Writing, teaching, and learning in the disciplines* (pp. 231–244). New York: Modern Language Association.

Kelly, G. (1963). *A theory of personality: The psychology of personal constructs.* New York: W. W. Norton.

Kelly, K. A. (1985). *Writing across the curriculum: What the literature tells us* (Report No. CS21–0–045). Wellesley, MA: Babson College. (ERIC Document Reproduction Service No. ED 274 975)

Kinneavy, J. L. (1983). Writing across the curriculum. *ADE Bulletin, 76,* 14–21.

Kinneavy, J. L. (1987). Writing across the curriculum. In G. Tate (Ed.), *Teaching composition: Twelve bibliographical essays* (pp. 253–377). Fort Worth: Texas Christian University.

Maimon, E. P. (1986). Knowledge, acknowledgement, and writing across the curriculum: Toward an educated community. In D. A. McQuade (Ed.), *The territory of language: Linguistics, stylistics, and the teaching of composition* (pp. 89–102). Carbondale: Southern Illinois University Press.

Maimon, E. P. (1988). Cultivating the prose garden. *Phi Delta Kappan, 69*(10), 734–739.

Maimon, E. P. (1990, January). Remarks made at *Writing and Thinking Across the Curriculum.* Conference held at Rhode Island College, Providence, RI.

Maimon, E. P. (1991). *Errors and expectations in writing across the curriculum: Diversity, equity, and the ideology of writing across the curriculum* (Report No. CS21-2-80-9). Paper presented at the conference on College Composition and Communication (CCCC), March 21, Boston, MA. (ERIC Document Reproduction Service No. ED 331 092)

McCarthy, L. P. (1987). A stranger in strange lands: A college student writing across the curriculum. *Research in the Teaching of English, 21*(3), 233–265.

Odell, L. (1992). Context specific ways of knowing and the evaluation of writing. In A. Herrington & C. Moran (Eds.), *Writing, teaching, and learning in the disciplines* (pp. 86–100). New York: Modern Language Association.

Russell, D. R. (1991). *Writing in the academic disciplines, 1870–1990: A curricular history.* Carbondale: Southern Illinois University Press.

Russell, D. R. (1992). American origins of the writing-across-the-curriculum movement. In A. Herrington & C. Moran (Eds.), *Writing, teaching, and learning in the disciplines* (pp. 22–44). New York: Modern Language Association.

Schwegler, R. A., & Shamoon, L. K. (1982). The aims and process of the research paper. *College English, 44*(8), 817–824.

Shaughnessy, M. P. (1977). *Errors and expectations: A guide for the teacher of basic writing.* New York: Oxford University Press.

Shaughnessy, M. P. (1987). Basic writing. In G. Tate (Ed.), *Teaching composition: Twelve bibliographical essays* (pp. 177–206). Fort Worth: Texas Christian University.

Shaughnessy, M. P. (1988). Diving in: An introduction to basic writing. In G. Tate & E.P.J. Corbett (Eds.), *The writing teacher's sourcebook* (pp. 297–302). New York: Oxford University Press.

Sheridan, J. (1989). Collaborative learning: Some notes from the field. *College Teaching, 37*(2), 49–53.

Sills, C. K. (1991). Paired composition courses: Everything relates. *College Teaching, 39*(2), 61–64.

Smit, D. W. (1991, September). *Improving student writing (Idea paper no. 25).* Manhattan: Kansas State University, Center for Faculty Evaluation and Development.

Stevenson, J. W. (1984). Writing as a liberal art. *Liberal Education, 70*(1), 57–62.

Thaiss, C. (Ed.). (1983). *Writing to learn: Essays and reflections on writing across the curriculum.* Dubuque, IA: Kendall/Hunt.

Thaiss, C. (1988). The future of writing across the curriculum. In S. H. McLeod (Ed.),

Strengthening programs for writing across the curriculum (pp. 91–102). San Francisco: Jossey-Bass.

"Why Johnny Can't Write." (1975, December 8). *Newsweek,* pp. 58–62, 64.

Zinsser, W. (1986, April 13). A bolder way to teach writing. *New York Times,* pp. 58–63.

ADDITIONAL READINGS

Berlin, J. A. (1987). *Rhetoric and reality: Writing instruction in American colleges, 1900–1985.* Carbondale: Southern Illinois University Press.

Bernhardt, S. A. (1985). Writing across the curriculum at one university: A survey of faculty members and students. *ADE Bulletin, 82,* 55–59.

Blair, C. P. (1988). Opinion. Only one of the voices: Dialogic writing across the curriculum. *College English, 50*(4), 383–389.

Brodkey, L. (1987). *Academic writing as social practice.* Philadelphia: Temple University Press.

Bruner, J. S. (1960). *The process of education.* New York: Vintage Books.

D'Angelo, F. J. (1987). Aims, modes, and forms of discourse. In G. Tate (Ed.), *Teaching composition: Twelve bibliographical essays* (pp. 131–154). Fort Worth: Texas Christian University.

D'Angelo, F. J. (1988). Imitation and style. In G. Tate & E.P.J. Corbett (Eds.), *The writing teacher's sourcebook* (pp. 199–207). New York: Oxford University Press.

Davis, D. J. (1987). Eight faculty members talk about student writing. *College Teaching, 35*(1), 31–35.

Dewey, J. (1938). *Experience and education.* London: Collier Books.

Eblen, C. (1983). Writing across the curriculum: A survey of a university faculty's views and classroom practices. *Research in the Teaching of English, 17*(4), 343–348.

Elbow, P. (1988). Embracing contraries in the teaching process. In G. Tate & E.P.J. Corbett (Eds.), *The writing teacher's sourcebook* (pp. 219–231). New York: Oxford University Press.

Eschholz, P. A. (1980). The prose models approach: Using products in the process. In T. R. Donovan & B. W. McClelland (Eds.), *Eight approaches to teaching composition* (pp. 21–36). Urbana, IL: National Council of Teachers of English.

Freisinger, R. (1982). Cross-disciplinary writing programs: Beginnings. In T. Fulwiler & A. Young (Eds.), *Language connections: Writing and reading across the curriculum* (pp. 3–14). Urbana, IL: National Council of Teachers of English.

Gebhard, A. O. (1983). Teaching writing in reading and the context areas. *Journal of Reading, 27*(3), 207–211.

Griffin, C. W. (1983). Using writing to teach many disciplines. *Improving College and University Teaching, 31*(3), 121–128.

Hall, D. (1973). *Writing well.* Boston: Little, Brown.

Hoff, K. T. (1992). *WAC policies: Winning friends and influencing people* (Report No. CS21–3–303). Cincinnati, OH: Conference on College Composition and Communication. (ERIC Document Reproduction Service No. ED 344 234)

Knoblach, C. H., & Brannon, L. (1983). Writing as learning through the curriculum. *College English, 45*(5), 465–474.

Langer, J. A. (1992). Speaking of knowing: Concepts of understanding in academic disciplines. In A. Herrington & C. Moran (Eds.), *Writing, teaching, and learning in the disciplines* (pp. 69–85). New York: Modern Language Association.

Larson, R. (1982). The research paper in the writing course: A non-form of writing. *College English, 44*(8), 811–816.

Limerick, P. N. (1993, October 31). Dancing with professors: The trouble with academic prose. *The New York Times Book Review,* pp. 3, 23–24.

Magistrale, T. (1985). Writing across the curriculum: From theory to implementation. *Journal of Teaching Writing, 5*(1), 151–157.

Maimon, E. P. (1979). Talking to strangers. *College Composition and Communication, 30,* 364–369.

Maimon, E. P. (1982). Writing across the curriculum: Past, present, and future. In C. W. Griffin (Ed.), *Teaching writing in all disciplines* (pp. 67–74). San Francisco: Jossey-Bass.

Maimon, E. P., Belcher, G. L., Hearn, G. W., Nodine, B. F., & O'Connor, F. W. (1981). *Writing in the arts and sciences.* Cambridge, MA: Winthrop Publishers.

McCrimmon, J. M. (1976). Writing as a way of knowing. In R. L. Graves (Ed.), *Rhetoric and composition: A sourcebook for teachers* (pp. 3–12). Rochelle Park, NJ: Hayden Book Company.

Moffett, J. (1968). *Teaching the universe of discourse.* Boston: Houghton Mifflin.

Moore, L. E., & Peterson, L. H. (1986). Convention as connection: Linking the composition course to the English and college curriculum. *College Composition and Communication, 37*(4), 466–477.

Murray, D. M. (1980). Writing as process: How writing finds its own meaning. In T. R. Donovan & B. W. McClelland (Eds.), *Eight approaches to teaching composition* (pp. 3–20). Urbana, IL: National Council of Teachers of English.

In A. Herrington & C. Moran (Eds.), *Writing, teaching, and learning in the disciplines* (pp. 22–44). New York: Modern Language Association.

Smith, L. Z. (1988). Opinion: Why English departments should house writing across the curriculum. *College English, 50*(4), 390–395.

Stout, B. R., & Magnotto, J. (1988). Writing across the curriculum at community colleges. In S. H. McLeod (Ed.), *Strengthening programs for writing across the curriculum* (pp. 21–30). San Francisco: Jossey-Bass.

Strenski, E. (1988). Writing across the curriculum at research universities. In S. H. McLeod (Ed.), *Strengthening programs for writing across the curriculum* (pp. 31–42). San Francisco: Jossey-Bass.

Tchudi, S. N. (1986). *Teaching writing in the content areas: College level.* Washington, DC: National Education Association of the United States.

Vygotsky, L. S. (1962). *Thought and language.* Cambridge, MA: M.I.T. Press.

Walker, A. (1988). Writing across the curriculum: The second decade. *English Quarterly, 21*(2), 93–103.

Walvoord, B. E., & McCarthy, L. P. (1990). *Thinking and writing in college: A naturalistic study of students in four disciplines.* Urbana, IL: National Council of Teachers of English.

Weiss, R. H. (1980). Writing in the total curriculum: A program for cross-disciplinary cooperation. In T. R. Donovan & B. W. McClelland (Eds.), *Eight approaches to teaching composition* (pp. 133–149). Urbana, IL: National Council of Teachers of English.

Winterowd, W. R. (1986). Brain, rhetoric, and style. In D. A. McQuade (Ed.), *The territory of language: Linguistics, stylistics, and the teaching of composition* (pp. 34–64). Carbondale: Southern Illinois University Press.

Winterowd, W. R. (1987). Literacy, linguistics, and rhetoric. In G. Tate (Ed.), *Teaching composition: Twelve bibliographic essays* (pp. 265–290). Fort Worth: Texas Christian University.

Chapter 2

Talking the Discourse: Composition Theory

Ross LaBaugh

It is Thursday night at 9:30. The semester ends tomorrow. Two students wearing $30 baseball hats, backwards, come to the desk.

"Where are, like, the laws?" they ask me.

Most librarians know that when students come to the library, they are on a mission. They need to photocopy an article on reserve for a business ethics class or find a couple of books on *Henry IV* for English. Maybe they just need a place to review lecture notes or do homework. Many come to the library because an instructor has told them they have to write a paper and the library seems the most likely place to do that. After all, the library is pretty much an academic supermarket—it has wide aisles, shelves, convenient hours, and probably stuff on, "like, the laws."

Most librarians know, too, that people do not always ask for what they want. "Where are, like, the laws?" could mean anything from "Where can I find Public Law 101–345?" to "Can an independent contractor depreciate the cost of a cellular phone if she claims her automobile as her principle place of business?"

Ever-sensitive to their nonverbal cues, the timing of their query, and their wardrobe, I figured they were English 101 students with a five- to seven-page, documented, persuasive paper due in hours. This was not the time to be parental.

"What are you writing about?" I asked.

"Legalization of marijuana," they said.

"Yawn," I thought and led them over to SIRS (the CD that has full-text mediocre articles on a wide variety of topics).

"Type 'marijuana' and press return," I said. Article after article zoomed onto the screen.

"Press F7 to print. Good luck guys," I said and went home.
Was my guidance inappropriate?

In the best of times, we imagine students inspired by their professors, or themselves, using the library to learn more about quarks or Falstaff. They go from broad ideas to more specific controversies and trends. They look for the interrelationships between knowledge domains and seek out critical investigations. Their papers are well constructed, thorough, and exquisitely documented. In the worst of times, we have Beavis rushing in, the night before due date, to print out some "Ask Beth" articles from *Parade* magazine. His greatest challenges are how to turn a couple of paragraphs into 2,500 words and how to cite *High Times*. Of course, these scenarios are extreme, and neither type of student represents even a strong minority. What the students share, however, is a common mission: they have to write something.

Writing is hard work. It is hard work for the professional, for the amateur, for the basic writer, for the novice writer, for the scholar, and for the student. They may all struggle with different gorillas, but they all own one. A half dozen teachers have tried their best to teach students, during their secondary education, how to master, or at least get along with the beast, but on the whole their efforts have been ineffective.

Library research is also hard work. Beginning in elementary school, and continuing on through college, librarians and teachers have taken students on library tours and assigned trivia questions from the end of the research chapter in the English handbook as a way to teach library skills. Despite these efforts (or perhaps because of them), most students enter college without knowing how to do library research. These students have rough times ahead of them.

My belief is that writing and library research are inextricably linked. Both are about discovery, questioning, organization, and process. However, whereas writing has ancient theoretical underpinnings, bibliographic instruction's history is more a twentieth-century chronicle of methodology (Beaubien, Hogan & George, 1982, p. 66). BI's (Bibliographic Instruction) practitioners have discussed the ways and means, and theorists, such as Mellon, Beaubien, George, and Roberts, do well in laying a foundation for BI, but still there is not much there. By looking more closely at what composition theory has to offer, librarians can further their own causes and befriend a long-lost first cousin. Let me explain what I mean by giving you a brief overview of rhetorical theory, explaining why it is important for librarians to know this theory, and leaving you with some ideas to ponder.

THE THREE Rs: RHETORIC, (W)RITING, AND REFERENCE

Rhetoric is rooted in the oral tradition. That means that a couple of thousand years ago, only a couple of people could read and write, and everybody else just talked. They talked mostly about what people talk about today: news, politics, the weather, and so forth. And like people today, not everyone agreed with what everyone else was talking about. Arguments broke out, and people began suing each other. The courts listened to the arguments. Remember, there were no legal briefs, depositions, reporters, stenographers, or fax machines, so the lawyers had to say everything really well, and they only had one crack at it. Aristotle, Cicero, Quintilian, and other enterprising rhetoricians, looking to cash in on a burgeoning market, analyzed winning speeches and began traveling around the countryside touting the magic formula. Basically, they said the trick was to find something to say, arrange it in some kind of logical sequence, use a style that suits the purpose, and play to the audience.

As more and more people learned to read, however, the touters had to change the formula. So, by the late seventeenth century, they got together and decided, "Talking is one thing, but if people want to start writing, we better have some rules." They scrapped the notion that writers needed anything good to say, as long as they used good grammar to say it, and declared that writers write to narrate, expose, describe, or persuade—and nothing else. Although a few gadgets, such as punctuation and a really good dictionary, did pop up as a result of these developments, these were pretty dry times.

For the next couple hundred years, teachers did not teach much writing. They were too busy giving grammar quizzes and blabbing about great works of literature. When a bunch of them started their own club, the Modern Language Association (MLA), in order to hobnob with their fellow wizards, they forever entwined writing with literature and denigrated writing instruction to second-class citizenship.

Within our recent memory, a few rhetoric renegades said, "Wait a minute, boys. There are a lot of people on this planet, and the reason we haven't slaughtered each other off is that we usually use words (instead of spears or plutonium) to get our message across. Maybe, we need to take off these blinders and look around."

And that is what they did. Buddying up with sociologists, psychologists, information theorists, and others, they began to see writing as a social phenomenon. "Sure, rules are okay," they said, "but they should be helpful not intimidating. Besides, does anybody know if they really work?" It didn't take much to figure out that the rules didn't work.

Because the word "rhetoric" has developed such a pejorative connotation, people who talk about teaching writing today use terms such as "discourse" or "composition." But, for all practical purposes, they mean rhetoric in much the same sense that people did back on the hills of Athens and Rome.

Librarians must understand that when teachers send students to the library, they are following a rhetorical tradition that was established several millennia ago. The intent is to have students persuade teachers that they understand what's going on. Maybe that means writing a paper, or presenting an oral report, or leading a group discussion, or answering an essay question. No matter which, the outcome must be persuasive, and persuasion is the basis for classical rhetoric.

We need to keep this tradition in mind when students approach us with a reference question. Whenever possible, we should remind students that the five-page paper is more a test of their persuasiveness than a test of their research abilities. Thirty books and a hundred articles on the reform of narcotics laws are of little use to those who are ill equipped to start with.

Secondly, it is very likely that few, if any, of the teachers assigning these papers have any background in rhetoric, writing instruction, or library research. They pass on what they know, in the same ways they were taught. They are not knowledgeable about methodology, theory, or current practice. At the reference desk or in the BI class, we do have an opportunity to correct some of these wrongs in quick and effective ways. For example, the student writing about the legalization of marijuana needs to spend a significant amount of time refuting arguments. (Cicero's refutations are proofs disputing his opponent's arguments.) The librarian, therefore, should make sure the student understands this and help him find information explaining why marijuana is illegal. Or the librarian can suggest to the student writing a paper on solid-waste disposal to use cause and effect (from Aristotle's topoi) to make a point about the health consequences of allowing untreated sewage to infiltrate an aquifer. A look, then, at the medical literature would be most appropriate.

COMMUNICATION THEORY

Finally, remember that writers write because they have something to say to someone about something. Those three elements (sender, message, and receiver) make the classic triangle of the communication process. There are myriad other variables involved, such as channel, noise, and encoders, but for our purposes, let us agree that writing is a form of communication and that students often do it.

1. *Sender.* Every sender carries his or her own baggage to the word processor. In an academic setting, such as a college or university, many students come with writing backgrounds stunted by compulsive grammarians obsessed with the horrors of split infinitives and tragic comma splices. These unfortunate students were brainwashed into believing that the objective of writing was to produce a neat, orderly paper, complete with outlines, note cards and bibliography.

Other students come from backgrounds where articulation is considered a disadvantage, or where English (standard, or otherwise) is a second language. Now they are thrown together in basic English 101 and told, on the first day of class, they must produce a term paper by the last day of class. Disparate as they may have been, these students are now united by a single rhetorical problem.

Or, as Erika Lindemann writes in *A Rhetoric for Writing Teachers,* "Before writers can respond to a particular task, they must define a rhetorical problem. Defining the problem requires, at least, assessing the writer's relationship to the subject and the reader" (Lindemann, 1987, p. 192). As librarians, we must understand that it is the synergy (or conflict) between writers' rhetorical needs and their backgrounds that brings them to the library. When we see them, they are engaged in the writing process, whether they know it or not, and our interaction with them can have a profound affect on their success.

If we recognize that the student is the sender of the message and focus more on who she is and what she knows, the clearer our response can be. For instance, when I am asked for information about a specific disease or medical treatment, I instinctively assume the person asking the question has very personal reasons for wanting the information. I tread cautiously.

2. *Message.* When Rhett damns Scarlet on that foggy Atlanta night she pleads, "But where shall I go, what shall I do?" I see a lot of students crying out in the same way. Assaulted by the insurmountable task of writing a research paper, many students simply collapse on the sidewalk. (I am exaggerating, but you understand my meaning.) Not only must they wrestle with choosing and narrowing a topic, but their teacher wants them to be creative and imaginative. In courses where content is primary (e.g., astronomy or American history) students are too busy digesting new information to pay much attention to the controversies about the subject. In courses where content is secondary (e.g., freshman composition), many students are so ambivalent about so many things that even deciding on a topic is a challenge. Unfortunately, too many students do what Scarlet did and "worry about it tomorrow."

Librarians can play a pivotal role in helping students find their voice. Our training, experience, and position in academia give us a clear view of the big picture. We can help students fine tune their message by showing them how to shape their ideas. In bibliographic instruction classes or at the reference desk, we can say, "Here's how I would narrow that topic, what do you think?" or "I did some similar research on this and found. . . ." By being specific and practical, we prove ourselves knowledgeable and helpful allies.

3. *Receiver.* This may seem obvious, but our penchant for showing students how to find books or journal articles often overshadows our need to ask students why they think they need them to begin with. For instance, a student asks at the desk where he can find some information about solid-waste disposal. After a superb reference interview, you find out that he is working on a paper for his technical writing class. You judge the level of your response to meet his level of expectation, but remember his receiver, his audience, is also part of the formula. If his paper is a persuasive piece for a citizen advisory committee, the kind of information he needs (and you help him find) is different from what he needs if he is writing for a group of municipal engineers. In the first case, you would do him well by showing him some great Boston *Globe* articles covering the state's struggle to locate an incinerator in a wealthy suburb; in the second case, he needs to spend some quality time with *Pollution Abstracts* and EPA regulations. By involving the receiver in the research process, you have helped that student get what he really needs.

WHAT WRITING IS

1. Writing is about writing, not about rules. In 1963, composition researchers Richard Braddock, Richard Lloyd-Jones, and Lowell Schoer conducted a study which proved that teaching students grammar did little, if anything, to improve their ability to write. (They even suggested that spending time on grammar was actually a detriment because it left too little time for the students to actually write.) The best way to teach writing, they concluded, was to have the students write and write and write. Unfortunately, this breakthrough has not quite trickled down to the classroom. Too many elementary and secondary school teachers still believe that mastering grammar rules, punctuation, parts of speech, and spelling is a precursor to learning how to write and insist that children spend twelve years of their life doing just that.

2. Writing is a process. In 1964, researchers Rohman and Wlecke analyzed journals students had kept as part of their writing assignments. They identified three stages in the writing process: prewriting, writing, and rewriting. Though by today's standards their analysis is a bit linear, it did dispel a common belief that writing begins when pen meets paper and set off a barrage of investigations into composition theory.

Though a few fossils cling to the belief that the research paper itself is a goal of the course, most teachers consider the term paper assignment a vehicle for their students to demonstrate their understanding of the course content, to organize ideas, and to express themselves in clear and concise English. But how the students view the paper seems more to the point, especially when the syllabus says the research paper is worth 50% of the grade and there is little, if any, class time devoted to it.

3. Writing is recursive. People do not think about what they are going to write, write, and then revise what they have written. Though many people have their own theories about exactly what recursive means, Janet Emig (1971) was among the first to bend the linear model into a circle. Writers think about what they are going to write, write, think some more, rewrite, write, think some more, and so forth.

We see this at the reference desk all the time. Students start with vague questions and pop back and forth between ideas, sources, topics, statistics, quotations, facts, and opinions. In the course of an evening, it is not unusual to interact with the same student five or six times, and each time he or she can be at a different place in the process.

4. Writing is discovery. How many times have you heard people say ''I didn't know what I was going to write until I wrote it?'' This is probably true for most of us, but varies by degree. The student writing a paper on marijuana reform laws knows the paper is going to be about marijuana reform laws, not about the Unix operating system. He may not know specifically what words or ideas are going to show up on the paper, but his personal experiences and task

are already playing a major role in what he will say. Peter Elbow (1973) and others have gone so far as to propose that writing is art and though it can be learned, it cannot be taught. Donald Murray (1978) and Sondra Perl (1979) are also proponents of the "writing equals discovery" theory.

This concept parallels the "library equals discovery" concept so often discussed in the BI world. Many of our instructional programs are founded on the belief that knowing how to use libraries is a liberating, lifelong skill and that in our search for some bit of information, we stumble upon (or seek out) other bits of information we didn't originally know we needed or wanted.

5. Writing is a cognitive activity. One of the first attempts at explaining the cognitive nature of writing was made by Flower and Hayes in the early 1980s. In a series of articles, this composition researcher and psychologist team watched and recorded every movement and thought of writers writing. They analyzed the data and concluded that writing is extremely complex. The writing process, they said, involves protocols (activities) for: (a) planning (generating ideas from memory), organizing (the most useful bits), and setting goals (to get the job done); (b) translating what is planned into sentences; and (c) reviewing what is written to improve its quality. What makes the process tick is a "monitor" (a sort of cerebral switch house) that keeps everything on track.

Later, less mechanical explanations emerged from developmental psychologists, including Piaget. His idea was that people develop higher order thinking skills (such as for testing hypotheses and evaluating and analyzing information) as they mature. To advance from one stage to another, individuals must be challenged by tasks which demand higher levels of thinking. While he guessed that by the age of eighteen or so, most would have reached what he calls the "formal operational level," we know this is not the case. Perhaps this is why many students find it so difficult to identify a thesis or formulate a sound research question.

6. Writing is a social act. In *The Hitchhiker's Guide to the Galaxy* (1980), D. Adams puts a babbler fish in his ear to translate Vogon into English. This little fish, he explains, has the remarkable ability to translate every language in the universe into every other language in the universe. On this planet, there are not only hundreds of languages, but many "discourse communities" as well. Psychologists talk like psychologists, and lawyers like lawyers, and engineers like engineers. Some composition theorists believe that language is epistemic, that it shapes the domain; others believe it expresses the domain. Regardless, the more specialized the domain becomes, the more foreign the language sounds to an outsider. Pick up a copy of *Tetrahedron Letters* and see what I mean.

Students often stumble into these foreign worlds without a babbler fish. Hopefully, an attuned librarian will use this opportunity to show them how to use a specialized dictionary and thesaurus and to explain that, even though some data bases are more appropriate for their topic than others, going outside the field often gives a much clearer perspective.

SO WHAT?

If anything, composition research in the last decade has proved that although no one knows how or why people learn to write, lots of people wonder about the phenomenon. Lately, poststructural deconstructionism and artificial intelligence are in the forefront of the debate. Although the flutter has produced no answers, it has prompted a great interest in the question. And this is good. Biology professors wonder why freshmen cannot write decent lab reports. Political science instructors wonder why sophomores fail essay exams. Engineers wonder why juniors cannot put together a research proposal. In the past, due mostly to its rhetorical traditions and history, the onus of writing instruction has fallen on English teachers. But given what we know about knowledge domains and the demands of today's information-driven lifestyle, this responsibility belongs to all of us—even librarians.

Considering that we already collect, organize, and make accessible the recorded knowledge of all humankind, this last little bit should not be so difficult. Unfortunately, however, librarianship is stronger on the back swing (acquiring, classifying, and circulating) than it is on the follow through (interpreting and analyzing). Piaget would say we are still at the concrete operational level, and he would be right.

Our collections, reference works, bibliographic instruction, systems, and software were created to unite the searchers with the searched. And we have done that really well. Now we need to help the searchers make sense of what they have found. I am not suggesting that we do this on our own, but through collaborative efforts with teaching faculty, academic computing personnel, and other support services. We can help teachers create assignments that challenge their students' ability to access and evaluate information. We can make sure the data-base search that the student downloads from the CD in the library is compatible with the word-processing software used in the computing labs. We can cosponsor, with other campus services, workshops in grant writing, learning styles, diversity, management, and public relations. These initiatives not only further our own concerns, but contribute to the overall objectives of the institution.

REFERENCES

Adams, D. (1980). *The hitchhiker's guide to the galaxy.* New York: Harmony Books.

Beaubien, A. K., Hogan, S., & George, M. (1982). *Learning the library: Concepts and methods for effective bibliographic instruction.* New York: Bowker.

Braddock, R., Lloyd-Jones, R., & Schoer, L. (1963). *Research in written composition.* Urbana, IL: National Council of Teachers of English.

Elbow, P. (1973). *Writing without teachers.* New York: Oxford University Press.

Emig, J. (1971). *The composing processes of twelfth graders.* Urbana, IL: National Council of Teachers of English.

Flower, L., & Hayes, J. R. (1981, December). A cognitive process theory of writing. *College Composition and Communication, 32,* 365–387.

Lindemann, E. (1987). *A rhetoric for writing teachers* (2nd ed.). New York: Oxford University Press.

Murray, D. M. (1978). Internal revision: A process of discovery. In C. R. Cooper & L. Odell (Eds.), *Research on composing: Points of departure* (pp. 85–103). Urbana, IL: National Council of Teachers of English.

Perl, S. (1979). The composing processes of unskilled college writers. *Research in the Teaching of English* (December) *13,* 317–336.

Rohman, D. G., & Wlecke, A. O. (1964). *Pre-writing: The construction and application of models for concept formulation in writing* (U.S. Office of Education Cooperative Research Project No. 2174). East Lansing: Michigan State University.

Chapter 3

Connected Communities: Encouraging Dialogue Between Composition and Bibliographic Instruction

Barbara Fister

Most colleges and universities today recognize that there are certain skills that need to be taught if students are to make much of the content they are attempting to master. Programs designed to inculcate these skills have most often been focused on in first-year courses, but a growing number of institutions have taken steps to integrate these necessary skills into the curriculum, to place them into a more meaningful context, and to make clear that they are a shared value and responsibility among all departments. These efforts emphasize learning a process, rather than evaluating a finished product. They assume that learning is, at best, active and student centered, rather than what Paulo Freire (1970) calls a "banking process" of depositing knowledge from teacher into student. These programs recognize that academic discourse is baffling to many students, that modes of knowledge production and dissemination are mysterious social constructions that are not transparent to the uninitiated, however obvious they seem to the faculty. They consciously unpack the institutional culture and its enigmas and invite students to learn the ropes of academic inquiry by participating as active members in a community of inquiry. These programs tend to be powered by bright, energetic, and dedicated people who make teaching a priority; they hope their enthusiasm will be contagious because, without enthusiasm, the programs tend to ossify.

The downside of these programs is that they are administratively problematic—they are outside the traditional political economy of the academy and are not protected by a single academic department or backed by a long disciplinary tradition. At best, they rely on theoretically shared ownership and are led by a consultant/expert. At worst, they become a stepchild, a time-consuming, additional task shared by many, but are no one's primary focus. Politically, too, these programs are risky; they suffer from fuzzy lines of authority, depend on the goodwill of participants, are less valued than content-area expertise, and yield little payoff at tenure and promotion time. The teaching is generally done by young, entry-level enthusiasts who, if they are successful, go on to more rewarding things. Even when these programs are successful, they are time-consuming, need constant infusions of new energy, and are conducive to burn-out.

Of course, this is a description of course-related bibliographic instruction programs. Or is it a description of the writing-across-the-curriculum movement? These programs share so many characteristics that it is hard, in the abstract, to tell them apart. Both are attempts to infiltrate the curriculum with basic academic and lifelong learning skills and to embed those skills meaningfully in the disciplines. Both are ways of making the values, assumptions, and methods of scholarship accessible to students. Both acknowledge that, even though disciplines and their methods of inquiry and discourse differ, those differences can be examined, penetrated, and claimed by students if some attempt is made to explore them. Though one focuses on finding and using information and the other on composing written knowledge, they both engage students in performing a basic activity of academia—scholarly inquiry. In order to improve our chances of making that activity meaningful to students, it is worthwhile to examine similarities and differences between the two approaches, explore common problems, and seek ways in which we can learn from one another to collaborate for stronger linkages among the highly interrelated activities of reading, writing, and research.

THE RESEARCH PAPER AS ARTIFACT

Writing instruction and bibliographic instruction grew from the same soil. In the nineteenth century, American education shifted from a British style of learning, based on apprenticeship under a master for whom the student practiced written or oral thesis building and defense, to a German model of text-based scholarship, in which knowledge was displayed in empirically flavored writing and followed strict conventions of textual documentation. As scholarly authority was displaced from individual scholars to a discipline's texts, the practice of scholarship came to rely more and more on both written displays of knowledge and on a collegium of texts rather than on individual erudition and rhetorical skill. The undergraduate research paper assignment was invented to initiate the apprentice scholar into these new methods of scholarship, just as the research collection was built to support those methods.

Though by the end of the 1880s the research paper assignment was a widespread practice in American higher education, it soon atrophied as a vehicle for research as such. The increasing specialization of disciplines ensured that students could not genuinely contribute to new knowledge in a field in which they were novices. Though the activity called "research" remained, it became increasingly marginalized; it became something the English department could teach in the freshman year at the service of other departments. "Real" research, research that formulated new knowledge as opposed to displaying knowledge found in other texts, became postponed to graduate study or undertaken as a dry run in the senior seminar or senior thesis. As its potential as a vehicle for inquiry in the disciplines atrophied, it began to fossilize into a distinct genre of its own, one with an elaborate code of regulations governing note taking and documentation (Russell, 1991).

Critiques of this genre abound and are nothing new. David McCaslin (1923) looked to libraries for help in a mode that will sound familiar to librarians who argue the case for information literacy as a basic skill for the twenty-first century. "It is surprising to find how little the average student in his Freshman year knows about the way around in a library and how abashed he is in the presence of a card-catalogue and how loath to accost a librarian to ask questions" (p. 592); but with proper instruction "the student understands enough of the methods of scholarly research that he can go at his college work with more system and better result and . . . he will be equipped to use a library as he needs to in his active life" (p. 596). A. L. Bader (1936) found the trouble to be not in finding sources, but in students' tendency to report on topics rather than engage in reflective thinking. He urged that students should write instead about "the really vital subjects [which] are those which concern the students' living and thinking in the world today" (p. 670). George Arms (1943) argued that research offered the opportunity to engage in meaningful inquiry, but that opportunity was lost in most research paper assignments. According to Arms, "to invoke the name of research when this is not actually done is to impose a boring task upon the student and at the same time to discredit the research activities of their teachers' research" (p. 25). He held librarians to account as part of the problem: "Students who will otherwise succeed will weaken before the seductions of librarians, whose very idea of scholarly investigation often seems to be that, as a writer remarked to Frank Case of the Algonquin, cribbing from one source is plagiarism but cribbing from enough sources is research" (p. 24).

While librarians still echo McCaslin's dismay at students' inability to negotiate libraries, composition teachers are vocally dissatisfied with the genre of the research paper. James Beck (1981) calls it "the uncritical amassing of correctly-documented facts" (p. 1), while James C. McDonald (1990) identifies it as "an exercise in researching and reporting what others have written to produce a paper that conforms to the course's conventions governing documentation" (p. 5). Sharon Crowley (1987) complains that "within the academy, expository writing is thought of as a sort of transcription skill, like shorthand" (p. 179). She points out in deconstructionist terms the irony of *expository* writing *covering* a subject, since it is contradictory to expose and cover at the same time, and suggests that the research paper encourages students to erase themselves and create papers that have no interior, only correct shells. "Serious students will try to work their way out of this dilemma by retreating to the library in order to read up on abortion, the war in Nicaragua, or whatnot. In Derridean terms, they try to enter the chain of signification which surrounds, and amounts to, discourse about their subjects'' (p. 176), entering that chain of signification while disappearing as subjects, reproducing those discourses without producing anything critical or new or their own. They simply borrow the discourse from the library. Richard Larson (1982) has launched the most spirited attack on the research paper, which he labels "a non-form of writing," suggesting that "the generic term 'research paper' is for practical purposes meaningless. . . . I would argue that the so-called 'research paper' as ordinarily taught by the kinds of texts I have reviewed, implicitly equates 'research' with looking up books in the library and taking down information from those books. . . . when we tend to present the 'research paper' as in effect a paper based upon the use of the library, we misrepresent 'research' '' (pp. 813–815). He raises two particular concerns: first, that designating only some writing assignments as "research" assignments suggests research is called for in only special, limited circumstances; and second, that research differs from discipline to discipline and from one situation to another, so it cannot be taught as if it is a singular genre by the English department. Both are concerns that helped launch the writing-across-the-curriculum movement.

CURRENT/TRADITIONAL ASSUMPTIONS

Critics do not believe students should abandon research—or the library—but rather think that the research paper, as represented in virtually all writing handbooks and as taught in most first-year composition courses, does not engage students in a meaningful research activity and may actually hinder an understanding of how academic inquiry is conducted. Yet, in spite of decades of complaint, the generic research paper is still a standby of the first-year writing course taught in most colleges and universities. A survey published in 1982 found that over 80 percent of writing courses included instruction in the research paper (Ford & Perry), and anecdotal evidence suggests that this is still largely the case. The recommendations given in most writing handbooks still dwell on finding and taking notes from written sources. Though some make a nod toward interviewing experts or contacting organizations, the chief activity of research, as it is described in the writing handbooks, is still gathering and synthesizing expert, textual information (Crowley, 1990; Trzyna, 1983). Presumably, teachers who use these handbooks in their classrooms share those assumptions to a large extent, or at any rate teach them.

The features of the current/traditional research paper assignment have significantly shaped bibliographic instruction programs, which tend to focus on ways to search efficiently for textual material that will then form the basic raw material of a research paper. As one current library instruction handbook puts it, "the research paper, by definition, is based primarily on evidence gathered from authorities and scholars" (Bolner, Dantin, & Murray, 1991, p. 308). Assumptions that underlie current/traditional pedagogy in writing instruction are mirrored in bibliographic instruction and its beliefs about writing, which guide its approach to research instruction. The list of attitudes below demonstrates these parallels:

Attitudes in current/traditional writing instruction (Hairston, 1982)	Parallel attitudes in current/traditional bibliographic instruction
• The product is more important than the process.	• Finding information by using bibliographic tools correctly is more important than the processes of decision making and problem solving.
• Discourse comes in distinct formal types—descriptive, narrative, expository, and argumentative.	• Knowledge comes in distinct forms—books, articles, reference materials, documents, and so forth—and the structure of knowledge is defined by its textual packaging.
• Correct style and usage are the proper subjects of a writing course.	• Correct search strategy and tool use are the proper subjects of a bibliographic instruction session.
• The informal essay and research paper are the dominant activities.	• Preparing students to find materials so they can write research papers is the dominant activity.
• Invention is not addressed in the classroom.	• Invention is not addressed as part of the research process—it is assumed that students will come to the library with a topic in mind.
• It is assumed all writers describe the same reality.	• It is assumed that information is the same to all researchers.
• Competent writers know what they are going to say before they begin to write.	• Competent researchers know what they are looking for before they begin to search.
• The writing process is linear, moving from planning, to drafting, to revision.	• The research process is linear, moving from planning, to locating and abstracting information, to writing and revision.
• Teaching editing is teaching writing.	• Teaching the use of bibliographic access tools is teaching research.

These attitudes are not startling or even particularly controversial if the main activity engaged in by undergraduates is finding and reporting on information gathered from textual sources. However, they do not prepare students for research as scholars define it. As George L. Dillon (1991) points out, ''Undergraduate majors do not write papers contributing to knowledge, but remain on the margins, as much observers as participants. One of the great, gaping holes in current academic self-understanding is any positive model of the undergraduate as a knowing or learning subject; we tend simply to think of undergraduates as beginners or proto-graduate students, and undergraduate teaching as some sort of professional recruiting (when it is not generalized consciousness-raising or horizon-broadening)'' (pp. 151–152). Sharon Crowley (1990) considers the research paper to be based on a rhetoric that discourages imagination and originality and that puts students into a ''vicious double-bind'' (p. 164) because it suggests that knowledge is a commodity unconnected with the knower, and is thus a legal tender for exchange—yet it is one which they may well be accused of stealing if they misinterpret the mysterious rules of documentation. They are asked to ''invent the university'' (Bartholomae, 1986) before they have been there long enough to know what it is all about—so they remain marginalized outsiders mimicking academic noises; ''learning, at least as it is defined in the liberal arts curriculum, becomes more a matter of imitation or parody than a matter of invention and discovery'' (p. 11). Because the current/traditional research paper denies that the student is a ''knowing or learning subject,'' ''research'' is a matter of copying an activity without actually engaging in it, just as copying text, rather than constructing it, becomes its defining activity.

ALTERNATIVE PEDAGOGIES

While current/traditional pedagogies are common in both writing and bibliographic instruction, there are also challenges offered to those pedagogies by practitioners in both fields. If responses to the problems of current/traditional pedagogy were sorted into camps, they might be mapped to the points of the rhetorical triangle, some emphasizing a change in the way we treat the speaker/writer role, some concerned with the text as a transaction between the speaker and the audience, and some focused on the role of the audience in shaping writing. (For other perspectives on the history of composition theory, see Berlin, 1987; Faigley, 1986; and North, 1987.) For each of these challenges, there is a counterpoint in the practice of bibliographic instruction.

The first group were early challengers to current/traditional pedagogy and emphasized the development of a personal voice as an antidote to the disengagement felt by students who were asked to write depersonalized, pseudo-omniscient prose for academic purposes. (See Macrorie, 1970; and Elbow, 1973, for examples of this approach.) Though this challenge to current/traditional composition pedagogy appeared at about the same time that ''relevance'' became a rallying cry for change in higher education and was no doubt connected with that trend, it has had a long-lasting effect on pedagogy. It challenged the dominance of form and concern for product and brought a focus on the writing subject that has had a shaping influence ever since. (See Elbow, 1991, for a current argument against valorizing academic discourse in the writing classroom; and Macrorie, 1988, for a recent example of this school of thought applied to the research assignment.) There have since been challenges to the assumptions made by those who uphold personal voice as a focus for writing instruction—charges that it rests on a neo-romantic notion of the creative individual and that it neglects to take into account the political and social context of the classroom (Faigley, 1986)—but advocates of personal voice have instituted such ubiquitous practices as free writing exercises and journal writing, now common in classrooms across the curriculum from elementary school through graduate school. Some of these pedagogies have been used in bibliographic instruction. (The free writing exercise has been used by Constance Mellon, 1986, and Marjorie M. Warmkessel, 1992, to assess student attitudes toward the library, and research journals have been used in course-integrated bibliographic instruction to focus students on the process of research.) Additionally, the claim that information literacy is a life-long skill that can be imparted in college and retained throughout life, making BI an agent of empowerment outside the academic context, sounds very like the notion that individual expression and fulfilment are more important than learning the ropes of academic discourse.

Interest next shifted to the space between writer and reader, to what transpires as a writer writes, with the empirical methods of the cognitive sciences being put to work in exploring and modeling the writing process. Janet Emig started the trend with her dissertation research (1971), in which she used protocol analysis to chart the stages student subjects went through as they tackled a writing task. A number of process studies followed (see Flower & Hayes, 1981, and Bereiter & Scardamalia, 1987, for important examples of this research), giving rise to the now standard notion that writing is a complex, recursive process and that teaching should address the process, rather than merely modeling an ideal product in the hope students will be able to imitate it after trial and error and much drill on sentence combining and grammar. This strand of composition theory has further challenged current/traditional pedagogy by focusing on process, opposing the idea that process in writing is linear, encouraging the discussion of invention in the writing classroom, and dislodging editing from its preeminence as a classroom concern. These process models of writing are now embedded in the teaching of writing (though they are too often oversimplified into a "prewriting—drafting—revising" regimen) and have been picked up on by such bibliographic instruction practitioners as Mellon (1984) and Kuhlthau (1988). They lend themselves to integration of a search strategy with a writing process.

Underlying the process model are two dubious ideas: that empirical observation will yield a model of the composing process and that students will learn to write better if they understand that model. It situates writing problems as problems in cognition, ignoring the cultural environment in which writing (and cognition) takes place (Bizzell, 1982) and further assumes that writing is an activity that comes after thought and that expression of ideas comes after ideas are formed. In short, it preserves some current/traditional assertions: that writers describe the same reality; that writers think of what they want to say before they write; and that they translate ideas into language only after they are thought. These assumptions are challenged in the current critical/theoretical climate, which questions a separation of thought and its articulation and which situates all discourse in a social context. Here, the audience point of the rhetorical triangle becomes an important factor, informing and shaping both the conditions of producing an utterance and the individual's control of that production; the individual, and his or her writing, and his or her writing process and situation, are all largely constituted by the audience and purpose of his or her writing act and furthermore are conditioned and shaped by those discourses that come *before* he or she writes. In Faigley's words, ''when students write in an academic discipline, they write in reference to texts that define the scholarly activities of interpreting and reporting in that discipline. . . . In a social view, any effort to write about the self or reality always comes in relation to previous texts'' (Faigley, 1986, p. 536).

This new concern with the social construction of knowledge and how it shapes and is shaped by discourse was influenced by Thomas Kuhn (1970), Richard Rorty (1979), and Stanley Fish (1980)—all working in different academic fields, but all viewing knowledge in their fields as socially mediated. Knowledge, in this view, is not formed by solving problems and working toward a unified truth, but by negotiating commonly accepted descriptions of truth that are always subject to revision. It is antifoundationalist, as Patricia Bizzell (1986) puts it, and adheres to the belief that ''an absolute standard for the judgement of truth can never be found, precisely because the individual mind can never transcend personal emotions, social circumstances, and historical traditions'' (pp. 39–40). And it places socially negotiated discourse at the heart of knowledge.

Curiously, this puts rhetoric, one of the original liberal arts, back in the center of knowledge construction, for it is through discourse and in discourse that we create knowledge. Knowledge, then, becomes a rhetorically conditioned construct. When we teach the content of a discipline, we are inevitably teaching the language of that discipline and determine that content based on the texts which constitute it. Rhetoric, which had become an embarassing poor relation to literary criticism in the English department and was taught only at the service of other departments, is coming back into its own.

Much research on writing has taken its departure from the notion that discourse and knowledge are socially constructed and mutually constituting entities, acting on one another inextricably, and are inextricably entwined with social forces. Charles Bazerman (1988) and Greg Meyers (1990) have examined science writing from this angle; others have followed Shirley Brice Heath's example in adopting ethnomethodological methods in exploring language in the classroom and as a methodology for research (1983). The political forces that shape the writing classroom have been explored by Miller (1991) and Bullock and Trimbur (1991), and the historical contexts by Russell (1991), Berlin (1987), and Murphy (1990). And, revisiting cognitive theories of the writing process, Linda Flower et al. (1990) and Doug Brent (1992) have been exploring the ways in which reading influences the social construction of the writer's reality, while Deborah Brandt (1992) suggests that the cognition *is* social, that when writers draw on prior knowledge or research in their writing, that marshalling of knowledge both enables and constitutes the act of understanding. Thus, the attention given to social forces at work in writing has inevitably changed the writing classroom.

Some of the pedagogies that arise from this social turn in writing instruction are particularly applicable to bibliographic instruction. Collaborative learning (Bruffee, 1984; Bizzell & Herzberg, 1987) has been adopted by many librarians in the BI classroom (Sheridan, 1992; Fister, 1990) as well as by teachers across the curriculum. The notion of discourse communities socially generating texts has been the subject of much discussion—it is a concept that is powerful for library instruction, which has for some time been interested in teaching the structure of literature in the disciplines. Tying that publication and dissemination process to the production and reproduction of discourses could broaden the concept and tie it more firmly to the students' own production of research. Historicizing and politicizing discourse production offers a chance to deepen students' understanding of the ways the texts in the library are produced and organized. Deborah Fink (1989) has enriched our understanding of these matters with her textbook *Process and Politics in Library Research.* The potential for rethinking BI in the light of these social theories of knowledge is enormous and has, as yet, been barely tapped.

Research assignments could make students not only familiar with how to find information, but aware of the structure and reproduction of knowledge. Students could explore political, economic, or historical influences on some aspect of publishing as a social, historical, and economic process, in an assignment that would not only familiarize them with publication forms and how the library organizes them, but would allow them to interpret and critique the circulation of ideas in a social framework. Another way to examine a discipline's means of creating and revising knowledge would be to ask students to explore the formation of a body of theory or the reception of a classic text in a field. They would thereby come to understand the intertextuality demonstrated in the citation practices of scholarship and the ways in which a discourse community negotiates knowledge and learn that knowledge is not an inert substance, but a changing and constantly reinterpreted view of things. Library systems themselves provide excellent opportunities for exploring the ways in which collection building, cataloging, and classification reflect, in slow motion, changes in social practice. Libraries glacially adopt new subject headings long after the language has picked up and moved on, organize materials on the shelves in ways which betray the cultural assumptions of the dominant class, and privilege certain forms of discourse as worthy of inclusion while excluding others. Because libraries are conservative and archival institutions, they preserve within their walls the traces of where knowledge has been and how it has changed. Students could learn the system as they use it, but rather than just learning the rules of access (like the rules of grammar—in themselves often arbitrary and downright dull), they could critique them and make them more meaningful by understanding them in context (as writing is taught more effectively as an activity in context). If the library were reimagined as a socially constructed artifact of our culture, it could become a laboratory for learning the ways in which we engage in knowledge construction, instead of being seen as a peculiarly organized storehouse of ready-made and infinitely reusable knowledge.

Of course, these ideas are merely pipe dreams if learning the library is a fifty-minute occasion, as it remains in so many of our institutions. Not only would we have to reimagine the library, we would have to reimagine bibliographic instruction and its place in the curriculum. And since we know that imagination is not all that is required—truly course-integrated instruction has been an unrealized ideal almost since BI acquired an identity—we need to keep a sharp eye out for opportunities. Writing-across-the curriculum programs offer the best hope we have had yet for true collaboration and involvement in the curriculum.

An institution's writing-across-the-curriculum program constitutes a campuswide discussion about and commitment to teaching and provides an opportunity for conversation about common needs among departments. It refocuses attention on such basic matters as how best to introduce students to academic methods and discourse, how to give students active learning experiences that make course content meaningful, and how to promote and assess student learning. Faculty share ideas on how to make writing part of the learning process, how to create assignments that work, and how to engage students in an academic enterprise that may seem baffling and foreign. Certainly the role of the library and of student research should be part of this conversation.

Of course, some of writing-across-the-curriculum's strengths are also its weaknesses: because it is interdepartmental, it is not defended by strong territorial instincts; because it requires conversation and change, it takes time and effort; and because it focuses on teaching, it is not part of the dominant academic reward system. These drawbacks all sounds very familiar to anyone who has been charged with "marketing" a BI program. But at least writing-across-the-curriculum represents a chance to combine our strengths and find common ground with faculty in all disciplines.

COMMUNITIES IN DIALOGUE

Just how much do we know about writing programs at our institutions? A survey of continuing education needs described in the American Library Association's *Bibliographic Instruction Section Newsletter* in 1992 found that more than two-thirds of the responding BIS members were interested in learning about writing-across-the-curriculum and its impact on BI. At any rate, there is a healthy curiosity among librarians about writing programs.

That same year, a free writing exercise conducted at a session of the Association of College and Research Libraries Sixth National Conference (Fister, 1992a) elicited an interesting mix of responses. Audience members were asked to characterize in a short statement their library's relationship with their institution's writing program or to comment on some aspect of that relationship. Informal responses, jotted on index cards, were shared with other audience members, discussed, and then collected. Those comments, written as off-the-cuff remarks, provide some interesting insights into writing programs and libraries.

Many writers commented on the strength of their ties to a first-year writing class; others indicated that the relationship depended on personal contacts ("we work well with those instructors who value documented writing"). One writer observed that programs were in a state of change, but that change was constant and positive: "our relationship is collaborative and evolutionary; change is the norm as new resources present theselves." Another writer found it somewhat baffling: "our writing program is changing in ways that we don't always understand." While one mused that "we seem to be getting along . . . but I suspect we don't really understand each other and are not working in collaboration," several felt defensive, reporting problems such as sending students to BI sessions without topics in hand or without adequate consultation about assignments, or simply "sending students to the library like a plague of locusts." Some writers reported their library had no relationship with the writing program while others indicated they weren't sure if their institutions even had a writing program.

Some exciting innovations were reported, however, including grant support for collaboration with teachers in three disciplines to increase writing effectiveness, a plan to develop a BI program for writing center staff, and the use of free writing and journaling in writing classes geared toward developing research skills. On the whole, these free writing responses suggest that writing programs have ad hoc, but frequently cordial, relationships with libraries and that there is both a need to communicate with one another and fertile ground for collaboration.

A survey conducted in 1992–1993[1] suggests that librarians and writing instructors share many assumptions and attitudes about student research. A series of statements about undergraduate research was sent to writing program directors and bibliographic instruction coordinators at randomly selected institutions of all sizes and types. Participants were asked to what degree they agreed or disagreed with the statements. Both groups largely agreed or agreed strongly with the idea that research was an important form of experiential education in the undergraduate curriculum, that it gives students skills for lifelong learning, and that it is an essential form of learning for undergraduates. They shared concern that students fail to give their research projects adequate time, that they fail to narrow a topic sufficiently, and that they have the misperception that answers will be found easily and in simple packages. According to both groups, learning what constitutes a good research question is a challenge for undergraduate researchers. And there was general agreement that a good research assignment should invite personal engagement, should build toward research with sequenced tasks, should make clear what constitutes good evidence in the context of the task, and should encourage students to develop and defend an argument. Significantly for BI librarians, there was general agreement among both groups that some class time should be spent in the library learning how to find and use information. There was general disagreement with the statement that the research paper is a form of writing that has little meaning outside of academia and, as such, is not very important and with the statement that the traditional research paper stifles creativity and invites plagiarism. On the whole, then, both BI librarians and writing teachers agree that research writing is important in the undergraduate curriculum and that assignments need to be well designed and the students' progress carefully nurtured to ensure success.

There were a few points on which the two groups differed significantly. Writing instructors were slightly more likely than librarians to feel that initiating students into academic discourse communities is the major purpose of undergraduate research writing and that a problem students have when they perform research is that they tend to quote authorities rather than develop and defend their own point of view. Librarians were somewhat more inclined than writing instructors to feel that research assignments are the most important writing assignments in college, that they provide skills for lifelong learning, and that information literacy is the most important outcome of student research. They were more likely to think student failure is due to problems in interpreting bibliographic citations and tools, that students do not understand the difference between primary and secondary sources, and that they do not check the *Library of Congress Subject Headings* list before searching for materials. Perhaps those problems are simply more visible in a library than in the classroom or in a finished paper. Interestingly, there was disagreement over whether students fail because they do not ask for help. Librarians were far more likely to agree with that statement than were writing instructors, which implies that students could afford to ask librarians for more help than they typically do. Perhaps they are bringing some of their questions to the wrong people—a situation that closer collaboration between librarians and writing instructors might alleviate. Librarians are also, not surprisingly, more likely than writing instructors to agree with the statement "a librarian should be given a chance to critique a research assignment before it is given to students." Again, there appears to be a certain resistance to the sharing of power and ownership, which might be lessened if both fields work more closely together.

Three questions about the research process which were responded to differently raise some interesting questions. Librarians are more likely than writing instructors to agree with the statement that the research process begins with defining a topic, then involves finding information, and ends with writing up conclusions. They also are more likely to feel that when students have problems with research tasks it may be because they fail to use a systematic search strategy, which moves from general information sources (such as encyclopedias) to specific sources (such as journal articles). Finally, they are more likely to connect problems in performing research with a student's failure to proceed in a systematic, step-by-step fashion. These results suggest that librarians on the whole have a somewhat different view of the research process than do writing instructors and that for librarians the process is, ideally, a logical and controlled one with a sequence of distinct tasks. Writing instructors may be more inclined to view the research process as a recursive and exploratory one.

Generally speaking, there appears to be agreement that research assignments are important and that, if attention is given to assignment design and teaching, students will gain valuable skills. The disagreements that showed up in the survey suggest that communication and joint exploration of issues could help improve students' research abilities.

There have been some instances of collaboration in the literature of both fields. Lori Arp (1990) suggests that since both fields have common interests there needs to be increased communication between the library and writing departments, an effort in which librarians can take the lead. Dee Cameron (1986) has published sensitive suggestions for improved library assignments in a journal directed toward writing teachers. Phyllis Reich (1986) has explored ways to teach invention in a BI session in a way which would fit well into many writing teachers' plans. She points out how difficult it is for freshmen to choose appropriate topics for research and suggests techniques for working through that part of the research process. She argues persuasively that BI sessions should focus on the difficult tasks of developing a research question worth posing, designing a search strategy, refining a search, and choosing evidence, rather than on the specifics of tool use. Students can learn to use tools effectively only by using them. Jean Sheridan (1992) and Donald Barclay (1992) have both introduced concepts from composition theory and practice to librarians, urging that through closer collaboration and better understanding, we can improve student learning.

Though at first glance the literature of the field of composition seems to have paid scant attention to the research assignment (there are few citations listed in the annual *CCCC Bibliography of Composition and Rhetoric* on the topic), there have been some publications which offer sound advice. Mary Jane Dickerson (1989) offers a sympathetic critique of BI efforts:

Our librarians had devised many useful ways to make it as painless as possible for composition teachers to introduce hundreds of students to the library through an array of services such as staff-directed tours, self-guided exercise tours, and videos starring other students as well as librarians. But no matter how diligently we went through the various well-intentioned programs, my students' eyes glazed over in a numbness that only seemed to distance them further from using the library with some understanding of its function to them and their need for its empowerment in their educational lives. . . . They entered the library as passive objects and they left without the means to become actively engaged as subjects learning and questioning how knowledge is categorized and organized. (pp. 6–7)

Dispiriting though this critique may seem, Dickerson goes on to offer the suggestion that the library itself can become the subject of collaborative research so that students can explore and understand the way the library organizes and categorizes knowledge in a deeper way than if they simply learn how it works. Virginia Chappell (1990) is another composition teacher who recommends that collaborative research projects are particularly helpful in making students familiar with libraries while grounding their writing activity in group reading and inquiry. Diane Quantic (1981) recommends that librarians and composition specialists work more closely together and that while most first-year instruction emphasizes the most boring aspects of research—notecards, documentation forms, and library skills—it should focus on using sources to solve problems, emphasize process rather than product, and help students become accustomed to college-level expectations. Cooperation could lead to a more integrated library skills program, with librarians helping teachers develop materials for the classroom and composition teachers developing materials on the writing process for the library.

One area in which our interests converge is in understanding the research process. Though writing classrooms have addressed the writing process for some years now, the usual schema does not address critical stages in the research writing process and, in fact, may misrepresent it (Stotsky, 1991). Nelson and Hayes (1988), in the field of composition, and librarians Kuhlthau (1988) and Fister (1992b) have examined the research process from different angles, each finding research writing to involve recursive, nonlinear strategies, without hierarchically distinct and separable steps. In Michael Klein's words, "it is *the absence of a direct and linear route* through the research/writing process that is most characteristic of solid, and honest, work" (Klein, 1987, p. 160). The implications for both bibliographic instruction and writing instruction are clear: if the library search process is treated as a separate activity, fit in somewhere between forming a topic and reading and writing about it, we are not preaching what we practice.

INTERCONNECTED PROCESSES IN RESEARCH

The interconnectedness of reading, writing, and thinking processes in research has been the focus of some recent investigations across both disciplines. In composition literature, Kennedy (1985), Klein (1987), Haas and Flower (1988), Kantz (1990), and Brent (1992) have examined how reading and writing are necessarily recursive parts of the research process, not stages performed separately before and after research. Ray McInnis and Dal Symes (1991) have included reading and writing as basic functions that should be integrated into bibliographic instruction frameworks and argue that understanding scholarship as discourse is necessary for understanding the research process. Researchers in both fields are finding that reading, writing, and research are recursive and mutually sustaining processes, and further are demonstrating that our efforts at teaching research in the writing classroom and in the library are inevitably connected, whether we are working together deliberately or not.

Collaborating with composition researchers offers bibliographic instruction practitioners an opportunity to rethink research instruction, integrating the search aspect with the knowledge-generating and rhetorical dimensions of reading and writing. The insights of librarians into the search process could, in turn, help build a more accurate model of the research writing process than the current one. The writing-across-the-curriculum movement, which places writing in the context of knowledge generation in the disciplines, may be a particularly valuable site for initiating a dialogue on the nature of student research, without privileging either the writing process or the search process, but rather placing both within knowledge communities. To carry on this dialogue, we will need to work on communication and collaboration, paying particular attention to the following:

• We need to trust one another and have a sense of shared ownership. Librarians have traditionally tried to retain control of instruction on library use. They have been known to be irritated if teachers take charge of that function, bringing students into the library themselves to show them around, and convinced they will get it all wrong. Perhaps we should pay attention to one factor that is critical to the success of writing-across-the-curriculum programs—ownership must be shared if it is to work at all (McLeod and Soven, 1992). Librarians need to respect the expertise of classroom teachers in the disciplines and make use of it as they broaden the teaching of research skills to embrace reading and writing as well as searching. In turn, writing instructors will have to be convinced that librarians' expertise and concerns play a part in a shared enterprise if they are to work together.

• We need to articulate our goals and purposes together. Currently our goals tend to focus on our own piece of the puzzle—librarians strive to make students more information literate, and composition teachers focus on improving students' writing skills. If we can come together through the auspices of a writing-across-the-curriculum program, we may be able to combine these emphases with a concern for disciplinary knowledge in each field, thus enriching our conception of what we are trying to accomplish.

• We need to share our insights, both practical and theoretical. We can help one another both be better teachers, by sharing ideas for assignments and exercises and combining our resources for better classroom teaching. We can also enrich our research lives by working on common theoretical problems, bringing to them our different capabilities. There are many parallel inquiries underway in the fields of bibliographic instruction and writing instruction. We need to become familiar enough with one another's knowledge communities that we can fruitfully collaborate on common problems.

• We need to make research experiences a valued part of the entire curriculum. In the recent past, the English department provided writing instruction as a service to other departments; that service could be dispensed in the first year, after which students were expected to write adequately in every academic situation. Librarians, in turn, took on the job of teaching information-retrieval skills, with which students were increasingly unfamiliar. Beyond a freshman-year research assignment and the occasional fifty-minute bibliographic instruction session, students were expected to manage on their own. Too often these skills have become generic and divorced from the rhetorical and epistemic frameworks of the disciplines, resulting in the debasing of undergraduate research into a nonform of research. Writing-across-the-curriculum places the site of writing instruction in the disciplines, which is also where research skills belong. As writing is reclaimed as a shared responsibility, so should research.

If we can pull it off, if we can reimagine the role and the locus of student research in the undergraduate curriculum, if we can collaborate with teachers committed to active student learning across the disciplines, if we can connect, we will have accomplished a great deal, and bibliographic instruction may never be the same.

NOTE

1. This work, conducted by the author, involved a comparison of attitudes and assumptions about student research, first by looking at the literatures of both BI and composition, then by collecting extensive narrative responses to a few questions from a small number of innovative practitioners in the fields, and finally by using those responses to generate a survey sent out to a random population of practitioners in both fields working in colleges of all sizes and types. Two hundred and sixteen surveys were sent out, and 97 useable ones returned. These were compared using a chi-square test to see if there were significant differences in responses. The project was funded by a research scholarship and creativity grant from Gustavus Adolphus College. The author is grateful to those who participated in the study, particularly those who took the time to compose thoughtful and thorough responses to rather difficult questions.

REFERENCES

American Library Association. (1992, Fall). Association of College and Research Libraries. Continuing education needs and interests survey. *ACRL Bibliographic Instruction Section Newsletter, 9*(2), 5.

Arms, G. (1943, October). The research paper. *College English, 5,* 19–25.

Arp, L. (1990, Fall). Vital connections: Composition and bibliographic instruction theory in the LRC. *New Directions for Community Colleges, 71,* 13–22.

Bader, A. L. (1936, October). Independent thinking and the "long paper." *English Journal, 25,* 667–672.

Barclay, D. A. (1992). Understanding the freshman writer: The pedagogy of composition and its relevance to bibliographic instruction. In *Proceedings of the Sixth National Conference of the Association of College and Research Libraries* (pp. 133–135). Chicago: Association of College and Research Libraries.

Bartholomae, D. (1986). Inventing the university. *Journal of Basic Writing, 5,* 4–23.

Bazerman, C. (1988). *Shaping written knowledge: Genre and activity of the experimental article in science.* Madison: University of Wisconsin.

Beck, J. (1981). *Upgrading the research paper toward "real writing" by using prewriting ploys, critical probe-questions, and audience-relating* (Report No. CS207-235). Whitewater: University of Wisconsin, English Dept. (ERIC Document Reproduction Service No. ED 222 907)

Bereiter, C., & Scardamalia, M. (1987). *The psychology of written communication.* Hillsdale, NJ: L. Erlbaum.

Berlin, J. A. (1987). *Rhetoric and reality: Writing instruction in American colleges, 1900–1985.* Carbondale: Southern Illinois University Press.

Bizzell, P. (1982). Cognition, convention, and certainty: What we need to know about writing. *PRE/TEXT, 3,* 213–243.

Bizzell, P. (1986). Foundationalism and anti-foundationalism in composition studies. *PRE/TEXT, 7,* 37–56.

Bizzell, P., & Herzberg, B. (1987, March). Research as a social act. *The Clearing House, 60,* 303–306.

Bolner, M. S., Dantin, D. B., & Murray, R. C. (1991). *Library research skills handbook.* Dubuque: Kendall/Hunt.

Brandt, D. (1992, July). The cognitive as the social: An ethnomethodological approach to writing process research. *Written Communication, 9,* 315–355.

Brent, D. (1992). *Reading as rhetorical invention: Knowledge, persuasion, and the teaching of research-based writing.* Urbana, IL: National Council of Teachers of English.

Bruffee, K. (1984). Collaborative learning and the ''conversation of mankind.'' *College English, 46*(7), 635–652.

Bullock, R., & Trimbur, J. (Eds.). (1991). *The politics of writing instruction: Postsecondary.* Portsmouth, NH: Boynton/Cook.

Cameron, D. B. (1986). Assigning the library. *College English Forum, 16,* 5–7.

CCCC Bibliography of composition and rhetoric. (1990). Carbondale, IL: Southern Illinois University.

Chappell, V. (1990, March). *Freshmen in the library: Making meaning out of diverse discourse communities* (Report No. CS212-410). Milwaukee, WI: Marquette University, Dept. of English. (ERIC Document Reproduction Service No. ED 321 260)

Crowley, S. (1987). Derida, deconstruction, and our scene of teaching. *PRE/TEXT, 8,* 169–183.

Crowley, S. (1990). *The methodical memory: Invention in current-traditional rhetoric.* Carbondale: Southern Illinois University Press.

Dickerson, M. J. (1989, March). *The implications of collaborative writing: A dialogue* (Report No. CS311-756). Burlington: University of Vermont. (ERIC Document Reproduction Service No. ED 305 644)

Dillon, G. L. (1991). *Contending rhetorics: Writing in academic disciplines.* Bloomington: Indiana University Press.

Elbow, P. (1973). *Writing without teachers.* New York: Oxford University Press.

Elbow, P. (1991, February). Reflections on academic discourse: How it relates to freshmen and colleagues. *College English, 53,* 135–155.

Emig, J. (1971). *The composing processes of twelfth graders.* Urbana, IL: National Council of Teachers of English.

Faigley, L. (1986). Competing theories of process: A critique and a proposal. *College English, 48,* 527–542.

Fink, D. (1989). *Process and politics in library research: A model for course design.* Chicago: American Library Association.

Fish, S. (1980). *Is there a text in this class?* Cambridge, MA: Harvard University Press.

Fister, B. (1990, Summer). Teaching research as a social act: Collaborative learning and the library. *RQ, 29,* 505–509.

Fister, B. (1992a). Common ground: The composition/bibliographic instruction connection. In *Proceedings of the Sixth National Conference of the Association of College and Research Libraries* (pp. 154–158). Chicago: Association of College and Research Libraries.

Fister, B. (1992b). The research processes of undergraduate students. *Journal of Academic Librarianship, 18(3),* 161–169.

Flower, L., & Hayes, J. R. (1981, December). A cognitive process theory of writing. *College Composition and Communication, 32,* 365–387.

Flower, L. Stein, V., Ackerman, J., Kantz, M. J., McCormick, K., & Peck, W. C. (1990). *Reading-to-write: Exploring a cognitive and social process.* New York and Oxford: Oxford University Press.

Ford, J. E., & Perry, D. R. (1982, December). Research paper instruction in the undergraduate writing program. *College English, 44,* 825–831.

Freire, P. (1970). *Pedagogy of the oppressed.* New York: Herder and Herder.

Haas, C., & Flower, L. (1988, May). Rhetorical reading strategies and the construction of meaning. *College Composition and Communication, 39,* 167–184.

Hairston, M. (1982, February). The winds of change: Thomas Kuhn and the revolution in the teaching of writing. *College Composition and Communication, 33,* 76–88.

Heath, S. B. (1983). *Ways with words: Language, life, and work in communities and classrooms.* New York: Cambridge University Press.

Kantz, M. (1990, January). Helping students use textual sources persuasively. *College English, 52,* 74–91.

Kennedy, M. L. (1985, October). The composing process of college students writing from sources. *Written Communication, 2,* 434–456.

Klein, M. (1987, Spring/Summer). What is it we do when we write articles like this one—and how can we get students to join us? *The Writing Instructor, 6,* 151–161.

Kuhlthau, C. (1988, Winter). Developing a model of the library search process: Cognitive and affective aspects. *RQ, 28,* 232–242.

Kuhn, T. (1970). *The structure of scientific revolutions* (2nd edition). Chicago: University of Chicago Press.

Larson, R. (1982, December). The "research paper" in the writing course: A non-form of writing. *College English, 44(8),* 811–816.

McDonald, J. C. (1990, April). *The research paper and postmodernist pedagogy.* Paper presented at the Annual Meeting of the College English Association, Buffalo, NY. (ERIC Document Reproduction Service No. ED 322 536)

Macrorie, K. (1970). *Telling writing.* Upper Montclair, NJ: Boynton/Cook.

Macrorie, K. (1988). *The I-search paper.* Portsmouth, NH: Boynton/Cook.

McCaslin, D. (1923, November). The library and the department of English. *English Journal, 12,* 591–598.

McInnis, R. G., & Symes, D. S. (1991, Winter). Running backwards from the finish line: A new concept for bibliographic instruction. *Library Trends, 39,* 223–237.

McLeod, S. H., & Soven, M. (Eds.) (1992). *Writing across the curriculum: A guide to developing programs.* Newbury Park, CA: Sage.

Mellon, C. A. (1984, November). Process not product in course-integrated instruction:

A generic model of library research. *College and Research Libraries, 45,* 471–478.

Mellon, C. A. (1986, March). Library anxiety: A grounded theory and its development. *College and Research Libraries, 47,* 160–165.

Meyers, Greg. (1990). *Writing Biology.* Madison: University of Wisconsin.

Miller, S. (1991). *Textual carnivals: The politics of composition.* Carbondale: Southern Illinois University Press.

Murphy, J. (Ed.). (1990). *A short history of writing instruction from ancient Greece to twentieth century America.* Davis, CA: Hermagoras.

Nelson, J., & Hayes, J. R. (1988, August). *How the writing context shapes college students' strategies for writing from sources.* Berkely, CA: University of California, and Pittsburgh, PA: Carnegie Mellon, Center for the Study of Writing. (ERIC Document Reproduction Service No. ED 297 374)

North, S. (1987). *The making of knowledge in composition: Portrait of an emerging field.* Upper Montclair, NJ: Boynton/Cook.

Quantic, D. D. (1981, June). *Developing a cooperative library skills program* (Report No. EA 013 915). Wichita, KS: Wichita State University, Dept. of English. (ERIC Document Reproduction Service No. ED 206 001)

Reich, P. (1986, Fall). Choosing a topic in a research-methods-oriented instructional program. *Research Strategies, 4,* 185–189.

Rorty, R. (1979). *Philosophy and the mirror of nature.* Princeton: Princeton University Press.

Russell, D. R. (1991). *Writing in the academic disciplines, 1870–1990: A curricular history.* Carbondale: Southern Illinois University Press.

Sheridan, J. (1992). WAC and libraries: A look at the literature. *Journal of Academic Librarianship, 18(2),* 90–94.

Stotsky, S. (1991). On developing independent thinking and responsible writing: What we can learn from studies of the research process. In S. Stotsky (Ed.), *Connecting civic education and language education: The contemporary challenge* (pp. 99–128). New York and London: Teachers College Press.

Trzyna, T. (1983, May). Approaches to research writing: A review of handbooks with some suggestions. *College Composition and Communication, 34,* 202–207.

Warmkessel, M. M. (1992). Assessing the need for bibliographic instruction in honors sections of freshman composition. In *Proceedings of the Sixth National Conference of the Association of College and Research Libraries* (pp. 175–178). Chicago: Association of College and Research Libraries.

Part II

Writing-Across-the-Curriculum: Making the Library Connection

Chapter 4

Research Skills Across the Curriculum: Connections with Writing-Across-the-Curriculum

Craig Gibson

Recent changes in writing instruction in American public schools, colleges, and universities are influencing the very way in which education is conceived. A paradigm shift from a "transmission model" of education to a student-centered, constructivist model is much in evidence at many institutions. Traditional assumptions about learning, teaching, and knowledge are being challenged by contemporary writing instruction through its influence across traditional academic structures. The movement known as writing-across-the-curriculum, according to its advocates, offers the potential to transform education—to make all students active learners, to renew faculty commitment to teaching, and to create communities of learners, including both students and faculty, dedicated to the pursuit of knowledge and lifelong learning skills across the disciplines. Though hardly an innovation in the 1990s, writing-across-the-curriculum has shown sustained growth and continues to face new challenges in implementation, funding, and assessment (McLeod, 1992).

Educational innovations occur in cycles. There is much in writing-across-the-curriculum that can be attributed to the influence of John Dewey, or, more accurately, be seen as refinements of Dewey's ideas about practical, active, student-centered learning. Contemporary writing instruction itself owes much to the ideas of Piaget, Bruner, and Vygotsky; the amalgam of theory and practice growing out of the ideas of these thinkers can broadly be termed "constructivist." A central assumption behind contemporary writing instruction is that students actively construct or make meaning, and that the process of making meaning overcomes the traditional problem of much traditional didactic instruction, which sees students as passive learners who receive what Alfred North Whitehead called "inert knowledge." The constructivist perspective is central to the ideas behind writing-across-the-curriculum; the belief that writing is a tool for learning (Emig, 1977), that writing develops critical thinking and problem-solving skills (Flower, 1989), and that process, not product, should be the core of writing instruction (Hairston, 1982) all figure importantly in the extension of writing instruction beyond the confines of English departments to other sectors of academia.

COMPOSITION THEORY AS BACKGROUND

Writing-across-the-curriculum must be considered against the general background of composition theory and practice if we are to understand its radical pedagogical implications, and to make potential connections between it and another important, though often less visible, curricular movement, which involves information problem-solving, information skills, or, more traditionally, library research skills. The emphasis on problem-solving as a primary component of the writing process, long espoused by Linda Flower (1989), is one important connection between writing-as-process and research-as-process. Using an information-processing model of the mind (for which other composition theorists have faulted her), Flower hypothesizes that proficient writers are goal directed, are actively aware of their own thought processes, and employ a repertoire of problem-solving strategies to manage the complexity of writing tasks (p. 190). Thus rhetorical problem-solving is, for Flower, an accurate description of what expert writers actually do. Flower's use of social science research methods, such as think-aloud protocols and protocol analysis, her emphasis on the mental events occurring in the mind of the individual writer, and her neglect of affect or emotion clearly identify her as one of the leading cognitive-process researchers in composition theory. Alternative theorists include Kenneth Bruffee, who asserts that writing proficiently is primarily an act of joining a social conversation (1989, p. 215). This point of view has created the concept of ''discourse communities'' both inside and outside academia—groups that share common assumptions about appropriate conventions and behavior for communicating.

Both the cognitive and social constructionist viewpoints are present in contemporary writing instruction and may, in some cases, find common ground in actual practice. The social constructionist influence is seen most obviously in the use of peer editing groups in writing classes and in the attempts to create miniature ''discourse communities'' out of those same classes. The rhetorical problem-solving model espoused by Flower evinces itself in the teaching of problem analysis. Both perspectives see writing as a struggle to make meaning within a given rhetorical context, though of course the cognitive perspective emphasizes the primacy of the individual student writer in problem solving. Both see the importance of dealing with authentic rhetorical situations and of emphasizing the process of writing rather than the surface correctness of a finished product. Flower's emphasis on problem solving, however, most clearly illuminates connections with the activities student researchers are expected to perform;

problem-solving processes inherently involve the juggling of many facts, knowledge bases, skills, and constraints, whether in composing or researching, and thus can be considered among the most complex tasks students are expected to perform.

CONNECTIONS BETWEEN WRITING SKILLS AND RESEARCH SKILLS

Many reference and instruction librarians will find Flower's perspective and ideas appealing because of the emphasis on "purposeful cognition." Student researchers, like student writers, are assumed to have goals that direct their inquiries and investigations in library-based research. Solving an information problem, like solving a rhetorical problem, involves careful development of goals and strategies. The process approach common to both requires a complex orchestration of knowledge construction, procedural skills, and self-monitoring. Problem solving in information skills has long been promoted by thinkers in bibliographic instruction such as Cerise Oberman (1984); such problem-solving abilities assume even greater importance because of the increasingly complicated and amorphous information environment, replete with multitudinous information sources both inside and outside of libraries. Developing the ability to "think like a searcher"—that is, to become proficient as an information problem-solver (Rubens, 1991, p. 276)—is analogous in many ways to becoming a more mature writer. Both depend on the ability to begin with high-level goals and strategies, to revise and discard strategies when appropriate, and to take control of one's thinking processes.

Just as composition theorists and teachers suggest that the traditional teaching of grammar and manuscript preparation skills is not adequate to help students become proficient writers, many librarians believe that narrowly considered "library skills," traditionally taught as tool-based instruction, are no longer sufficient to develop in students the skills they will need to deal with the information glut of the foreseeable future. In this view, high-level goals and strategies, combined with flexible reasoning, critical thinking, and sound models for understanding the contemporary information environment, will become essential parts of the student researcher's toolkit. Such knowledge and skills find their analogue, again, in contemporary writing instruction. Problem solving in both writing and research is inherently nonalgorithmic and cannot, or should not, be reduced to formulaic rules or search strategies (Fister, 1993). It is not a narrow set of rote skills, but a repertoire of interrelated thinking processes. Both writing and information seeking involve "ill-structured" rather than "well-structured" problems because they constrain the student to plan and orchestrate goals, strategies, and procedures without knowing guaranteed solutions in advance. If Flower's "problem analysis," involving clarification of goals, central issues, audience, and rhetorical context, is one model of problem solving for student writers, then "question analysis" and search-strategy formulation, as delineated

by Oberman, Beaubien, Hogan, and others in the bibliographic instruction literature (Oberman, 1984; Beaubien, Hogan & George, 1982), is an analogous
problem-solving model. Both models assume that problem solving is a flexible,
goal-directed, strategizing process that depends on knowledge and conscious
control of one's own thinking.

Another central concern for both writing instructors and instruction librarians
is critical thinking. For writing instructors, thinking and writing are indivisible:
the latter is a concrete representation of the former. Moreover, in the view of
composition theorists, it is not just "thinking," but critical thinking, that writing
develops. Critical thinking is defined in this perspective as higher-order thinking,
which involves the skills of analyzing, synthesizing, evaluating, and revising.
One noted expert on critical thinking, Richard Paul, advocates writing as one
of the primary means for developing critical thinking in students (1993, p. 312).
He also writes of the "perfections of thought," attributes such as clarity, precision, specificity, relevance, depth, and significance (p. 421). By any other
names, these are qualities of mature writing as well. Critical thinking is thus a
special kind of thinking, a rigorously self-aware, higher-order thinking that asks
questions, seeks proofs, constructs meaning, finds patterns, discovers knowledge,
and holds itself to demanding standards of fairness and accuracy. That writing
can be a process for helping students develop some of these critical thinking
skills and attributes, which hardly come naturally, is not a new idea; it is one
of the basic claims for writing instruction as currently practiced and is one of
the major emphases of the writing-across-the-curriculum movement.

Although critical thinking skills are now seen by many reference and instruction librarians as crucial to the research process (Oberman, 1991), such skills
have not always figured prominently in traditional library skills programs. Sonia
Bodi was one of the first to discuss the connections between critical thinking
and the research process (Bodi, 1988). The fundamental premise that the research process, like writing, is also a thinking process allows us to consider
research as more than a set of rote skills. Critical thinking entails posing good
questions, developing and modifying search strategies, and evaluating arguments
in sources by using certain criteria such as currency, authors' credentials, and
the level of authority of a publication. Jacobson (1992) has discussed the problems facing librarians who must teach an ever-larger array of information retrieval tools, such as CD-ROMs, to naive, unquestioning students. Finding
contexts for tools and relating them to appropriate information-seeking strategies
will require critical-thinking skills in greater measure than in the past. Even
larger issues loom in the electronic information deluge facing students now,
with too much information available through the Internet, as well as through
more traditional sources. Developing the ability to self-regulate, to use skepti-
cism about the ostensible infallibility of information appearing on computer
screens and printouts, and to find standards for judging appropriateness and
relevance of information wrenched from context by retrievals in "cyberspace"
are major, difficult challenges for student researchers (indeed, for more mature

researchers) in the amorphous and always complex electronic information environment. Hence Paul's (1993) standards for excellence in critical thinking—fairness, accuracy, completeness, self-awareness, self-questioning, and integrity—apply to the research process in ways we have not often considered. In this rapidly changing environment, there can be no substitute for the critically evaluating mind, just as there can be no substitute for internalized critical-thinking standards developed by the writing process. Paul's ideas about critical thinking apply equally well to writing and researching; they are likely to become even more important in dealing with such issues as the ethics of information use, the integrity of unverifiable data sources, and the management of information overload.

Hence the shared intellectual roots of current composition theory and current information skills theory offer much common ground for librarians and writing teachers. Fister has offered a thorough schematic of commonalities, which, in addition to the concern with process, problem solving, and critical thinking, also include the empowerment of the student as both writer and researcher and the concern with social context (discourse communities) in both writing and research (1992). Librarians seeking to establish dialogue with writing teachers at any level will want to keep these intellectual roots in mind when planning library involvement in programs.

CHALLENGES IN DEVELOPING A RESEARCH PROCESS PERSPECTIVE

Librarians who wish to find common ground with writing teachers and who begin exploring linkages with writing-across-the-curriculum programs will do well, politically, to focus on the commonalities in the process approach shared by both librarians and writing faculty. Some conceptual ambiguities and practical difficulties may emerge, however, in curriculum committee meetings and other forums, with librarians, writing teachers, and faculty from various disciplines engaged in discussions about writing and research instruction. Representatives of these groups often share some of the same assumptions, but librarians may learn that writing teachers, though frequently their firmest allies, often possess different ideas about "library skills" and "the research process." These different ideas may evince themselves even more clearly in discussions with faculty in the disciplines.

Writing teachers and faculty in the disciplines may hold a reductive notion of "library skills." Writing teachers sometimes assume that learning to use the library is only a matter of hands-on practice, emphasizing narrow procedural skills, with on-line catalogs, CD-ROMs, and other tools. Although hands-on work with tools is essential for students to gain confidence with information systems, an overemphasis on this particular kind of skill, removed from a larger rhetorical or critical-thinking context, shortchanges real learning of the type many librarians have been espousing in recent years. As LaBaugh observes, these skills are analogous to rote grammar drills—certainly not the primary type of learning that writing teachers want students to acquire in "making meaning" (1992, p. 35). If it is true that students learn to write by writing, it does not necessarily follow that they learn to use the library (much less the larger information landscape) by simply "using the library" in a rote manner. Hands-on activities in research skills classes, taught by librarians, should emphasize critical thinking, question analysis, search-strategy development, evaluation of sources, and other, more fundamental issues. Librarians should remember the critical-thinking, problem-solving approach and insist on using this approach in teaching effective library use to students, who can all too easily become fixated on procedural skills, whether keyboard skills on a CD-ROM terminal or rules for manuscript preparation in a writing workshop.

Faculty in the disciplines may not as often reduce "library skills" to this particular notion of narrow procedures, but will often, as librarians know, possess idiosyncratic ideas about learning to use the library. The time-honored "library tour" as a primary vehicle for learning to do research is one such example. The equally time-honored "scavenger hunt" exercise is another. Many faculty in the disciplines assign artificial exercises that fail to connect students with understanding the information structure in a particular discipline, or with the larger issues discussed in a discipline. In other cases, faculty send students to the library with assignments requiring disciplinary knowledge that the students do not possess (and must possess to complete the assignment). Librarians who work with faculty in the disciplines will want to develop a repertoire of strategies for changing some of these practices, including offering workshops, developing model assignments, asserting themselves on curriculum committees, and studying the research habits of students and faculty alike so that they can make more informed judgments about the need for instructional intervention. The central problem remains that many faculty in the disciplines do not see learning information skills as a valuable activity in its own right, with an important place within, or across, the curriculum. The traditional faculty view that "library skills" can be learned by osmosis, haphazardly, experientially, and without much time or attention given to the real *teaching and learning* of such skills, much less to a campus-wide program of development for them, is the instruction librarian's greatest problem—and opportunity.

Another likely barrier to understanding is that writing teachers and faculty in the disciplines may differ from librarians in their ideas about the "research process." Because many writing teachers are now influenced by social constructionist ideas, which see knowledge as socially constructed, librarians at the reference desk should be prepared to see much more student collaboration and many more group assignments. Writing teachers believe that the benefits that accrue from this kind of activity are manifold: students gain from peer teaching/ learning, show greater motivation, and, most important, acquire a sense of how knowledge grows through collaboration, which mirrors the process seasoned scholars and researchers in many fields employ. Librarians should explore and honor the advantages of collaborative learning whenever possible. What this idea about the research process suggests, however, is that the social context for research, for writing teachers, may assume greater importance than the cognitive goals librarians often associate with search-strategy formulation, data-base selection, and information evaluation and management. Librarians will need to articulate the need for cognitive goals, similar to those discussed by Flower and captured well in her phrase "purposeful cognition" (1989, p. 205), to complement the social constructionist practices many writing teachers now employ in teaching students the research process.

The concept of research process itself is the main problem arising in misunderstandings between librarians, writing teachers, and faculty in the disciplines. Investigations into the literature of composition theory and bibliographic instruction suggest some of the ambiguities involved. If librarians are to make an effective case for research-skills-across-the-curriculum, these ambiguities need to be acknowledged and clarified. When the term research process is used by composition theorists in an undergraduate writing context, it can take on a variety of colorations. Susan McDonald, for example, has discussed the traditional view of the research process as learning a set of rote skills, which students must suffer through in developing "objective" writing as opposed to "subjective" reliance on the voices in their heads (1984, pp. 39–40). She points out the commonalities between writing and researching, chiefly the hierarchical processing involved in both, whether refining a thesis statement or searching for narrower or broader subject headings when performing a catalog search. Carmen Schmersahl (1987) sees writing and researching as an intertwined set of thinking processes, with the research process largely subordinate to the writing process, or as just another occasion for rhetorical invention. Other voices in the field of language theory, however, offer a different perspective. Sandra Stotsky, for example, hypothesizes that the research process should be considered distinct from the composing process. She cites Carol Kuhlthau's ethnographic studies of college-bound high school seniors to show that the "search process" itself is a crucial point for thinking and developing a thesis or controlling idea for a research paper (Stotsky, 1991, pp. 107, 112–113). Stotsky believes that insufficient attention has been given to the research process itself, as opposed to the writing process. She even suggests that, for purposes of studying the complexities of writing and research, it may be most useful to subsume both writing and reading within a larger, global research process. These are just some of the variations on the idea of research process among composition and language theorists; librarians may find others at their own institutions.

Among faculty in the disciplines, the notion of research process gets very complicated. Faculty in the disciplines are trained in various schools of thought and in differing research methodologies. Many faculty will mean "doing a literature review" within their field when they refer to the research process. Others will almost certainly mean conducting primary, as opposed to secondary, research: the sociologist will design surveys; the psychologist will design experiments; the biologist will conduct field trips and write reports; and the historian will examine artifacts and documents. The range of possible elements and processes for research in the disciplines is limited only by the assumptions about knowledge and how it is developed in those disciplines. Because they are familiar with the literatures of those disciplines and have access to those literatures, librarians are well suited to introduce students to secondary research, which is one means of helping students understand the assumptions and values of a discipline. The well-known habit of faculty of ignoring or neglecting secondary or tertiary research tools within their own fields (Stoan, 1991) suggests that librarians have a role as advocates for student research in the disciplines. If faculty rely on their local colleagues, a few favorite journals or private monograph collections, and the "invisible college" for crucial information in their field, it is small wonder that they do not always design effective student research assignments.

For librarians to become advocates of improved student research in the disciplines, they would do well to work with the ACRL (Association of College and Research Libraries) Model Statement of Objectives for Academic Bibliographic Instruction. This planning document offers great flexibility for librarians to design programs that support WAC programs because one of its central objectives deals with disciplinary expertise and the idea that students should learn how information is communicated among experts—scholars and researchers within the disciplines. The model statement provides a framework for librarians to think about relationships between their ideas about the research process, search strategies, and the electronic information environment and the potential for curricular planning within a particular institution when a WAC program is initiated.

RESEARCH SKILLS AND THE WAC MOVEMENT

When librarians answer for themselves some of the key questions about library skills, research process, and similar ambiguous terms commonly used in academia, they will be in a better position to articulate the need for research skills programs that support and complement writing-across-the-curriculum programs. Librarians must first understand the assumptions of composition teachers; these two groups together, if they understand each other, will be able to make a stronger case to disciplinary faculty for research skills programs throughout appropriate parts of the curriculum. Librarians and composition teachers can form a powerful coalition because they both believe in "process" and share a concern for critical thinking and problem solving; their challenge is to find ways of promoting these ideas and practices with their colleagues in the disciplines.

Librarians will find two central ideas in WAC programs. First is the tenet that writing is a mode of learning, that it develops and extends thought. This is the "expressivist" writing used to promote greater understanding of an issue or topic. Free writing and "journaling" are good examples of writing used as a mode of learning, in the sense in which Emig uses the phrase (1977, p. 85). Second, writing in the disciplines is assumed to possess rhetorical and formal conventions specific to those disciplines. Writing of this type may be classified as "transactional" or informative writing, in the sense in which James Britton uses the term (1975, p. 88). The purposes of these two types of writing are very different; advocates of writing-across-the-curriculum, however, promote both types. Librarians will need to understand the varying purposes of faculty who assign writing requiring use of the library's resources. Expressivist writing assignments may not involve the use of library resources, but those that do will likely have very different goals and assumptions behind them than more transactional or informative writing assignments. In any event, both writing to learn and writing to inform in a disciplinary context pose special challenges for students unfamiliar with the structure of information in disciplines, the specialized vocabularies of those disciplines, and the problems of literature control and "scatter" in those disciplines. Patricia Peroni points out the problem of faculty in the disciplines making unwarranted assumptions about the abilities of students to conduct research in their fields, and argues for intervention by librarians to teach students the structures of literatures and access to those literatures (1981, pp. 6, 8).

Writing in a disciplinary context, as Chris Anson (1988) points out, is actually more than just writing to learn or writing to inform. Writing may have both academic and nonacademic goals, may cross the boundaries of discourse communities, and can be considered from these three perspectives: the *professional* uses of writing in a field; the *curricular* uses of writing in discipline-specific courses; and the *developmental* uses of writing that help initiate students into the conventions, assumptions, and behaviors of a discourse community of scholars or researchers (p. 4). Anson points out the complexity and inconclusiveness of much of the research on writing in academic disciplines and suggests as complicating factors such elements as teacher ideology, institutional context, and the frequent lack of clearly defined conventions for writing in professional discourse communities (pp. 13–15, 19).

Anson's framework for academic writing—the professional, the curricular, and the developmental—suggests a similar framework for librarians and faculty alike to consider in thinking about student research in the disciplines. If faculty rationales for assigning library assignments are not always well conceived, librarians can use Anson's framework for thinking about library assignments according to purpose, understanding those assignments, and offering suggestions to faculty when appropriate.

The *professional* purpose for student research skills is most often prominent in courses such as Business Writing, Technical Writing, or other forms of professional writing, offered by either English departments or business or engineering schools. In such courses, student research linked to writing projects takes on a strongly utilitarian flavor, like the writing itself in those courses. Students may be expected to use both formal (library) and informal (interviews, or phone calls to government agencies, foundations, or grant sources) information sources. Teaching research skills in such courses may be more the province of the course instructor than the librarian because of the highly specific goals for student research in professional or preprofessional writing. However, librarians espousing "information literacy" can often find common ground with instructors in these courses because of a shared practice in identifying and assessing information wherever it is found, inside or outside of libraries.

The *curricular* uses of student research are wide-ranging, but take two different forms according to their course-related context. In general education courses, student research is often seen as a tool to expand and enrich student knowledge of the key issues in a course. The curricular uses of student research, which are similar to the resource-based learning promoted by Breivik (1992), seek to transcend information delivered to students through textbook and lecture. The curricular uses of student research in discipline-specific or major courses, on the other hand, will acquaint students with the forms of academic discourse and, to some extent, with common research practices and norms within a specific discipline. Research skills taught in these courses will ordinarily focus on the structure of the literature in the discipline and major disciplinary research tools, whether in print or computerized, as well as such concepts as publication sequence. Librarians cannot overlook the problem that the research skills students in major courses need may differ sharply from the actual research practices of faculty teaching those courses. This paradox is resolved most readily if student research in major courses is thought of as a cognitive apprenticeship to a discipline. That is, students are trained in, and acculturated into, the norms and conventions of beginning researchers in a discipline, who lack ties into an invisible college and are familiarizing themselves with the cognitive territory of their field as reflected in its information structure and research practices. The apprenticeship model for student researchers asks students to observe how experts in a field proceed with research and uses the secondary literature and bibliographic apparatus to introduce search vocabularies, research practices, and the structure of the literature in the field; this model links well with acculturation into the writing practices of a discourse community. The knowledge gained through an apprenticeship model for student research helps students bridge the gap between the often too-generalized, context-free research skills taught in freshman or general education courses and the highly contextualized research skills and tacit knowledge of the expert researcher in an academic discipline.

The *developmental* use of research skills most closely parallels the emphasis on writing to learn in a discipline-specific context. Researching to learn may be considered the expressivist function of student research within the curriculum. Such research emphasizes personal discovery and exploration of ideas through information resources. Ken Macrorie's famous "I-Search" assignment exemplifies this approach to student research because it asks students to research an issue of personal significance (1988). Researching to learn can, of course, be an ancillary goal of any library use assignment.

Regardless of the purpose behind a library research assignment, students need to place that assignment within a rhetorical context, as Fister (1993) suggests. Assignments that merely call for rote information retrieval do not engage students' minds and help them understand the research process as it is connected to professional, disciplinary, or personal information needs—the sense that information is sought and used in highly contextualized, specific ways by accountants and bankers, pharmacists and veterinarians, microbiologists and art historians, and even undergraduate students.

RESEARCH SKILLS ACROSS THE CURRICULUM: PROGRAMMATIC, SUPPORT, AND POLITICAL ISSUES

With these conceptual underpinnings in mind, librarians can begin to plan research skills programs that complement WAC programs. Planning such programs will necessarily involve careful study of how the WAC program on one's own campus has evolved—its traditions, successes, problems, structure, administrative support, and links with other curricular initiatives.

Programmatic Issues

WAC programs have varying structures and models. Fulwiler and Young's casebook, *Programs That Work: Models and Methods for Writing Across the Curriculum* (1990), offers descriptions of widely varying programs at institutions large and small, public and private. Some familiar curricular/programmatic elements for WAC programs include a foundation writing course offered by the English department to introduce students to academic writing, followed later by writing-intensive courses or seminars at the upper-division level. Additional requirements may include writing proficiency exams, writing portfolios, and disciplinary writing courses.

Librarians can learn valuable lessons from the WAC movement and borrow some practices from WAC programs in developing research skills programs. Key questions librarians should ask include the following:

• How much library use is appropriate in introductory (freshman) writing courses and other general education courses? Many freshman writing courses contain a library assignment of some type. Just as this type of course serves to introduce first-year students to forms of academic writing, it can also introduce them to research skills that transcend the requirements of one or two specific assignments given in the course. The real question for research skills at this level, however, may well be how many library experiences should be integrated into the curriculum within freshman course requirements overall. Librarians should give serious attention to the problem of perceived duplication of library use assignments among first- and second-year students. It is possible that requiring too much library use too early in students' academic careers will place unreasonable demands on both the students and the library. Peroni believes that ''library instruction should be provided only for those parts of a writing curriculum which require research.'' (1981, p. 9)

• Should a separate research skills course be offered for credit? The advantages of such a course involve giving serious, sustained attention to developing student research skills, skills that are often haphazardly developed through isolated assignments and one-shot library instruction classes. The disadvantage is that a separate course, unconnected to other parts of the curriculum, will suffer politically and will have little organic relation to the professional, curricular, and developmental rationales for student research discussed earlier. One possible model for combining disciplinary instruction, writing instruction, and research skills is the integrated studies model of Evergreen State College, described by Joan Graham (1984). This model coordinates disciplinary instruction and "skill" instruction across the curriculum so that students enrolled in biology, history, or anthropology also take writing courses designed to introduce students to writing in those fields. Linking a separate research skills course in the integrated studies model is an obvious possibility.

• What kinds of links should be developed between the library and upper-division writing courses, especially writing-intensive courses or disciplinary writing seminars? Librarians should consider proposing library research components in courses of this type because of the opportunity to build on more basic research skills taught in freshman writing courses and other lower-division courses. Some upper-division courses could be designated research intensive within a given program or academic major, to parallel the writing-intensive model. Research-intensive courses can be the same as writing-intensive courses, or be linked with them in terms of major requirements for students in an academic program.

• How should a research skills program be assessed? Mary George has pointed out the limited, anecdotal nature of much of the evaluation of bibliographic instruction programs. She calls for longitudinal studies that give us a clearer picture, over time, of the effectiveness of instruction programs offered by libraries (1990). Librarians may want to borrow an idea from the WAC movement and ask for campus-wide assessment of students' research abilities through a "research portfolio," similar to a "writing portfolio" (the two could contain many of the same student papers and research projects). These portfolios would give a richer, more complete picture of student research abilities, over time, than would standardized tests.

Support Issues

Librarians should ask the following questions about support issues:

• How can libraries support WAC programs in times of declining budgets and increasing costs of materials? The impact of WAC on library collections is not well understood, though we can assume much greater use of collections if a particular WAC program emphasizes use of information resources. Tying collection development to a library's instruction program, as Lori Arp and Jay Schafer (1992) have shown, is an important management technique in a time of declining resources.

• What kinds of teaching technologies are important to support research skills instruction and its links to WAC programs? Librarians should explore the concept of "collaborative computing" because of the emphasis on collaborative learning in contemporary writing instruction at all levels; they should also investigate the advantages of computer-assisted instruction to support those parts of a research skills program that have traditionally had expensive personnel costs.

- What kinds of reference training and support are necessary to support WAC programs? Are alternative reference models appropriate to help cope with large increases in library use across the curriculum? Peer tutoring in basic research skills by students, term paper clinics, and a "tiered" approach to reference service may be appropriate to deal with the highly differentiated information needs shown by students in institutions with intensive library use resulting from WAC programs.

Political Issues

Key questions librarians should ask about political issues include the following:

- What will be the role of librarians on curriculum committees, including planning committees for implementing WAC programs? This opportunity for librarians cannot be overemphasized because of the campus visibility involved and the influence the library will gain in affecting other curricular initiatives.
- What can librarians do to transform isolated successes with their instruction programs into campus-wide acceptance? Holding faculty workshops over a period of years, finding allies in key departments across the campus, persuading key administrators of the importance of the library's instruction program, and showing a willingness to link assessment of the program with larger campus-wide assessment programs, will do much to institutionalize the library's role in curricular reform movements such as WAC. Faculty must, of course, be persuaded of the program's importance and must feel some ownership of it, even if they are not directly involved in the instruction itself.

SUSTAINING RESEARCH SKILLS PROGRAMS

Instruction programs offered by libraries will survive and prosper to the extent that they support their institution's mission and goals, including the improvement of student writing at all levels and in all disciplines. Librarians, composition teachers, and disciplinary faculty all share common concerns about improving student learning, even if their assumptions about appropriate methods and strategies for teaching and learning may differ. The role of librarians in this age of information overload cannot be ignored. In this environment, the ability to think critically and to manage information appropriately, to make informed choices about one's professional, curricular, and personal information needs, poses enormous challenges even for the most motivated and diligent student. With their ability to see the entire curriculum from a unique interdisciplinary perspective, librarians can offer special advantages to their institutions in planning the curricula for all the discourse communities across the curriculum.

REFERENCES

Anson, C. M. (1988). Toward a multidimensional model of writing in the academic disciplines. In D. A. Jolliffe (Ed.), *Advances in writing research, Vol. 2: Writing in academic disciplines* (pp. 1–33). Norwood, NJ: Ablex Publishing.

Arp, L. & Schafer, J. (1992). Connecting bibliographic instruction and collection development: A management plan. *RQ, 31,* 398–406.

Beaubien, A. K., Hogan, S. A., & George, M. W. (1982). *Learning the library: Concepts and methods for effective bibliographic instruction.* New York: R. R. Bowker.

Bodi, S. (1988). Critical thinking and bibliographic instruction: The relationship. *Journal of Academic Librarianship, 14,* 150–154.

Breivik, P. S. (1992). Education for the information age. In M. Kramer (Series Ed.) & D. W. Farmer (Vol. Ed.), *Information literacy; Developing students as independent learners* (pp. 5–13). San Francisco: Jossey-Bass.

Britton, J. (Ed.). (1975). *The development of writing abilities.* London: Macmillan.

Bruffee, K. A. (1989). Thinking and writing as social acts. In E. P. Maimon, B. F. Nodine, & F. W. O'Connor (Eds.), *Thinking, reasoning, and writing* (pp. 213–222). New York: Longman.

Emig, J. (1977). Writing as a mode of learning. *College Composition and Communication, 28,* 122–128.

Fister, B. (1992). Common ground: The composition/bibliographic instruction connection. In *Proceedings of the Association of College and Research Libraries Sixth National Conference* (pp. 154–158). Chicago: American Library Association.

Fister, B. (1993). Teaching the rhetorical dimensions of research. *Research Strategies, 11(4),* 211–219.

Flower, L. (1989). Taking thought: The role of conscious processing in the making of meaning. In E. P. Maimon, B. F. Nodine, & F. W. O'Connor (Eds.), *Thinking, reasoning, and writing* (pp. 185–212). New York: Longman.

Fulwiler, T., & Young, A. (Eds). (1989). *Programs that work: Models and methods for writing across the curriculum.* Portsmouth, NH: Boynton/Cook.

George, M. W. (1990). Instructional services. In M. J. Lynch & A. Young (Eds.), *Academic libraries: Research perspectives* (pp. 106–142). Chicago: American Library Association.

Graham, J. (1984). What works: The problems and rewards of cross-curriculum writing programs. *Current Issues in Higher Education, 3,* 16–26.

Hairston, M. (1982). The winds of change: Thomas Kuhn and the revolution in the teaching of writing. In R. L. Graves (Ed.), *Rhetoric and composition: A sourcebook for teachers and writers* (pp. 3–15). Portsmouth, NH: Boynton/Cook.

Jacobson, T. E. (1992). "All I need is in the computer": Reference and bibliographic instruction in the age of CD-ROMs. In S. G. Blandy (Ed.), *Assessment and accountability in reference work (The Reference Librarian, No. 38)* (pp. 221–228). New York: The Haworth Press.

LaBaugh, R. T. (1992). BI vignettes: BI is a proper noun. *Research Strategies, 10,* 34–39.

McDonald, S. P. (1984). Writing program administrator's view. *Research Strategies, 2,* 33–44.

McLeod, S. H. (1992). Writing across the curriculum: An introduction. In S. H. McLeod & M. Soven (Eds.), *Writing across the curriculum: A guide to developing programs* (pp. 1–11). Newbury Park, CA.: Sage.

Macrorie, K. (1988). *The I-search paper,* Portsmouth, NH: Boynton/Cook.

Oberman, C. (1984). Patterns for research. In T. G. Kirk (Ed.), *Increasing the teaching role of academic libraries* (pp. 35–44). San Francisco: Jossey-Bass.

Oberman, C. (1991). Avoiding the cereal syndrome, or critical thinking in the electronic environment. *Library Trends, 39,* 189–202.

Paul, R. (1993). *Critical thinking: How to prepare students for a rapidly changing world.* Santa Rosa, CA.: Foundation for Critical Thinking.

Peroni, P. A. (1981, July). *The second kind of knowledge: The role of library instruction in writing across the curriculum.* Paper presented at the Meeting of the National Endowment for the Humanities/Beaver College Summer Institute for Writing in the Humanities, Glenside, PA. (ERIC Document Reproduction Service No. ED 217 487)

Rubens, D. (1991). Formulation rules for posing good subject questions: Empowerment for the end-user. *Library Trends, 39,* 271–298.

Schmersahl, C. (1987). Teaching library research: Process, not product. *Journal of Teaching Writing, 6,* 231–238.

Stoan, S. (1991). Research and information retrieval among academic researchers: Implications for library instruction. *Library Trends, 39,* 238–257.

Stotsky, S. (1991). On developing independent thinking and responsible writing: What we can learn from studies of the research process. In S. Stotsky (Ed.) *Connecting civic education and language education* (pp. 99–128). New York: Teachers College Press.

Chapter 5

Making the Library Connection with Process Writing

Jean Sheridan

Librarians have a lot to tell students and writing instructors about process. For years they have been teaching that research is a process composed of many different steps that are often repeated. And they are the first to say that it is not easy, this process, that it is characterized as much by dead ends as by successes, and that it is messy and frustrating. They will also say that it is helpful to tell someone else what you are doing because that person may be able to direct you to other avenues of inquiry. And librarians know that it is never over, that there will always be something else to discover, some unexplored twist, some new avenue of exploration you never thought of. Sometimes you have to go back to where you began and start over.

If this sounds familiar, it is. The characteristics we have been describing are also typical of process writing, a concept of writing instruction folded into writing-across-the-curriculum. The underlying premise of process writing is that the preparation of a written document, far from being a neat linear activity created by an isolated single writer and consisting of a clear beginning, middle, and end, tied up neatly in perfect grammar and edited to a shine, is instead a sometimes untidy, step-by-step endeavor, often shared throughout with others.

Library research and process writing, then, especially when applied to long projects such as term papers, are similar in a number of respects. Indeed, it is possible to match certain steps in both. The comparison cannot be absolute, however, as research stops (at least temporarily) when actual writing, draft sharing, peer review, and editing are undertaken. Therefore, it is more reasonable to look on the research process as complementary to the writing process, similar in some respects, but not all.

As we make this comparison, it is also important to note that library research and the use of library resources in general are important only when appropriate.

While many writing instructors never see the connection or scrupulously avoid it, librarians, on the other hand, must be careful not to err in their own behalf by promoting the use of library resources at unsuitable points in the writing process. The connection should not be contrived lest it lose its credibility.

This chapter is a practical one. Process writing and the process of writing, subtly different, will be discussed at some length, and the discussion will be followed by specific down-to-earth suggestions for introducing library resources at appropriate points. Both generic and discipline-specific assignments will be suggested.

THE COGNITIVE PROCESS OF WRITING

The concept of process writing stems from the recognition of writing as a cognitive skill which enables learning in unique ways. When a person makes a decision to write, said James Britton in 1975, it is not an involuntary but "a deliberate act," an act of selecting from other possibilities. This is his "conception stage," the first part of the process. The second stage, the "incubation stage," is the time for planning, a time when the student writer becomes focused on "the marshalling of significant data, logical ordering, precision, exclusion of the irrelevant, justification of assertion and possibly formal proof" (p. 27). During this stage, the writer is supposed to remove any subjective involvement with the material and the use of expressive writing should be rejected. The third and final stage, when the document is being produced, is the point at which "the writer is essentially alone with his thoughts, his pen, and his paper" (p. 32). There are four primary forces at work throughout—collecting, connecting, writing, and reading—and these are always at some degree of juxtaposition.

Although we can and do speak of "forces at work," writing is not a magic art, even if it has often been revered as such. The voice of the muse, inspiration, and inherited talent are often invoked to explain fluency in writing. In actual fact, professional writers are very deliberate about their process. Having read extensively, they develop a sense of what constitutes good writing and model their own work on the best. They are aware of their own processes and see themselves actively solving problems as they write (Flower, 1989). These writers are aware of the complexities of writing, including the aspects of audience, purpose, and context. They write in response to the needs of the audience, are fully committed to the job, and rewrite and revise extensively.

Although some see the writing process as consisting of hundreds of processes or strategies (Odell, 1980a, p. 49), most agree that competent writers engage in three major processes throughout, namely, planning, translating, and reviewing (Hayes & Flower, 1980). During the planning phase, practiced writers generate ideas by retrieving information from long-term memory, begin to organize it, and set tentative goals. Following that, they begin to "translate" their concepts and information into language. In the reviewing process, their document is re-

read and edited to improve its quality. In this way, these writers come to a fuller understanding of the subject.

Although the process is understood in general terms, it still appears to have an amorphous quality which makes it difficult to define. This, however, has not deterred many theorists and practitioners from attempting to do just that. We will now consider how some "authorities" in the field describe it.

PROCESS WRITING

For Donald Murray (1980), producing a written document is something like giving birth or parenting. During the phase he calls "rehearsing," the writer is totally absorbed in the subject, but remains open to new stimuli. In the drafting phase, a process of separation begins, and the piece of writing assumes its own form and character or identity. This, according to Murray, is the central activity in the process and a time when writing and writer become separated one from the other so that by the time the writer is revising, he or she is interacting with a thing apart. In Murray's words, "the writing has detached itself from my intentions and instructed me" (p. 5). For him, writing is a living organic process.

The stages of the writing process, as Elaine Maimon (1988) sees them, are these: (1) prewriting, or readiness, a time when many discovery processes, such as brainstorming, reading, and imagining, along with exercises such as mapping, outlining, and journal writing are encouraged; (2) drafting, during which students should have in mind a specific purpose and audience; (3) sharing, when the writer, seeking distance, reads aloud to peers, when listeners respond, and when conferring with a teacher is fruitful; (4) revising, when the writer works toward clearer meaning and brings in supporting ideas; (5) editing, when attention is paid to spelling, syntax, punctuation, and structure, with help from thesaurusi, dictionaries, style manuals, and other reference materials. For Maimon, a sixth step, publishing one's written work, is an essential component in the process, but one not often attended to. She insists that there are many opportunities for student writers—school newspapers and magazines, compilations of class writings, and today, even e-mail—to share their work beyond the classroom. Writing a statement of acknowledgment can also be a very creative exercise for student writers.

Some of the stages in Maimon's (1988) model—prewriting, drafting, sharing, revising, editing, and publishing—connect well to the library, especially prewriting, which demands the acquisition of sufficient content material. The revision stage often requires finding additional material to support a thesis.

In the initial stages, topic selection can be assisted through a perusal of subject headings in indexes and CD-ROM data bases, the *Library of Congress Subject Heading List,* the indexes and tables of contents of books, and the use of general and subject encyclopedias and other reference sources. It is also the time when the writer chooses an audience and decides on the appropriate tone and language or vocabulary for the intended audience. A study of the many varieties of books and periodical literature unquestionably facilitates these decisions.

For S. N. Tchudi (1986), the stages of the writing process are: (1) preparation to write, (2) organizing to write, (3) writing, (4) revising, (5) proofreading, and (6) presenting (p. 35). Each phase has its own attendant energy level. The preparation phase, for instance, should not be a passive experience for the teacher, but rather a time to teach actively through the use of short practical writings (p. 26). During this time students should be encouraged to freewrite about the topic, taking into consideration the following questions: what do you already know, what information sources provided this knowledge, what do you not know and need to find out, where can you find the answers?

Students should next be guided through a process of organizing (Step 2). One way of doing this is to develop a series of questions in small discussion groups. Other methods of organizing include "concept mapping," described by Hanf (1971, p. 225) as "a graphic representation of the intellectual territory traveled or to be traveled via reading" (p. 225), and more traditional ways of gaining control of a subject, such as formal outlining and the use of index cards. Whatever the style of organizing chosen, it should acknowledge each student's personal preferences.

To begin Step 3 and "trigger the flow of writing," Tchudi (1986, p. 32) suggests several strategies. Students should first of all review their notes, "maps" or outlines, and journal writings. They can talk in small groups about how to begin, freewrite in class, or write and share several opening paragraphs. Some students find it helpful to skip the beginning and dive right into the middle, or to use a dark screen on their word processors so as not to be distracted by what they have already written. During revision (Step 4), they should take into consideration the organization, structure, accuracy, style, and correctness of the written document.

Shamoon (1986) suggests a process model with the following components: "getting to know your subject matter close up and from several perspectives; visualizing the audience, or judging who is listening and what they need to hear; writing a first draft, or getting it down on paper and creating order; rewriting, or tinkering with words, sentences, and paragraphs to make the writing shine; editing, or getting the details of spelling and grammar correct" (p. 2). It is a recursive operation, which moves back and forth and allows individual writers to develop alternative processes unique to their styles and personalities.

WRITING INSTRUCTION

Inevitably, these new approaches necessitate the rejection of certain past assumptions on writing instruction, some of which are: that the errors in a piece of writing are clear indications of the cause of a problem and its remedy, an assumption which implies that students should not proceed until the skill has been mastered; and that the order of reading—thesis, discussion, conclusion—

is the order in which the paper should be written (Maimon, 1988, p. 733). Writing instructors and those who teach students how to write in the content areas need to realize instead that the main focus should be on coaching student writers through the writing process rather than evaluating the outcome. The instructional method should take into account the steps or stages of the writing process as described above.

THE RESEARCH PAPER

Process writing is especially appropriate in the preparation of long documents such as research or term papers, which, in spite of assaults on their value, are still considered to be suitable assignments for testing many skills, among them the ability to conduct a research inquiry, to formulate and organize ideas, and to produce those ideas in language. The research paper can take many forms. As it is commonly seen today, it is a construct which strikes a compromise between the rhetorical forms taught in Comp 101 and the highly stylized forms used in the content areas or disciplines. According to Schwegler and Shamoon (1982), the most typical is the literature review, followed in frequency by the application of a theory, commentary on or reworking of prior research, and testing of a hypothesis (p. 822).

Instructors who insist on assigning a term paper are advised to make it an incremental, carefully monitored project, and to incorporate short writing tasks throughout. All effective assignments should represent stepwise development of skills, focus on real problems and issues, and be introduced with clear and unambiguous instructions. Students should be given a clear thesis to defend or refute, guidelines about what sources to use, and specific, carefully monitored tasks—to summarize, for instance, or to draw inferences, select evidence, define an original thesis, evaluate authorities, compare or contrast, define terms, describe. Instructors should write these assignments in clear, concise, candid, and complete language. Every assignment should have a clear and relevant purpose.

A COLLABORATIVE MODEL

In the collaborative process model promoted by Walvoord (1986), instructors follow five steps: (1) they present several models of process—drafts, outlines, freewriting, and so forth; (2) they pair students off in a buddy system; (3) they get input from successful students in past classes; (4) they present case studies of other writers' experiences; and (5) they invite writers to the class (p. 33). When the time comes for students to select a topic, they begin by reading in a general area, asking themselves what questions remain unanswered and what aspects may be controversial (p. 33).

This model suggests several points of entry for library use. First, Walvoord (1986) has suggested that instructors show students several models of process—drafts, outlines, freewriting, and so forth. While these are being described, it is important to consider the origin of the content material. Did these outlines and drafts emerge whole from the imaginations of their creators, or were they supported by other written texts and documents? Are there examples of early drafts, especially in the field of literature, which show the evolution of an idea? This step in Walvoord's process affords an opportunity for the librarian to talk about publication sequence and about how an idea, especially in the sciences and the social sciences, evolves, being introduced first informally through presentations at departmental seminars, then to national conferences, and eventually as published journal articles. This is an appropriate time for the instructor and librarian to share the professional publishing experiences they have had in refereed journals.

Second, Walvoord suggests pairing students off in a buddy system, an excellent idea for doing library research. Students either work on the same project collaboratively or help one another on separate searches. Either way, a spirit of shared responsibility is engendered.

Finally, Walvoord suggests inviting writers to the class. The invitation could be expanded to include content-area faculty and subject-specialist librarians. The idea that the instructor take on the role of coach suggests the concept of a team approach, ideally including a librarian.

TERM PAPER ALTERNATIVES

Alternatives to the term paper are useful and many times preferable. Many are described in the column by that name edited by Thomas G. Kirk in issues of *Research Strategies.* The "documented essay," described in Chapter 6 and used at the University of Massachusetts-Amherst (see case study, in Part IV) is a graceful way to move students toward more sophisticated writing.

Marilyn Lutzker (1988), a librarian, suggests the "structured assignment," a process which fits the writing-across-the-curriculum model nicely. In a structured (process) assignment, the work is not left until the deadline is near. Instead, multiple tasks and deadlines are assigned throughout, ensuring that problems are identified early. Between the stages of the project, there is time to reflect on its progress and prepare for the next stage. Within this framework, there is room for students to learn and to experiment with many different forms of writing, among them "analysis, classification, comparison, contrast, criticism, definition, evaluation, paraphrasing, illustrating, justifying, reviewing, and summarizing" (p. 10).

At certain points in the development of the document, basic library research skills can be introduced. These, of course, include use of the catalog, indexes and abstracts (and, now, CD-ROM data bases), serials holdings information, knowledge about interlibrary loans, the use of complicated reference tools, newspapers, bibliographies, statistics, government publications, and biographical sources, and the application of evaluative criteria.

Lutzker's procedures, all of which suggest some use of the library, are summarized as follows: (1) after explaining the assignment, ask students to summarize their understanding in their own words; (2) ask students to read and summarize in writing two encyclopedia articles, at least one of which is from a subject encyclopedia; (3) advise students about the kinds of library materials they are to use and instruct them in their use; (4) ask students to submit a bibliography and a written evaluation of their research experience; (5) ask students to compare and analyze two of the articles on their bibliographies; (6) generate class discussion by having all students read the same articles, of which some will prepare summaries and others will write analyses; (7) ask students to prepare an additional bibliography which includes other kinds of library resources, such as government publications; (8) require a preliminary outline and list of questions the paper will answer; (9) require an additional outline and a written explanation of each section; (10) ask students to prepare a set of note cards for summaries and another for analyses of the same items; and (11) ask students to submit a draft for comment and corrections—a draft that is to be appended to the final paper (Lutzker, 1988, p. 10). Although these procedures are directed toward instructors, librarians can apply them to courses they teach themselves, if they have the opportunity, or to their collaborations with classroom teachers.

EXPRESSIVE WRITING

To many practitioners, writing-across-the-curriculum implies a subjective relationship between the student writer and the material being written or written about. This relationship is effected primarily by assigning short expressive writing tasks. Brevity and rapid writing are encouraged, and excessive preoccupation with grammar and technicalities is ignored, except in the case of final drafts. Typically, instructors may ask students to write a few sentences or a paragraph, to create a concept map, or to paraphrase, summarize, or make a journal entry reflecting their feelings about the subject or the assignment. They may interrupt a lecture and ask students to write briefly about its content or to outline the lecture material. Prior to class, students may be asked to freewrite about a chapter in their textbook, about the previous lecture, or in response to a question posed by the instructor.

Writing-across-the-curriculum proponents strongly encourage the use of journals so that students can reflect on the process of writing. Journal entries are typically personal and informal and are used to help students develop their ideas about subject matter. They are used equally well to describe the experience of conducting library research.

SOURCES OF CONTENT MATERIAL

While the subjective or personal writing task has value in and of itself, the issue of content must eventually be addressed. In traditional teaching, this has been accomplished through an inordinate reliance on textbook reading and lectures. The use of the library may have been discouraged or restricted to those materials selected by the instructor and placed in a reserve collection.

As most textbooks are written in a bland factual style that gives the student no real sense of the vital issues in the disciplines, their use should be limited or supplemented by other kinds of reading. It would be better for students to read more of the scholarly literature, such as journal articles, and thus become aware of the conventions of academic writing. As we all know, however, immersion in scholarly writing, especially in journals, can become an obstacle course. Such writing, developed by scholars to make the results of their research look absolute, is often turgid and is usually constrained by highly specialized jargon. Fortunately, this style of writing is gradually falling out of fashion, but an assignment which requires students to read it gives instructors an opportunity to open up a discussion of scholarly writing and promote an understanding of it. Content specialists and subject-specialist librarians can add a great deal to this discussion, illuminating the variety of written forms and describing access points for them.

THE LIBRARY CONNECTION

Librarians who wish to make the connection with writing-across-the-curriculum need to be aware that the keeping of journals, short expressive writing, and longer content-laden documents written in a process mode are characteristic of it. In their conversations with writing instructors or instructors in the content areas who are incorporating writing into their courses, they can ask to make presentations to whole classes at strategic points in the course work. Acting as consultants or coaches, they can meet with individual students or groups of students. This "real-life" approach is in itself a model for the information-gathering activities students will be engaged in during their professional and personal lives.

In discussions of library research and writing instruction, the emphasis should be on the discipline and its content material. The writing-across-the-curriculum movement is founded on this principle. Therefore, it is important to look at how the writing process is viewed in the disciplines. In this section, both generic and discipline-specific suggestions for writing assignments that bring the library into the picture will be presented. Some will promote a subjective response, most a more traditional or academic one. Broad definitions of the disciplines will precede each section. Hopefully, these will not offend by being overly simplistic.

THE DISCIPLINES

Traditionally, college and university course work has been divided into strict classical categories, the liberal arts encompassing all except the professional and technical fields. The liberal arts include the humanities (literature, language, philosophy, the fine arts, and history), the social and behavioral sciences (anthropology, economics, political science, psychology, and sociology), and science (physical and biological) and mathematics. In recent years, this schema has given way to interdisciplinary approaches, and preparation for entrance into the professional and technical fields, such as business, journalism, nursing, and education, is weighed equally with the liberal arts, especially in public institutions.

Each of the disciplines, as librarians well know, is supported by a unique body of literature—reference and statistical sources, journals and indexes, and book collections. Many lists of these sources have been compiled. Subject encyclopedias are listed in *First Stop* (Ryan, 1989), and reference books of all types in the *Guide to Reference Books* (Sheehy, 1986), to name only two of many. Textbooks, style manuals, and guides to the literature often list representative titles. (See Lester, 1990, *Writing Research Papers: A Complete Guide,* and the *Writer's Guides* series for examples.)

The Humanities

In the humanities, the purpose of most writing and writing assignments is to analyze a piece of art or literature in order to determine its meaning and uncover new insights about life, humanity, and the field of literature. In the humanities, in contrast to the social sciences, personal insight is preferred over method, and the writer is strongly encouraged to get involved with the work being analyzed. The use of the personal subjective ''I'' is allowed.

A typical piece of humanities writing starts with consideration of a piece of art, music, dance, or writing. A thesis is developed and is followed by an analysis of the parts of the work that ''proves'' the thesis with persuasive garnering of evidence. The writer becomes intimately engaged, ''probing'' the work by listing the parts (different for art, music, dance, and literature), or elements, which compose it. This probing requires observation, note taking, and research on the historical, sociological, and biographical environment within which the work was created. The analysis is often concluded with a ''statement of significance'' which synthesizes the parts into a whole (Shamoon, 1986, p. 62).

Literary research is different from other kinds of research (Maimon et al., 1981, p. 130). The critic reads and takes notes, eventually arriving at a ''controlling question,'' uniquely different from those which can be answered from a close reading of the work. Typically, the question involves sociological, historical, geographical, and biographical elements. The writer then chooses one or several aspects of the novel, poem, play, or story—a character, scene or setting, method, point of view, or scope—for analysis. This process may include brainstorming, free association, development of an analogy, and, eventually, consultation of library sources, such as books, encyclopedias, and indexes. Next, the writer/critic decides on a point of view and imagines a specific audience, writes a thesis sentence and first draft, and proceeds to revise and edit. The Modern Language Association (MLA) has created a unique form of documentation for scholarly papers in the field of literature.

Humanities scholars typically work alone and use libraries more, prefer retrospective over current sources, and rely more on primary material than on journal literature than do scholars in other fields. They are less interested in conference papers than are scientists or social scientists. The secondary sources they are likely to use are book reviews, biographical materials, bibliographies, and literary periodicals, indexes, dictionaries, handbooks, and encyclopedias. They often find literature surveys and research guides very helpful for their research.

The Social Sciences

The social and behavioral sciences, once separated, are now considered together, although behavioral science employs more experimental approaches. Many new fields are emerging, but those traditionally included are sociology, economics, political science, social psychology, cultural anthropology, and psychology. The formal literature of the social and behavioral sciences reflects a preoccupation with methods of investigation.

Sociology is the study of the individual in relationship with others and within groups. Social conventions and institutions are also considered. Psychology studies the mental processes of humans and animals. It is composed of many subfields concerning the emotions, sexuality, cognition, personality, and clinical practices. Political science is concerned with the study of governmental structures and political activity, including legislation, voter behavior, and political organization. The goal of economics is to understand how wealth is produced, distributed, and consumed. Microeconomics is concerned with individual or corporate matters, macroeconomics with entire economies.

The form of a typical paper in the social sciences tells much about the writing process involved in its preparation. It is tight and highly stylized, unlike the analytical essay in the humanities, and little structural variation is allowed. A typical paper in the social sciences includes an introduction, a review of the literature, a description of the method (survey, interview, questionnaire, or observation) employed to do the research, a results section, discussion, and a conclusion which usually points to further questions that have been raised during the research.

Within the social sciences, psychology is one of the more complex and sophisticated disciplines (Thaxton, 1987). The American Psychological Association requires that empirical studies include the following sections: abstract, introduction, method, results, discussion, and references. Primary sources in psychology consist of original reports of research in journal articles, technical reports, and conference papers. Secondary sources include review articles that evaluate or restructure primary sources. The documentation style developed by the American Psychological Association has gained wide acceptance among most of the disciplines in the category. It is a name and year system, with commas separating items in the in-text references and an alphabetized list of citations at the end of the paper.

Science and Mathematics

Science is concerned with the physical world, both organic and inorganic, and mathematics is the study of numerical, quantitative and spatial relationships. Science relies on observations, which are to be collected and reported in an unbiased and systematic way. The scientific disciplines include the physical sciences, the biological sciences, medicine, and engineering.

The physical sciences, consisting of physics, chemistry, astronomy, and the earth sciences, are concerned with the study of the inorganic world. Physics is the basic science of the physical sciences; it is concerned with natural forces and the structure and behaviors of atoms. Chemistry is the study of the behaviors of molecules and their structure. Astronomy is the study of the entire universe beyond Earth, and the earth sciences study the solid part of the planet Earth, the atmosphere, the hydrosphere, and its environment in space. The biological sciences are concerned with the study of living organisms.

Scholarly scientific papers are generally tersely written and documented, but much beautiful and esthetic writing has also entered the literature. The format used almost universally for papers includes an introduction, a research hypothesis of a narrow subject, a literature review, a methods and materials section, results, discussion, and a conclusion, which is expected to point to new questions. A review paper in the sciences must be up to date, comprehensive, and authoritative.

Besides reviews of the literature and lab reports, students may be asked to prepare simulations of conference reports, to write book reviews, to make oral presentations, and to prepare poster sessions. In preparing these assignments, students may use the library for the purpose of uncovering models and supporting material. To conduct an efficient literature search, for instance, students may select appropriate keywords by using both general and subject-specific encyclopedias and handbooks, special indexing and abstracting services, books, periodicals, and review articles.

The preferred documentation style for the sciences is the number system, which employs numbers rather than years in the text and corresponding numbers in the ''works cited'' list. Some variations are prescribed by the American Chemical Society, the American Institute of Physics, the Council of Biology Editors, and the American Medical Association.

Professional and Technical Fields

The professional and technical fields, such as business, education, textile design, fisheries management, and journalism, are representative of the vast array of subjects taught in institutions of higher education today. Faculty in these areas have been especially open to the principles of writing-across-the-curriculum, clearly showing their recognition of the importance that writing skills will play in the professional lives of their students.

GENERIC ASSIGNMENTS

Generic sequences of literature searching, familiar to librarians, may be applied across the curriculum and linked to writing tasks. These may include introducing library resources by type, as part of a step-by-step strategy, by specific publication forms, as primary or secondary sources, as part of a publication sequence or citation pattern, or according to the index structures applied to them (Kobelski & Reichel, 1987). If the librarian has the opportunity to teach a credit course, the outline presented by Fink (1987) is recommended. But even without that opportunity, librarians can refer to specific items in the sequence, such as the topic-specific pathfinder, which readily suggest writing assignments. This is an excellent way to reframe the ubiquitous library treasure hunt popular among so many instructors. The course outline described in Chapter 6 is also recommended.

The conceptual frameworks concept, introduced in Reichel and Ramey's 1987 book by that name, presents numerous ways to merge the use of library resources with specific disciplines. In the conceptual frameworks model, students are introduced to library resources in sequences that acknowledge the structures and methods of the disciplines under study. In other words, they are presented only as they become relevant to the course material. A marketing research class, for instance, derives its structure from a strategy presented in its textbook (Ramey, 1987, p. 48).

Appendix B in this book lists many types of library resources that can be used as starting points for writing instructors. Appendix C is a list of discourse forms. By creatively ''mixing and matching'' between the two lists, instructor/librarian teams can easily bring library use into focus for the novice writer.

Assignments

—Interview a subject-specialist librarian in your field of interest. Ask about the kinds of writings typical of the discipline and the ways they are made accessible through CD-ROMs, indexes, and so forth.

—Look up a description of a major discipline in an encyclopedia. Bring to class an example of a book or article in the field. Make note of its Library of Congress classification number and write a correct citation for it.

—Describe how scholars in the major disciplines—the humanities, sciences, and social sciences—write up their research. What is similar? What is different? Include a discussion of documentation styles in your analysis.

—After instruction in the use of an on-line catalog, prepare an annotated bibliography on an assigned topic.

—Select and refine a topic using only annual reviews, subject indexes (paper or electronic), and chapter headings from your text.

—Draw up a list of indexes and CD-ROMs, abstracting services, representative journals, reference books, and subject headings relevant to your field of interest. Briefly describe how they would be helpful to you.

—Write a descriptive outline of a scholarly paper.

—Find examples of coverage of your topic in a scholarly journal, an international news source, a national newspaper, a local newspaper, and a popular magazine. What are the similarities and differences in the coverage?

—Look at an original paper and at its treatment in a secondary source, such as a book or review article. Look at a treatment in a tertiary source, such as an encyclopedia or textbook. What has happened to the interpretation of the idea?

—Compare and contrast a scholarly journal, a professional magazine, and a popular magazine in your area of interest. How do they differ? Consider your response in terms of layout, vocabulary, advertising, audience, editorial content, letters to the editor, and so forth.

—Write out an outline of a scholarly journal article and describe its structure and the function of each of its parts.

—Write three abstracts of articles in scholarly journals reporting original research.

—Contrast and compare several documentation styles.

SUBJECT-SPECIFIC ASSIGNMENTS

The Humanities

Literature

—In the Library of Congress classification system, every author is given a unique call number that embraces primary works as well as biography and criticism. "Browse" the collection for a specific author and write a report on the scope of the library's collection. Compare it to a bibliography of the author's works.

Philosophy

—Locate the *Philosophers' Index* and journals from several recent years. Identify two articles on a selected topic and write a brief paper on the topic. Include documentation.

(List and Plum, 1990, in their excellent guide to philosophy, introduce the student researcher to bibliographies and the recent literature. Their Appendix III lists representative journals and a topical list of basic sources.)

History

—Write a 25-page research paper. The class is divided into small groups. Using brain-storming techniques, the students develop topics and research strategies. Each student keeps a "research log" in which to record the experience of finding corroborating evidence from library sources (Steffens, 1989).

—Conduct a study of your family history using original documents, oral interviews, and ethnic and immigration studies found in books and journal articles.

—Trace the sources of a well-known historian using the footnotes from his or her works. Use some primary sources, i.e., correspondence or diaries, in your report (Cassara, 1985).

The Fine Arts

—Research a time in the life of an artist (musician, architect, choreographer) and write several diary entries describing the creative process. Document the sources used.

—Using basic reference sources and books on history, describe the social milieu of a chosen artist. Document your report using the footnote style.

The Social Sciences

General

—There are six parts to a classic social sciences methods paper: abstract, introduction, method, results, discussion, references. Through a search of the *Social Sciences Index,* identify three articles that conform to this model. Analyze and compare the six parts in each of the articles.

—Write up a description of the methodology used in several journal articles, the results, and the discussion. Describe the hypothesis in your own words.

—Select a basic reference source and write an analysis of its features—table of contents, indexes, organization, coverage, currency. Include a correct citation for the source.

Thaxton (1987) finds that a publication sequence framework is a good research process for this subject area. Similarly, Tuckett and Pryor (1983) present a strategy for political science, based on the differentiation between primary and secondary sources, which could be applied to several fields.

Sociology

—Trace the development of the field of sociology through the following stages, using the suggested sources and library tools.

1. Pioneering (early nineteenth century). *Sources:* minutes, letters, pamphlets, articles. *Tools:* indexes, bibliographies.

2. Elaboration (late nineteenth-early twentieth century). Sources: essays, memoirs, journals. Tools: journal reviews.

3. Proliferation (1910–1940). Sources: proceedings, annual reports, books, dissertations. Tools: guides, handbooks, encyclopedias.

4. Establishment (1940-). Sources: books, dissertations, government publications. Tools: special encyclopedias, bibliography of dissertations.

An excellent list of sources accompanies this model, which is recommended for advanced students (Ready, 1987, pp. 78–79).

For a research paper in sociology, Ready, a contributor to *Conceptual Frameworks for Bibliographic Education* (Fink, 1987), suggests a question analysis process composed of eight steps: (1) overview the topic and learn its terminology; (2) create subtopics; (3) decide on what types of primary and secondary sources will be searched; (4) decide how much material will be needed; (5) decide on what level of quality is necessary; (6) allocate sufficient time to complete the assignment; (7) list other perspectives or disciplines involved with the topic; and (8) decide on what types of reference tools will be used (p. 75).

The library research component she recommends for such a paper suggests that students first define and clarify the topic by using dictionaries, encyclopedias, and handbooks; next, identify journal articles in indexing and abstracting services and review current thinking on the topic as presented in annual reviews; third, support the hypotheses of current thought with bibliographies; fourth, examine the distillation of thought in books, through a search of the catalog of the library's holdings; and lastly, verify the validity of sources by citation analysis. An excellent list of sources is given at the end of her chapter. Another detailed example of a systematic literature search as applied to sociology is given by McDonough and Rothman (1983).

Psychology

—Write a three-page critique on a multivariate statistic often used in American Psychological Association journals.

—Using the library on-line catalog and indexes (on paper or CD-ROM) only, not encyclopedias or textbooks, locate three sources in the library on the topic of group behavior. Do any of them agree with your own personal experience?

—There are six parts to a classic methods paper: abstract, introduction, method, results, discussion, references. Analyze these parts in three articles you identify in a search of *Psychological Abstracts* or *Psychlit.*

—Trace the publication sequence of a current issue in psychology. Write a history of the idea as it evolved throughout the process. Consider it as a report presented within the department, as a paper presented at a regional conference and then a national conference, as a manuscript submitted to a journal, and as an abstract in *Psychological Reports* or *Psychlit.*

Reed and Baxter's (1992) excellent handbook on psychology is an ideal model on which to base creative library-based assignments. Especially informative are the bibliographies at the end of each chapter and the appendixes, especially Appendix C, "Exercises and Other Topics to Pursue."

Political Science

—Prepare a foreign policy brief on an Eastern European country, using government publications, books, and journal articles identified through a systematic library search. Describe your experience with the research process.

—Describe and define an issue of current national interest. Look at public opinion polls, news stories, party platforms. Find a biography of a political figure involved in the issue.

—Use primary sources (court opinions, congressional committee hearings, eyewitness accounts in newspapers, statistics) to investigate the history of a political issue. Discuss its background and evolution, using secondary sources (bibliographies, books, journal articles). Report on your research strategy—use of the on-line or card catalog (for example, subject tracings, author searches), indexes, CD-ROM data bases.

—Working in small groups, prepare a report on a recent Supreme Court opinion from the three perspectives of primary sources, secondary sources, and statistical data (Tuckett & Pryor, 1983).

Lowery and Cody's *Political Science: Illustrated Search Strategy and Sources* (1993) outlines a classic search plan which names specific journals, books, and reference tools. Using this excellent resource, librarians and instructors can create innumerable short expressive assignments.

The Sciences

General

—In a recent newspaper or magazine, find an article or story which reflects the importance of science in daily human life. Write about its impact on your own life. Document your essay with an article from a scholarly journal.

—Invite a reference librarian whose specialty is science to talk to the class about the structures of the literature and points of access to it (indexes, CD-ROM data bases, on-line searching, reference tools, and so forth). Students retrieve one item from each category and write critiques of them.

—Compare experimental data found in the literature with what you have collected in your own lab work.

Biology

—On a topic of special relevance to women, for example, reproduction, birth control, or career advancement, prepare a portion of a roundtable discussion. Support your aspect of the discussion with a list of from five to seven sources and an annotated bibliography.

—Write a proposal for a research project in animal behavior. Support it with data and information found in a search of the literature.

—Prepare brief summaries of three articles in the literature on an aspect of sexual reproduction.

—Select a concept of reproduction and trace its development through the research/publication cycle: department colloquium, meeting presentation, dissertation or patent, conference paper, journal article or technical report, review article, annual review or book, encyclopedia or handbook.

Chemistry

Kobelski and Reichel (1987) suggest an index structure framework as a research process. Students are invited to the library for an orientation which focuses primarily on the use of periodicals; teaches keyword searching in *Chemical Abstracts (CA), Current Contents, General Science Index,* and *Index Medicus;* introduces chemical nomenclature indexing in the *CA* Formula, Substance, and Registry Number Indexes, the *Merck Manual,* and so forth; and presents other specialized reference tools in the field. A knowledge of on-line systems is essential, as is citation searching in the *Science Citation Index.*

—Using the library, find one classical and one modern method for analyzing a given element from the periodic table (Atkinson, 1986).
—Do an evaluation of a new drug using information derived from scholarly journals indexed in *Index Medicus* on CD-ROM.

Mathematics

—Study and report on the biography of a well-known mathematician.
—Outline the evolution of a particular set theory, logic, or probability.
—In a recent magazine or newspaper, find a story that reflects the importance of mathematics to daily life. Write about its effect on your own life.

The Professional and Technical Fields

Business

Ramey (1987) emphasizes designing a bibliographic instruction presentation which follows the sequence of a typical marketing plan found in many textbooks. Library sources (statistics and financial data, reference tools, citation data bases and indexes, journals and books) are presented only when they become relevant in the information-gathering process. As they prepare their plans, students are required to cite some of these sources.

Over 250 research problems are listed in Appendix D of Charles Smith's *Guide to Business Research* (1991). All of them suggest using the library to find models of other research, to analyze secondary and tertiary sources for corroboration, and to gather supporting social, political, historical, and demographic data.

—Read a novel that deals with a matter of ethics in a business environment and write a paper on it (Pamental, 1990).
—Compare an article in a trade publication with one in a professional journal. Describe their visual layout. On what level of complexity is the writing style? Who are the target audiences? What is the depth of the presentation? Give specific examples.
—For a course in Media Law, find a state statute, read one of the cases listed in the notes in the *Reporters,* and summarize both.

Education

—Select a major educational theory and locate articles that explain or support the theory through a search of the ERIC database.

Fisheries Management

—Following a model found in *American Zoologist,* write a review of an aquaculture topic. Use primary sources found in the library.

—Write a one-paragraph topic statement on one of the following: site selection, species selection criteria, nutrition, disease. At least two references to journal articles must be attached.

Wildlife Management

A publication sequence process is recommended by Greenfield (1987). A new concept is traced from the time it was first conceived and presented as an informal report to a small group, as a conference poster or presentation, as a journal article, and as an indexed and cited item. Key articles that emerge as a result of its publication are identified as the concept is integrated into the discipline's accepted body of knowledge. Eventually it is written up in reference sources and referred to in the popular literature. An excellent list of representative reference sources accompanies the chapter.

—Assume that you are in a work situation in which you are expected to write up a life history of a specific species, for example, mountain lions or mule deer. Use articles in scholarly journals, government publications and conference reports. Document your report properly.

CONCLUSION

Examples such as those just listed are only provocative beginnings and point to myriad other possibilities. Although most are best applied to transactional/ informative writing, they can also inspire more subjective and expressive exercises. The opportunities for creating intersections between the rich resources of the library and course content are endless. Other ideas will surely suggest themselves.

Why, it might be asked, do librarians need to know these finer points about the structures of the academic literatures? Why, indeed, are librarians expected to know just about everything? And why do librarians have the same expectations of themselves? The answer lies in the inherent nature of our profession. We are the refuge of last resort—and first resort—the place and the person everyone, whether novice or expert, can turn to when they need to find out about something.

Writing-across-the-curriculum involves us in yet another ''continuing education program'' that we engage in to serve our constituencies better. In addition, as we will see in later chapters, it will enable us to become better teachers ourselves, to create a new vitality in our own classrooms. On a larger scale, the movement is part of an effort to democratize education and make it more socially responsible. This aspect gives it a dynamic and invigorating quality which invites us to participate. As librarians we have a unique part to play in this evolving drama. Let's join the company.

REFERENCES

Atkinson, G. F. (1986). Writing among other skills. *Journal of Chemical Education, 63*(4), 337–338.

Britton, J. N., Burgess, T., Martin, N., McLeod, A., & Rosen, H. (1975). *The development of writing abilities (11–18)*. London: Macmillan.

Cassara, E. (1985). The student as detective: An undergraduate exercise in historiographic research. *The History Teacher, 18*(4), 581–592.

Fink, D. (1987). Information, technology, and library research. In M. Reichel & M. A. Ramey (Eds.), *Conceptual frameworks for bibliographic education: Theory into practice* (pp. 24–38). Littleton, CO: Libraries Unlimited.

Flower, L. (1989). Taking thought: The role of conscious processing in the making of meaning. In E. P. Maimon, B. F. Nodine, & F. W. O'Connor (Eds.), *Thinking, reasoning, and writing* (pp. 185–212). New York: Longman.

Greenfield, L. W. (1987). Publication sequence: The use of a conceptual framework for library instruction to students in wildlife and fishery management. In M. Reichel & M. A. Ramey (Eds.), *Conceptual frameworks for bibliographic education: Theory into practice* (pp. 166–182). Littleton, CO: Libraries Unlimited.

Hanf, M. B. (1971). Mapping: A technique for translating reading into thinking. *Journal of Reading, 14*(4), 225–230.

Hayes, J. R., & Flower, L. S. (1980). Identifying the organization of writing processes. In L. W. Gregg & E. R. Steinberg (Eds.), *Cognitive processes in writing* (pp. 3–30). Hillsdale, NJ: Lawrence Erlbaum Associates.

Kobelski, P. G. (1987). Index structure as a conceptual framework for bibliographic instruction in chemistry. In M. Reichel & M. A. Ramey (Eds.), *Conceptual frameworks for bibliographic education: Theory into practice* (pp. 147–156). Littleton, CO: Libraries Unlimited.

Kobelski, P. G., & Reichel, M. (1987). Conceptual frameworks for bibliographic instruction. In M. Reichel & M. A. Ramey (Eds.), *Conceptual frameworks for bibliographic education: Theory into practice* (pp. 3–12). Littleton, CO: Libraries Unlimited.

Lester, J. D. (1990). *Writing research papers: A complete guide* (6th ed.). Glenview, IL: Scott, Foresman.

List, C. J., & Plum, S. H. (1990). *Library research guide to philosophy*. Ann Arbor, MI: Pierian Press.

Lowery, R. C., & Cody, S. A. (1993). *Political science: Illustrated search strategy and sources*. Ann Arbor, MI: Pierian Press.

Lutzker, M. (1988). *Research projects for college students: What to write across the curriculum*. Westport, CT: Greenwood.

Maimon, E. P. (1988). Cultivating the prose garden. *Phi Delta Kappan, 69*(10), 734–739.

Maimon, E. P., Belcher, G. L., Hearn, G. W., Nodine, B. F., & O'Connor, F. W. (1981). *Writing in the arts and sciences.* Cambridge, MA: Winthrop Publishers.

McDonough, K., & Rothman, B. K. (1983). The library research module in introductory sociology: The case study of a collaboration. *Research Strategies, 1*(3), 109–118.

Murray, D. M. (1980). How writing finds its own meaning. In T. R. Donovan & B. W. McClelland (Eds.), *Eight approaches to teaching composition* (pp. 3–20). Urbana, IL: National Council of Teachers of English.

Odell, L. (1980a). The process of writing and the process of learning. *College Composition and Communication, 31,* 42–50.

Pamental, L. (1990, January). Presentation given at *Writing and Thinking Across the Curriculum.* Conference held at Rhode Island College, Providence, RI.

Ramey, M. A. (1987). Adaptation of market research concepts for bibliographic instruction. In M. Reichel & M. A. Ramey (Eds.), *Conceptual frameworks for bibliographic education: Theory into practice* (pp. 48–62). Littleton, CO: Libraries Unlimited.

Ready, S. K. (1987). Search strategy in the research process; sociology. In M. Reichel & M. A. Ramey (Eds.), *Conceptual frameworks for bibliographic education: Theory into practice* (pp. 75–85). Littleton, CO: Libraries Unlimited.

Reed, J. G., & Baxter, P. M. (1992). *Library use: A handbook for psychology.* Washington, DC: American Psychological Association.

Reichel, M., & Ramey, M. A. (Eds.). (1987). *Conceptual frameworks for bibliographic education: Theory into practice.* Littleton, CO: Libraries Unlimited.

Ryan, J. (1989). *First stop: The master index to subject encyclopedias.* Phoenix: Oryx.

Schwegler, R. A., & Shamoon, L. K. (1982). The aims and process of the research paper. *College English, 44*(8), 817–824.

Shamoon, L. K. (1986). *Think/write: A guide to research writing across the curriculum.* Dubuque, IA: Kendall/Hunt.

Sheehy, E. P. (Ed.). (1986). *Guide to reference books* (10th ed.). Chicago: American Library Association.

Smith, C. B. (1991). *A guide to business research: Developing, conducting, and writing research projects* (2nd ed.). Chicago: Nelson-Hall.

Steffens, H. (1989). Designing history writing assignments for student success. *The Social Studies, 80*(2), 59–63.

Tchudi, S. N. (1986). *Teaching writing in the content areas: College level.* Washington, DC: National Education Association of the United States.

Thaxton, L. (1987). Conceptual frameworks for bibliographic instruction in psychology. In M. Reichel & M. A. Ramey (Eds.), *Conceptual frameworks for bibliographic education: Theory into practice* (pp. 63–74). Littleton, CO: Libraries Unlimited.

Tuckett, H. W., & Pryor, J. (1983). Research strategy for political science. *Research Strategies, 1*(4), 128–130.

Walvoord, B. E. (1986). *Helping students write well* (2nd ed.). New York: Modern Language Association.

Writer's Guide. The Heath writing across the curriculum series. Lexington, MA: D.C. Heath.

ADDITIONAL READINGS

Balay, R. (Ed.). (1986). *Guide to reference books* (Supplement to the 10th ed.). Chicago: American Library Association.

Barnet, S. (1989). *A short guide to writing about art* (3rd ed.). New York: HarperCollins.

Beaubien, A. K., Hogan, S. A., & George, M. W. (1982). *Learning the library: Concepts and methods for bibliographic instruction.* New York: R. R. Bowker.

Beyer, B. K. (1979). Pre-writing and rewriting to learn. *Social Education, 43*(3), 187–189, 197.

Blake, G., & Bly, R. W. (1991). *The elements of business writing.* New York: Macmillan.

Bruffee, K. (1985). *A short course in writing: Practical rhetoric for teaching composition through collaborative learning.* Boston: Little, Brown.

Bruffee, K. A. (1989). Thinking and writing as social acts. In E. P. Maimon, B. F. Nodine, & F. W. O'Connor (Eds.), *Thinking, reasoning, and writing* (pp. 213–222). New York: Longman.

Buehler, M. L. (1988). Writing the research paper step by step. *College Teaching, 36*(1), 20.

Clark, A. S., & Jones, K. F. (Eds.). (1986). *Teaching librarians how to teach: On-the-job training for bibliographic instruction librarians.* Metuchen, NJ: Scarecrow.

Croneis, K. S. (1989). Search strategies, the research publishing cycle: Bibliographic instruction for graduate students. *Research Strategies, 7*(3), 138–140.

D'Aniello, C. A. (1987). A sociobiological and sociohistorical approach to the study of bibliographic and reference sources: A compliment to traditional bibliographic instruction. In M. Reichel & M. A. Ramey (Eds.), *Conceptual frameworks for bibliographic education: Theory into practice* (pp. 109–133). Littleton, CO: Libraries Unlimited.

Day, R. A. (1988). *How to write and publish a scientific paper* (3rd. ed.). New York: Oryx.

DeVinney, G. (1987). Systematic literature searching as a conceptual framework for course related bibliographic instruction for college freshman. In M. Reichel & M. A. Ramey (Eds.), *Conceptual frameworks for bibliographic education: Theory into practice* (pp. 13–23). Littleton, CO: Libraries Unlimited.

Ditmar, T. (1985). An alternate sequence. In R. J. Kloss, J. Feeley, S. Hanks, M. O'Connor, H. Parker, & D. Perry (Eds.), *On writing well* (pp. 31-32). Wayne, NJ: William Paterson College.

Egan, P. J. (1992). Bridging the gap between the student and the library. *College Teaching, 40*(2), 67–70.

Emig, J. (1983). Writing as a mode of learning. In D. Goswami & M. Butler (Eds.), *The web of meaning: Essays on writing teaching, and thinking* (pp. 122–131). Upper Montclair, NJ: Boynton/Cook.

Encyclopedia Britannica (15th ed.). (1993). Chicago: Encyclopedia Britannica, Inc.

Erikson, B. L., & Strommer, D. W. (1991). *Teaching college freshmen.* San Francisco: Jossey-Bass.

Eschholz, P. A. (1980). The prose models approach: Using products in the process. In T. R. Donovan & B. W. McClelland (Eds.), *Eight approaches to teaching composition* (pp. 21–36). Urbana, IL: National Council of Teachers of English.

Farber, E. I. (1974). Library instruction throughout the curriculum. In J. Lubans, Jr. (Ed.), *Educating the library user* (pp. 145–162). New York: R. R. Bowker.

Farber, E. I. (1984). Alternatives to the term paper. In T. G. Kirk (Ed.), *Increasing the teaching role of academic libraries* (pp. 45–54). San Francisco: Jossey-Bass.

Fister, B. (1992). The research processes of undergraduate students. *Journal of Academic Librarianship, 18*(3), 163–169.

Flower, L. (1990). Negotiating academic discourse. In L. Flower, V. Stein, J. Ackerman, M. J. Kantz, K. McCormick, W. C. Peck (Eds.), *Reading to write* (pp. 221–252). New York: Oxford University Press.

Foster, D. (1992). *A primer for writing teachers: Theories, theorists, issues, and problems* (2nd ed.). Portsmouth, NH: Boynton/Cook.

Fulwiler, T. (1982). Writing: An act of cognition. In C. W. Griffin (Ed.), *Teaching writing in all disciplines* (pp. 15–26). San Francisco: Jossey-Bass.

Fulwiler, T. (1987). *Teaching with writing.* Portsmouth, NH: Boynton/Cook.

Fulwiler, T., & Biddle, A. W. (Eds.). (1992). *A community of voices: Reading and writing in the disciplines.* New York: Macmillan.

Gere, A. R. (Ed.). (1985). *Roots in the sawdust.* Urbana, IL: National Council of Teachers of English.

Gredel-Manuele, Z. (1991). The study of family history: Research projects in a senior seminar. *Teaching History, 16*(1), 27–31.

Haney-Peritz, J. (1989). Making a difference: Thought, signs, and the teaching of writing. In E. P. Maimon, B. F. Nodine, & F. W. O'Connor (Eds.), *Thinking, reasoning, and writing* (pp. 223–244). New York: Longman.

Hansen, K. A. (1992). Term paper assignments: Information for mass communication. *Research Strategies,* (Spring), *10*(2), 92–96.

Johnson, M. L. (1983). Writing in mathematics classes: A valuable tool for learning. *Mathematics Teacher, 76*(2), 117–119.

Kinneavy, J. L. (1989). Thinkings and writings: The classical tradition. In E. P. Maimon, B. F. Nodine, & F. W. O'Connor (Eds.), *Thinking, reasoning, and writing* (pp. 169–184). New York: Longman.

Kirk, T. G. (1974). Problems in library instruction in four year colleges. In J. Lubans, Jr. (Ed.), *Educating the library user* (pp. 83–103). New York: R. R. Bowker.

Kirk, T. G. (Ed.). (1984). *Increasing the teaching role of academic libraries.* San Francisco: Jossey-Bass.

Kirk, T. G., & Huber, K. R. (Eds.). Term paper alternatives (column). In *Research Strategies.*

Kloss, R. J., Feely, J., Hanks, S., O'Connor, M., Parker, H., & Perry, D. (1985). *On writing well: A faculty guidebook for improving student writing in all disciplines.* Wayne, NJ: William Paterson College.

Kuhlthau, C. C. (1993). *Seeking meaning: A process approach to library and information services.* Norwood, NJ: Ablex.

Luey, B. (1990). *Handbook for academic authors* (rev. ed.). New York: Cambridge University Press.

Maimon, E. P. (1982). Writing across the curriculum: Past, present, and future. In C. W. Griffin (Ed.), *Teaching writing in all disciplines* (pp. 67–74). San Francisco: Jossey-Bass.

Mellon, C. A. (1984). Process not product in course-integrated instruction: A generic model of library research. *College and Research Libraries, 45*(6), 471–478.

Meyers, C. (1986). *Teaching students to think critically.* San Francisco: Jossey-Bass.

Moss, A., & Holder, C. (1982). *Improving student writing: A guidebook for faculty in all disciplines.* Pomona, CA: California State Polytechnic University.

Murray, D. M. (1985). *A writer teaches writing* (2nd ed.). Boston: Hougton Mifflin.

Novak, J. D., & Gowin, D. B. (1984). *Learning how to learn.* New York: Cambridge University Press.

Oberman, C. (1984) Patterns for research. In T. G. Kirk (Ed.), *Increasing the teaching role of academic libraries* (pp. 35–44). San Francisco: Jossey-Bass.

Odell, L. (1980b). Teaching writing by teaching the process of discovery: An interdisciplinary enterprise. In L. W. Gregg & E. R. Steinberg (Eds.), *Cognitive processes in writing* (pp. 139–154). Hillsdale, NJ: Lawrence Erlbaum Associates.

Odell, L. (1983). Written products and the writing process. In J. N. Hays, P. A. Roth, J. R. Ramsey, & R. D. Foulke (Eds.), *The writer's mind: Writing as a mode of thinking* (pp. 53–66). Urbana, IL: National Council of Teachers of English.

O'Hanlon, N. (1991). Begin at the end: A model for research skills instruction. *Research Strategies, 9*(3), 116–123.

Pastine, M. (1987). Teaching the art of literary research. In M. Reichel & M. A. Ramey (Eds.), *Conceptual frameworks for bibliographic education: Theory into practice* (pp. 134–146). Littleton, CO: Libraries Unlimited.

Peroni, P. A. (1981). *The second kind of knowledge: The role of library instruction in writing across the curriculum* (Report No. CS20-7-050). Glenside, PA: Beaver College, National Endowment for the Humanities Summer Institute in the Teaching of Writing. (ERIC Document Reproduction Service No. ED 217 487)

Powell, A. (1985). A chemist's view of writing, reading, and thinking across the curriculum. *College Composition and Communication, 36*(4), 414–418.

Ramey, M. A., & Reichel, M. (1987). Literature searching in education: A sample approach. In M. Reichel & M. A. Ramey (Eds.), *Conceptual frameworks for bibliographic education: Theory into practice* (pp. 39–47). Littleton, CO: Libraries Unlimited.

Read, M., & Thomson, S. K. (1974). Instructing college faculty in the bibliographic resources. In J. Lubans, Jr. (Ed.), *Educating the library user* (pp. 191–201). New York: R. R. Bowker.

Saule, M. (1992). The new library. In T. Fulwiler & A. W. Biddle (Eds.), *A community of voices: Reading and writing in the disciplines* (pp. 904–958). New York: Macmillan.

Sayre, H. M. (1989). *Writing about art.* Englewood Cliffs, NJ: Prentice Hall.

Scanlon, L. (1983). Invention and the writing sequence. In J. N. Hays, P. A. Roth, J. R. Ramsey, & R. D. Foulke (Eds.), *A writer's mind: Writing as a mode of thinking* (pp. 95–101). Urbana, IL: National Council of Teachers of English.

Scheffler, J. A. (1980). Composition with content: An interdisciplinary approach. *College Composition and Communication, 31,* 51–57.

Schmersahl, C. B. (1987). Teaching library research: Process, not product. *Journal of Teaching Writing, 6*(2), 231–238.

Sensenbaugh, R. (1990). Process writing in the classroom. *Journal of Reading, 33*(5), 382–383.

Shamoon, L. K. (1993). *URI's writing across the curriculum handbook: Writing assignments and teaching tips from the WAC demonstration faculty.* Kingston, RI: University of Rhode Island.

Shaughnessy, M. P. (1977). *Errors and expectations: A guide for teachers of basic writing.* New York: Oxford University Press.

Simon, L. (1988). The papers we want to read. *College Teaching, 36*(1), 6–8.

Simon, R. A. (1984). The faculty/librarian partnership. In T. G. Kirk (Ed.), *Increasing the teaching role of academic libraries* (pp. 55–62). San Francisco: Jossey-Bass.

Steffens, H. (1988). Collaborative learning in a history seminar. *The History Teacher, 21*(10), 1–14.

Sternberg, R. J. (1991). *The psychologist's companion: A guide to scientific writing for students and researchers* (2nd ed.). New York: Cambridge University Press.

Strickland, J. (1986). The research sequence: What to do before the term paper. *College Composition and Communication, 37*(2), 233–236.

Thaiss, C. (Ed.). (1983). *Writing to learn.* Dubuque, IA: Kendall/Hunt.

Tierno, M., & Lee, J. H. (1983). Developing and evaluating library research skills in education: A model for course-related bibliographic instruction. *RQ, 22*(3), 204–211.

Walvoord, B. E., & Smith, H. L. (1982). Coaching the process of writing. In C. W. Griffin (Ed.), *Teaching writing in all disciplines* (pp. 3–14). San Francisco: Jossey-Bass.

Wason, P. C. (1980). Specific thoughts on the writing process. In L. W. Gregg & E. R. Steinberg (Eds.), *Cognitive processes in writing* (pp. 129–138). Hillsdale, NJ: Lawrence Erlbaum Associates.

Weiss, R. H. (1980). A program for cross-disciplinary cooperation. In T. R. Donovan & B. W. McClelland (Eds.), *Eight approaches to teaching composition* (pp. 133–150). Urbana, IL: National Council of Teachers of English.

Wiggins, M. E., & Wahlquist, E. (1985). Independent library usage: A research strategy. *Journal of Academic Librarianship, 11*(5), 293–296.

Wilkinson, A. M. (1985). A freshman writing course in parallel with a science course. *College Composition and Communication, 36*(2), 160–165.

Williams, J. M. (1994). *Style: Ten lessons in clarity and grace* (4th ed.). New York: HarperCollins.

Wingell, R. J. (1990). *Writing about music: An introductory guide.* Englewood Cliffs, NJ: Prentice Hall.

Young, A., & Fulwiler, T. (Eds.). (1986). *Writing across the disciplines: Research into practice.* Upper Montclair, NJ: Boynton/Cook.

Chapter 6

Making the Connection in the Classroom: A Model for a Library-Based Writing Course

Jean Sheridan

Writing-across-the-curriculum, as we have seen, incorporates new and somewhat revolutionary concepts, among them expressive writing, process writing, keeping of journals, and collaborative learning. Expressive writing—subjective responses to the material being taught—is preferred over transactional forms, which are designed with the sole purpose of imparting or transferring information. Process writing, another innovation, gives equal weight to both the finished product and essential intermediate processes such as information gathering and brainstorming, mapping or outlining, drafting, peer reviewing of drafts, revising for style, and editing, that ultimate step where punctuation, spelling, and grammar are finally considered. This is a radical shift from the traditional approach where students struggled with grammar and spelling rules during the initial stages of writing. The keeping of journals encourages students to reflect on their academic work and on their experiences doing library research. Some instructors encourage students to use their journals to record reflections about their personal lives as well.

Collaborative learning is part of a pervasive social and educational reform which is converting the classroom from traditional hierarchical ways of teaching and learning to more cooperative and democratic ones (Bruffee, 1987). In the collaboratively designed writing classroom, students are trained to critique the drafts of one another's work. This is called peer review. Students also collaborate in other ways—by brainstorming for ideas, by assisting one another in finding sources, and by working on group writing projects.

This collaborative model was utilized in a course taught to adult students at the University of Rhode Island's College of Continuing Education. The course, which was described as an intermediate writing course, was designed to introduce students to the varieties of academic writing. The instructor, a librarian, was interested in acclimating students to academic research and the forms of discourse unique to specific disciplines through the intensive use of only scholarly materials. Specifically, she sought to do this by insisting on immediate and regular use of library resources. As faculty and librarian subject specialists were invited to the class at appropriate times to discuss their disciplines, the forms of writing unique to them, and ways of finding them, the course became a collaboration of students, instructor, librarians, and faculty writers, in an interactive loop with the subject matter.

The syllabus was divided into four large units corresponding to the broad categories of the sciences, the social sciences, the humanities, and the popular or professional literature. There was no textbook. Instead, students were taught how to find, read, and analyze journal articles and other written forms characteristic of the disciplines. The instructor, however, used several resources, among them *Writing Research Papers* (Lester, 1990), which was especially useful for teaching in-text referencing and documentation styles, and *Think/Write: A Guide to Research Writing Across the Curriculum* (Shamoon, 1986). *The Journal Book* (Fulwiler, 1987) was also consulted. (Guidelines adapted from it are listed in Appendix F.)

The following course description was made available to students during registration.

COURSE DESCRIPTION

This course is designed to introduce students to the forms of writing—primarily academic—in the humanities, social sciences, and sciences. Professional and popular publications will be considered. Primary and secondary forms of academic and professional writing will be used as texts. Style manuals will also be used.

A great deal of emphasis will be placed on learning how to do research in the library. Although traditional techniques of literature searching will be taught, the new electronic technologies will also be introduced and their use encouraged. These include the on-line book catalog and other electronically produced resources such as CD-ROM indexes and data bases. All assignments must be prepared using word-processing software.

Students will be allowed a great deal of autonomy in selecting their writing projects and will learn to approach these projects as a process. This process will include information gathering, structuring, and drafting, along with learning the skills involved in editing and revision. Many of these processes will be entered into collaboratively with other students and the instructor.

There will be a high expectation of both independence and social responsibility. Grades will be awarded on the basis of the quality of the four major writing projects and the level of cooperation/collaboration exhibited by the individual student.

OVERVIEW

The semester was divided into two introductory classes and four units of three classes each, except for the social sciences unit, which required four classes.

—Each class began with a period of silence during which students and the instructor wrote in their journals in response to a question, written on the blackboard, which pertained either to the content of the unit or the current writing task.

—Also on the board was a "map," or outline, of a chapter from the resources used by the librarian/instructor.

—Following the quiet writing time, the instructor lectured from the material on the board.

—This was followed by open discussion and conversation about the lecture and the students' current writing projects.

—On most days the librarian/instructor then brought the class to the library for instruction in the use of the OPAC (on-line public access catalog) and various reference sources and indexing services.

—At the break, the students left their journals with the instructor, who read them with an eye to the ease or difficulty they were encountering in their writing and research. Each journal entry was given one or two check marks for degree of effort; the journal entries were not graded.

—During the break the instructor also looked over the homework, which, for every class, included a one-page analysis of an article from a journal of the students' choice. This one-page analysis always required paraphrasing, in-text referencing using quotations, and a citation properly formatted according to the documentation style appropriate for the subject matter. (See Appendix A for a description of this assignment.)

—Students then worked in small groups to review their writing assignments or practice difficult concepts, such as in-text referencing and grammar rules. Appendix E lists criteria for effective group behavior.

CLASS OUTLINE

Class 1: Introduction

—After a general introduction and discussion about requirements and expectations, the students are asked to write an in-class essay on a topic of immediate interest to them.

—After writing, they break up into groups of three to read their essays aloud.

—Following this, the instructor lectures on the process model of writing and encourages general class discussion.

—After the break, the students are taken into the library and given a brief introduction to the catalog and indexes.

—For homework, they are instructed to develop their essays further and to find and bring to class two books or articles relevant to the subject matter.

Class 2: Introduction

—For the preclass writing exercise, students are asked to write about either their library or their rewriting experience during the past week.

—The instructor lectures on the format they are to follow for peer review of each other's work (see Appendix D).

—Using the articles they have gathered in support of their (now) "documented essays," the instructor leads a general discussion about the forms and conventions of academic writing and about how it differs from professional and popular writing. (For a discussion of the documented essay, see the University of Massachusetts-Amherst case study in Part IV.)

—Students are then instructed on the preparation of the one-page journal article analysis that is expected for each class. Each analysis will include a citation for the article in the documentation style appropriate for the discipline, the name of the paper index or electronic data base used to identify it, a summary of the article and some paraphrasing, and at least one direct quotation, both appropriately referenced in the text (see Appendix A).

—In-class exercises reinforce the directions for this assignment.

Classes 3 – 5: The Sciences

In the science unit, students produce a brief annotated bibliography and literature review. In this unit, and in the succeeding units on the social sciences, the humanities, and the popular or professional literature, the librarian/instructor will include bibliographic instruction and hands-on use of library sources in each class.

—Students will work in groups to gather material and to critique drafts of one another's work.

—Reinforcement exercises will be incorporated into each class.

—A visiting scholar and a subject-specialist librarian will visit the class to speak about the conventions of scientific writing and the ways scholarly materials are organized and located in the library.

—In this same class, students will be expected to present material they have gathered and interviews they have conducted in order to find out about the nature and history of a discipline or one aspect of it, biology in the sciences for example. The conversation generated by these contributions demonstrates real collaboration.

Classes 6 – 9: The Social Sciences

This unit is a difficult one to teach because students are introduced to the concept of original research, a complex and complicated procedure. The paper they will produce includes a literature review (which they learned to write in the science unit), as well as the other sections required by the behavioral sciences—a descriptive title, an abstract, an introduction in which a thesis is presented, a description of the methodology, results, discussion, and a conclusion in which further questions are suggested. It is a challenging project.

—Students execute the project collaboratively, in small groups, which is a test of their social and organizational skills, and a test for the instructor who must train them (see Appendix E, "Guidelines for Effective Group Behavior"). The original research is conducted in teams or pairs. The introduction, thesis, and conclusion are written collaboratively. The remaining sections—methodology, results, and discussion—are assigned by group decision to individual students within each group.

—Some time in each class is devoted to presenting models from which to learn and to doing exercises for reinforcement. Helping students understand about methodology, especially, can be difficult and time-consuming. (What constitutes a good survey and how should one be distributed? How can one set up efficient observations and get reliable results? What constitutes an effective interview?)

—Throughout, students read and critique drafts of each other's work, including the abstracts.

—The final papers are presented both orally and in writing. Giving an oral presentation reinforces the message that, in writing, audience is critical and that written work, whether intellectual or creative (in the poetic sense), is meant to be communicated.

Classes 10 – 12: The Humanities

For some, if not all, students, this unit comes as a welcome relief, as the critical essay they will write is much less structured than either the literature review or the methods paper they have produced so far.

—Students are given a wide range of options from which to choose, but little instruction. At this point, they should be able to demonstrate the necessary skills to discover and follow the conventions of the art or discipline they choose and to apply the appropriate forms of in-text referencing and documentation.

Classes 13 – 15: The Popular Literature

While the popular literature assignment may look like the proverbial "piece of cake," the students quickly discover that there are many conventions of this material they need to learn. Scholarly and professional journals vary considerably in terms of presentation, documentation style, and audience, but not to the degree that popular, intellectual, and trade magazines do. Although the students themselves find their subject personally exciting and inspiring, their primary challenge is to sustain the interest of the audience they have chosen to please.

—This unit provides the instructor with an opportunity to introduce the reference tools the free-lance writer uses and the idiosyncrasies of the writing industry.

—Many students will be encouraged to market their piece or article, and the class as a whole may choose to publish its "opus," perhaps in a form that could be cataloged and added to the library collection.

CONCLUSION

Upon completion of this course, the student writers will have learned valuable lessons. Having started out by writing subjectively about a topic in the introductory class, they will have mastered the material of other, less personal "experiences" and learned to use writing techniques and methods to express that material in print. They will have a grasp of the varieties of research materials found in academic libraries. They will come away with a sense of the uniqueness of each discipline, as presented by the subject-specialist librarian and the professor. They will have an appreciation of what collaboration means, as they themselves will have worked collaboratively to prepare the social sciences methods paper and reviewed each other's work. They will be aware that writing is a process more than a talent and that library research is an exploration and not a mystery. Most of all they will know that, since they have done it once, they will be able to do it again.

The librarian/instructor benefits as well. This course is a forum which helps to demystify the library for students and to make clear both to them and to faculty in the content areas that there are strong connections between the library and written academic discourse, an achievement which has solid and lasting rewards. What the course ultimately proves is the efficacy of collaboration in all scholarly endeavors.

A PERSONAL REFLECTION

I had occasion to teach this course three times. In my classes, there were adult students ranging in age from twenty to seventy. Some of the twenty-year-olds were students from the main campus who had been unable to register there. They were an interesting contrast to the more typical continuing education student (including others also in their twenties), who came to class with a variety of life experiences. Since that time, my teaching experience has been with the traditional younger student, and I look back now on those days and those classes with considerable nostalgia. Every face and name I recall as I review old rosters carries a history, and each one of the students in these classes entered into a relationship with me, the instructor, which was dynamic and personal, and far different from what I have experienced with younger students.

That relationship was initially formal and tense, of course, as the majority of the students were burdened with fear of failure and memories of past unpleasant classroom experiences. Adding to their trepidation were exaggerated fears surrounding writing and the library. Encouraging these students to explore writing expressively was no problem and, in fact, was a mode they clung to tenaciously. Moving them away from this self-centered, subjective relationship with the material was difficult and in the case of some—the oldest and those taking the course for "self-enrichment"—largely unsuccessful. It was these same students who resented the peer review and small group work, insisting that the teacher be the sole authority in the classroom. Those who "got it," who began to understand what I was attempting to do, however, moved perceptibly toward a more mature understanding of what their writing tasks entailed.

A hurdle even more formidable than the writing itself was doing research in the library, but even here great strides were taken. The physical setting for the class, a self-contained building which housed all student services, including the library, was a definite asset. From the first class onward, I allocated some class time to the library and worked alongside the students as they learned to find books and journal articles on their topics. It was here, using the scholarly journals, that they unlocked the mysteries of documentation styles and learned to approach unfamiliar and sophisticated vocabularies courageously.

The outcomes were generally successful. Students frequently returned to say how much more comfortable they had become doing library research in other courses. One published her article on how to grow tomatoes in cutout automobile tires on a deck in the university's cooperative extension publication. The wet-behind-the-ears, somewhat arrogant business student produced a beautifully documented study on the drinking habits of his fellow fraternity brothers. He endeared himself to me and the rest of the class when it was time for him to present his paper, as he became overwhelmingly self-conscious and his voice shook throughout. On the other hand, Alice, a seventy-year-old who took three buses to get to school, had no trouble giving her impassioned argument for simplifying holiday customs so that women could enjoy themselves more.

A few years later, I encountered the young woman who had published her article. She had just completed a master's program in sociology and invited me to her graduation party. I was the one, she said, who got her over her fear of writing and libraries.

This experience reinforces my opinion that librarians are uniquely prepared to teach the conventions of scholarly writing. They have no prejudices toward any one of the disciplines and are immersed daily in the myriad literatures and their access points. Furthermore, from their vantage point behind the reference desk, they understand better than others the difficulties most often encountered by those attempting to conduct library research.

Teaching writing and research together has advantages for the librarian as well as the student. As we well know, it is impossible to develop lasting relationships with students in the one-shot lecture we are traditionally called upon to deliver. Being able to spend an entire semester with the same students, going through the process with them, seeing them develop competencies under your personal guidance, coming to know them as individuals with unique problems and personalities—these are refreshing experiences and lasting gifts which serve to develop us personally as well as professionally.

REFERENCES

Bruffee, K. (1987). The art of collaborative learning. *Change, 19,* 42–47.

Fulwiler, T. (Ed.). (1987). *The journal book.* Portsmouth, NH: Heinemann.

Lester, J. D. (1990). *Writing research papers: A complete guide* (6th ed.). Glenview, IL: Scott, Foresman.

Shamoon, L. K. (1986). *Think/write: A guide to research writing across the curriculum.* Dubuque, IA: Kendall/Hunt.

Part III

Writing-Across-the-Curriculum: Happy Endings

Chapter 7

What Writing-Across-the-Curriculum Instructors Can Learn from Librarians

Marilyn Lutzker

LIBRARIANS TALK TO WRITING INSTRUCTORS

Librarians need to talk to writing instructors. To put it bluntly, there are quite a few things librarians should be prepared to tell them.

WRITING INSTRUCTION AND LIBRARY RESEARCH

Instructors of writing who believe that expressive or process writing is the most effective pedagogical method frequently feel that including library research in their assignments is unnecessary or distracting. They feel this way because writing, rather than information, is their primary concern.

Within this context however, it is important for writing instructors, as well as librarians, to recognize that by combining writing instruction with the gathering and assessing of information both groups become key participants in the effort to foster information literacy among students. Librarians, as well as writing instructors, however, must recognize that the writing being practiced need not be in the standard academic mode.

The purpose of this chapter is to make clear that there need not be any conflict between expressive or process writing and writing based on library research. Although traditional term papers requiring formal, documented, academic writing frequently do not provide the latitude that is necessary to meet the objectives of the writing instructor, there are many other ways of combining research and writing that can provide the freedom and scope necessary to meet those objectives.

The alternative research/writing assignments that are discussed below have two additional advantages. Because of their innovative nature, they are almost certain guarantees against recycled or purchased term papers or other forms of intentional plagiarism. And, of even greater importance, because students often come to writing classes already convinced that they will never enjoy writing term papers, these alternative formats provide the opportunity to achieve another of the writing instructor's frequently expressed and most laudable objectives: to have students experience writing as an interesting and satisfying, as well as necessary, activity. Thus, writing instructors who have not previously considered research as appropriate or helpful within the context of their own teaching, should be urged to consider some of the alternatives discussed here.

RESEARCH-BASED WRITING: ALTERNATIVES TO THE TERM PAPER

The research-based writing assignments discussed below are extremely flexible in terms of the amount of research required and/or the amount of writing required. Most are appropriate for group work, for peer review, and for sharing research results and thus lend themselves well to use in cooperative learning situations.

Anthologies

Anthologies or books of readings are very familiar to students since they are frequently used in college classrooms in place of textbooks or as supplementary readings. "Editing" an anthology of their own can be a rewarding experience for students. The assignment is extremely flexible and lends itself to peer assessment.

Many types of material can be included in a student-produced anthology. The anthology can be of works of fiction or nonfiction; topics can range from current events to biographies; writing can be descriptive, analytical, personal, or a combination. Chapters could include:

—articles from scholarly journals, popular magazines, and newspapers

—primary sources, including poems, stories, government documents, letters, journal entries, and excerpts from autobiographies

—illustrations from books and journals, reproductions from museums, and photographs

—a bibliography of other related items that have not been included

—study questions

The following is a sample anthology assignment:

—Locate and read ten relevant articles, essays, poems, or stories on your topic or about your subject.

—Select and photocopy five to be the chapters in your anthology.

—Write an introduction to your anthology that gives an overview of the subject and then relates each of the chapters to the anthology as a whole.

—Write an introduction to each chapter that includes a summary of the key points (or an analysis of the key characters) and an explanation of why you have chosen it to be included in the anthology.

Such an assignment can provide students with the opportunity to make critical judgments, to write in several modes, and to create a substantial finished project. The student anthologies can themselves become part of the supplementary reading for the course. The completed projects can be kept on reserve in the library, and each student can be required to read a specified number. The knowledge that their peers will be actively using the results of their projects should bring an additional sense of importance to the work being done.

Scrapbooks

Compiling someone else's scrapbook, an activity similar to compiling an anthology, might be preferred when the instructor wishes to provide practice in a more personal, expressive type of writing.

The following is a sample scrapbook assignment:

—Pretend you are a suffragette, an urban reformer of the 1890s or the 1950s, an advocate of multicultural education in the 1990s, or the organizer of a campaign to ban smoking on campus.

—Prepare a scrapbook of information to assist you in your campaign. The scrapbook can consist of newspaper articles, magazine articles, journal articles, firsthand accounts, excerpts from biographies or autobiographies, illustrations, and so forth.

—Write a letter to a friend describing each item in your scrapbook. Tell your friend what your feelings are about each item and how you hope to use it in your campaign.

Scrapbooks, like anthologies, lend themselves to group work. Several students can collaborate in compiling each scrapbook, and the finished products can be shared with the class. The assignment can be extended by having students write essays or letters based on a classmate's scrapbook.

Exhibitions

Exhibitions—normally thought to be limited to the visual arts—can provide an innovative and flexible opportunity for writing in modes ranging from the most personal and expressive to the most formal. The exhibition can be an art exhibition of course, but it can also be devoted to topics as diverse as fashion, household implements, such as vacuum cleaners, or everyday objects, such as pencils or baseball cards. The exhibition can be devoted to a particular group of people (the Romanies) or to a single person, either famous (Gloria Naylor) or not (my grandmother). Appropriate historical topics include the history of your city, or a particular neighborhood within it, and the history of the college, as well as topics related to political or social history of the United States or any other place in the world. For some topics, library research would be essential; for others (my grandmother), it could provide enriching details.

In most instances, of course, students will not be able to bring to class the actual objects they want in their exhibition, but they can provide pictures of the objects or, if those are difficult to locate, write descriptions of the items. The assignment can then include any combination of the following:

—Describe the topic and discuss why you chose it.

—Write captions for each item.

—Write the material for the "wallboards" that are customarily used to introduce exhibitions to viewers. The wallboard material should provide an overview of the topic and point out particular highlights of the show. It can be personal and casual in style, or more traditionally formal.

—Write publicity releases for specific target audiences.

—Write reflections about the exhibition for a personal journal.

—Write critical evaluations of the exhibition for a newspaper.

—Write letters to friends, lovers, and family members describing highlights of the exhibition.

This assignment would also be appropriate for group work and for peer evaluations. The exhibition could be devised and "mounted" by one group of students, with another group serving as critics, evaluators, or reactors.

Illustrated Books

"Illustrating" books is another way to combine visual resources with writing. Such an assignment could include the following:

—Prepare an illustrated edition of the work of fiction you have just read. Your edition will include five (or ten or fifteen) illustrations. They can be photocopies of pictures in books or magazines, advertisements, drawings, photographs you have taken yourself, or postcards from museums or souvenir shops. However, do not be constrained by available illustrations. If you cannot find what you need, provide a written description of the picture you wish you could find.

—Explain why you feel the particular scenes should be illustrated.

—Write suitable captions for each illustration.

This assignment can provide the opportunity to think and write about a work of fiction in a somewhat different analytical and creative fashion. It provides the opportunity for some broad-ranging library (and museum) research, while requiring short, highly focused writing. It is well suited to both historical and contemporary topics.

Diaries, Journals, Letters

These are forms of writing that teachers and students of writing are thoroughly familiar with. In addition to using them in the traditional manner, however, writing instructors can challenge students to write a letter or a series of journal entries as if they were another person. This other person can be one of the following:

—a character in a work of fiction

—a person from history (Abraham Lincoln, or John Brown, as a young boy)

—an imagined person representative of a group or an era (a member of the audience at the Lincoln–Douglas debates, a young male slave who joined John Brown, or the daughter of a slave owner)

Instructors looking for opportunities for group work and peer interaction in the writing process can enrich the assignment by setting up "correspondence networks" in which the daughters of slave owners in Georgia can write to the sons of Quaker farmers in Pennsylvania, Irish or Chinese immigrants of the nineteenth century or Vietnamese immigrants of the 1980s can exchange letters with their families in the "old country," or college students in the United States can communicate with their peers in the former Soviet Union.

The possibilities in these types of assignment are obviously endless. The amount of research required will vary with the topic and the manner in which the assignment is structured. If several students are "playing" the same character then group research combined with peer evaluation of the results might prove stimulating.

Newspaper Articles and Newspapers

Writing for newspapers can provide opportunities for "role-play writing" of a more formal type than writing diaries and letters. The articles can describe actual events or fictional events based on real occurrences.

Writing for newspapers need not be limited to standard reportage. Students can write editorials, letters to the editor, columns addressed to women or children, obituaries, social columns, and so forth. Writing instructors interested in group work can ask the class to produce an entire newspaper. The newspaper produced can be from an earlier time, or be contemporary. It can be a general interest newspaper, or reflect a specific group (Quakers, the Democratic Party, a labor union, a reform group). It can emanate from the area in which the college is located, or come from another area within the United States, or from another country. The amount of research required will vary with the assignment.

Fiction

Although undergraduate fiction writing, for good reason, is usually rooted in the experience of the writers, it is possible to challenge students to sharpen their writing skills by producing short works based on experiences of others. The following are sample fiction-writing assignments based on research:

—Research three recent airplane crashes (or earthquakes or terrorist attacks) and write a story incorporating some of the information.

—Read about the Great Depression and write a story about a sixteen-year-old girl during that period.

PANDORA'S BOX, OR CHOOSING TOPICS FOR STUDENT RESEARCH

Writing instructors might be surprised to learn a fact which is well-known to librarians: choosing a topic is frequently the most difficult part of a student's research assignment. Librarians should take every opportunity to communicate this to those who are giving the assignments.

Students would benefit if writing instructors and librarians discussed together the objectives for student research/writing assignments. These objectives can include acquiring a specific body of information, learning library research skills, practicing writing skills, or practicing critical thinking skills. We need to remember that the topic is the vehicle through which to achieve the objective of the assignment. Classroom instructors do not know how often topics for students' papers have actually come from librarians rather than from the instructors who have set the objectives, or the students who are being asked to meet the objectives.

"Write on anything you want to" and "choose a topic that interests you" sound like instructions that will provide motivation for somewhat reluctant student researchers. However, most of these potential researchers are also comparatively young, have had fairly narrow life experiences, and generally have only limited information about history, geography, literature, fine arts, and politics, not to mention religion, archeology, anthropology, psychology, sociology, and law. This comparatively limited experience is one reason why, given total freedom of choice, probably 50 percent of all freshmen and sophomores will write on either AIDS, gun control, or abortion. A large number of the remainder will end up selecting topics like teenage pregnancy or teenage suicide, juvenile delinquency, capital punishment, racism, or discrimination.

It is reasonable that these topics are so popular: they are much in the news, they are of genuine concern to young adults, students have already thought and probably written about them in high school, and—in some instances—they can either reuse an earlier paper of their own or use one for which their friend got an A in another course or another school.

It is precisely because these topics are so often discussed, both in the news and among their peers, that they become rather dull as research topics. The arguments have already been heard by the instructors who must read the papers, as well as by those writing them, and even if a new line of thinking is unearthed, it will never be as exciting as discovering something completely new. Topics that make the researcher exclaim: "Wow, this is interesting; I never heard of such a thing! I never knew that happened!" are likely to result in writing that is better than a rehash of familiar facts and already formed opinions.

Because the instructor knows more about the world (and about available library resources) than the students do, because the instructor has set the objectives of the assignment, and because the instructor wants the assignment to be a positive experience for the students, the instructor should provide a list of topics. And, the topics should be annotated to stimulate student interest and to provide a starting point for research.

The following is a list of sample annotated topics:

—Bloody riots, spurred by a Civil War draft lottery, break out between blacks and Irish in competition for jobs, New York City, 1863

—Dozens of working women jump to their death in the Triangle Shirtwaist Fire, New York City, 1911

—Twenty-million people die in Europe and America in the influenza epidemic of 1918–1919

—A Bronx school teacher becomes prime minister of Israel, Golda Meier, 1898–1979

—First American woman to openly wear pants in public, Amelia Bloomer, 1818–1894

Writing instructors (and librarians) preparing such lists should not be afraid of hype; remember you might have the heritage of twelve years of boring assignments to overcome. (Of course, students who want to pursue their own ideas should be encouraged to do so, with guidance.)

"REAL" RESEARCH: USE OF PRIMARY SOURCES IN UNDERGRADUATE RESEARCH

Carefully selected topics and innovative formats for presenting information are two ways librarians have observed to be successful in stimulating student interest in research/writing projects; a third way is through use of primary sources. There are a number of reasons why teachers of writing might find use of well-selected primary sources helpful in achieving their objectives.

—Students who may balk at reading textbooks, monographs, and even short works of fiction, may approach primary sources with an open mind, if not necessarily with initial enthusiasm.

—When using primary sources, the way in which one reads is more important than how much one reads. Primary sources are thus useful in stimulating critical thinking.

—In their very appearance, primary sources are far removed from material that resulted in failures in high school or was used in previous boring research/writing projects.

We obviously do not expect students on this level to make original contributions to scholarship by the use of primary sources, but we can provide them with the opportunity to experience the sense of excitement that comes from experiencing another world or another time through the immediacy of primary sources. The types of sources most likely to be useful to teachers of writing are those that are fairly simple to access and to read and that do not necessarily require obtaining a great deal of prior information to allow for interpretation. Two of the best are likely to be newspapers and magazines from earlier periods and the school archives.

Newspapers and magazines from the nineteenth century, as well as the first half of the twentieth century, are widely available in our libraries. Even on microfilm, these sources are familiar to students, and at least the most popular are indexed from the mid-nineteenth century on. Even very limited reading assignments in these sources can give students a sense of immediacy and personal connection that reading a textbook can never achieve.

The school archives are likely to contain letters, yearbooks, samples of old curricula and examinations, student newspapers, and other memorabilia, as well as official papers from the administration of the institution. These could provide a limited, thus useful, introduction to the process of analysis needed to produce a coherent history based on diverse sources. College archives can often enable students to research topics related to the everyday life of their predecessors, to changes in the curriculum, to changes in the nature of the student body and the faculty, and to the relationship of the college to the larger community.

When assignments are made using primary sources, it is helpful to suggest that the writing instructor look at the sources first (or consult the librarian about them), and then devise the list of topics. Since writing instructors are not teaching a course in research methods, it is important to be sure that the sources suggested can actually provide the necessary information for the topic.

CONCLUSION

There are many ways in which the knowledge and experience of librarians can help writing instructors achieve their goals. This chapter has addressed several of them. Insuring that our students become information literate—that they know how to locate and assess information and communicate effectively—is a responsibility that is shared across the academy.

ADDITIONAL READINGS

More detailed discussions of student writing projects can be found in the author's books: *Research projects for college students: What to write across the curriculum* (Greenwood, 1988), and *Multiculturalism in the college curriculum: A handbook of strategies and resources for faculty* (Greenwood, 1995).

Chapter 8

What Bibliographic Instruction Librarians Can Learn from Writing-Across-the-Curriculum Instructors

Jean Sheridan

Librarians teach best what they know best. The same is true of people in every profession, whether it be law, medicine, psychiatry, religion, or government—all of us like to display our proficiencies, sometimes to the point of neglecting the needs of others, of failing to listen to others. In his landmark book, *The Reflective Practitioner,* Donald Schoen (1983) alerted all the professions to the pitfalls inherent in this way of practicing. Stand back from your work, he said, and consider your clients. Are you listening to them, or are you hearing only to the point where you can open your mouth to prescribe once again the same old remedies? Instead, he advises the professional, reflect upon the dynamics of the encounter. Allow your clients to enter into the process of solving the problems they present to you. Respect their inherent wisdom. Work on the problem together.

  The clients who present themselves to librarians today are looking for the same thing they have always been looking for—information. In the light of Schoen's perspective, what is the appropriate "reflective" response? Is it to insist on teaching the use of printed indexes so that "the students will know the 'right way' to do it?" Or is it to move them to the CD-ROM workstations, realizing that there is no longer any "right way," nor, for that matter, any time to debate the issue. Librarians who realize this will stay in the "loop." Those who resist will be bypassed. One case in point is the Internet, that tidal wave of electronic information that threatens to engulf us. Between the time this chapter was being written, in the summer of 1994, and the time of publication, enormous changes will have taken place in the way access to the Internet is conducted, and the number of destinations on the electronic "superhighway" will have expanded astronomically. The issues of keeping up, of managing, and of providing access will challenge librarians and information seekers in new ways.

There are any number of ways librarians are responding to these large issues. The one with which we are concerned is our teaching function, what we call bibliographic instruction (BI). Academic librarians have come to see their bibliographic instruction classes as once-in-a-lifetime opportunities, precious moments when time stops and the skulls of students are opened up, allowing the librarians to pour knowledge into their heads. What constitutes the substance of these classes? What are they about? The literature of bibliographic instruction tells. It is about the stuff that fills libraries—books, indexes, catalogs, and now OPACs, CD-ROMs, and the Internet as well. From this profusion of resources, librarians list and evaluate the best items to include in their presentations and, in fifty minutes or less, teach strategies for finding them. No wonder, then, that the atmosphere of the BI classroom is charged with tension, at least for the performer, the librarian. The audience, on the other hand, is generally passive.

In the modern collaborative classroom, such lectures are infrequent. Today, experts in the pedagogy of higher education unanimously agree that those orations impede rather than enhance learning. Retention is not facilitated by the unrelenting presentation of dense material. Such presentations only make students, who are itchy in their seats and far from being engaged or excited by the content, want to bolt. It is no wonder that they come back to the reference desk asking the same questions over and over again. They have not learned. In addition, not every student even has the "head-open-pour-in" experience, for many instructors will not schedule a library class. They are usually experimenting with interactive teaching techniques themselves and are reluctant to subject students to a dry, content-laden tour or lecture.

Clearly, bibliographic instruction librarians need to become more creative, to dare to experiment, to "reimagine" themselves and their tasks (Fister, 1992). This will entail a rejection of past principles and an incorporation of new ones. It calls for a revolution in bibliographic instruction and a new way of looking at the business of teaching library skills. It will require librarians to reject the "more is better" approach in favor of the "less is more" approach. It requires a relaxation of classroom protocols to allow for more interaction between student and instructor. It requires that librarians learn more about teaching methods and less about indexing structures (until that is relevant to the teaching). It calls for more articles in the literature about teaching techniques and fewer about research strategies. It asks librarians to become teachers in the same way that their colleagues in the disciplines are teachers. It asks librarians to consider the words of Thomas Kirk (1984), who said that bibliographic instruction "can be more than providing directions on how to use library resources to complete a specific assignment. It can also make a significant contribution to the aims of liberal education [because it works] to develop those abilities and qualities that characterize the rational mind" (p. 96).

REFLECTIONS AT THE REFERENCE DESK

In 1984, Charles Bunge wrote an article for the *Journal of Academic Librarianship* in which he spoke to the discouragement of reference librarians. They burned out, he claimed, because improved access to information was too expensive and complex, because their clients presented problems associated with diversity and were deficient in academic skills, and because their own performance was difficult to evaluate and their expertise was in question. Today's bibliographic instruction librarians are equally disquieted, overwhelmed by the avalanche of information and the new skills they are challenged to master on what seems to be a daily basis. This pervasive discouragement stems in large part from a perception that they cannot keep up with the work, that it is overwhelming—there are too many students, too much material to cover (including the gargantuan Internet), too many changes, and, of course, not enough money.

But librarians are not alone in their discomfort. Today, a general dissatisfaction plagues the academic environment, a dissatisfaction that is felt by all—administrators, instructors, librarians, and students. Classroom instructors are baffled by the ever-changing information environment and are more reluctant than ever to encourage library use. They are discouraged, as Anthes and Crowe (1987) have said, by the "enormous growth of printed materials and the complexity of the contemporary library" (p. 92), a viewpoint that has led to dependence on lecture and textbook teaching. Many, especially those not regularly engaged in research, may have lost their confidence in using traditional sources and may be reluctant to learn how to use the new electronic technologies. These faculty are understandably disinclined to assign library-dependent tasks. Instead, they send their students into the library to "learn how to use the computer." This attitude conditions skill-deficient students to demand immediate gratification of their information needs. Oriented to instant service by modern culture, they are irritated when the inevitable detours occur.

RESPONSES FROM THE REFERENCE DESK

How do librarians respond to this shifting landscape? Do they? Unfortunately, many do not. In contrast to the approach advanced by Schoen (1983), they still choose to "perform comfortably with old routines, presenting or using personal knowledge and skills" (Michaels, 1986, p. 320). They stick with the same styles—they teach index searching, trot out volumes of reference tools, and demonstrate their own skills and knowledge. And they continue to rely on the lecture method.

Some librarians have become technicians and have transformed bibliographic instruction classes into computer workshops in which students and faculty are shown how to manipulate the software that drives the electronic data bases. Instructors in greater numbers are demanding that librarians teach about the intricacies of the Internet as well. This shift to the technical is not intrinsically bad; the stuff of libraries has always been uniquely appropriate for computerization. And just as they were trained in the past to manage print formats, so must our clientele now be trained to use computer-driven information sources. These skills, however, can be taught in open workshops given on a regular basis. Once a few basic skills are learned, most people can master electronic media with ease.

What I suggest as a necessary and complementary effort is a reinterpretation of bibliographic instruction, a new approach which calls upon the librarian to teach rather than demonstrate. We need to collaborate more fully with composition and content instructors "so that our teaching will integrate well into the culture of the classroom" (Fister, 1992, p. 156). In addition, the librarian must present the material so that its value appears worthwhile (Reichel, 1986, p. 20) and must study the qualities of good teachers (Lutzker, 1986; Roberts & Blandy, 1989; Sheridan, 1990). This requires that librarians learn how to use the same pedagogies as their colleagues in the disciplines (Jacobson, 1993; Kaplowitz, 1993). It requires learning about specific methods employed in collaborative learning and in writing-across-the-curriculum. It requires developing team-teaching relationships with instructors in the content areas. It requires reading higher education journals that publish praxis and writing articles for higher education as well as for our own literature of librarianship. The benefits will be many—a stronger, more intimate relationship with students, greater respect from faculty, and a sense of personal accomplishment without the stresses resulting from labor-intensive presentations.

NUT AND BOLTS

Today, those who teach teachers how to teach stress that the development of critical skills should take precedence over rote learning. This presents a dilemma to the average instructor who may feel that he or she is betraying his or her beloved subject matter, having lived with it through the PhD process and happily ever after. However, even the diehards, if their ultimate goal is to transfer knowledge, realize that they must find the best ways to do it, and most have come to realize that note-taking and lecturing is counterproductive. Instead, they are beginning to see that students learn best when less material is presented, and it is presented in more interesting ways when instructors keep the class busy, insist on in-class recall, pose people-centered problems, divide the class into small discussion groups, and find other ways to connect prior knowledge with new material.

Writing tasks are especially valuable and, of course, relevant to this investigation. In classes that use writing as a heuristic, students are asked to summarize lecture or textbook material, define concepts, give examples, devise applications for the material, or, in the case of a library class, critique the sources just presented. Many instructors use note cards for such writing because they encourage brevity and can be handled easily.

Many of these techniques form the basis of collaborative learning, which was discussed at some length in Chapter 1. To recapitulate briefly, collaborative learning requires a reduced emphasis on leadership by the instructor and a giving-over of responsibility to the students, whether to individuals or to small groups. Students help one another in seeking out information, and competition in the traditional sense is rejected for an attitude of cooperation. Peers review and evaluate one another's work. (See appendixes for guidelines.) Student teams often work together outside of class or with the instructor or librarian.

In spite of the emphasis on student activity, however, collaborative learning does not imply any diminishment of effort on the part of the instructor. On the contrary, careful class preparation is required. Groups must be carefully monitored, and relevant learning tasks created, whether these be a series of challenging questions relating to the course material or guidelines for evaluating reference sources, to use an example relevant to library instruction.

Writing-across-the-curriculum has incorporated many collaborative learning techniques, especially peer review and small group work, into its model, but it is primarily about writing as learning. This writing is expressive as well as transactional; it is approached in a recursive rather than a linear fashion; it makes use of journals and writing portfolios (collections of student writings); and it invites students into the discourse communities of the disciplines.

Bibliographic instruction can do all this as well. Students can be asked to write about how they conducted library research and to share these observations with others in small groups. They can be encouraged to keep journals and be given "starter" questions that inspire fruitful speculation and demonstrate that research, like writing, is a recursive process. The librarian can present written examples from the disciplines—journal articles, conference papers, abstracts—to familiarize students with these forms and to promote discussion about access to them. Specific writing activities are outlined in writing program handbooks which your institution may already have. Other examples and listings will be found in Chapter 5 and the appendixes.

STANDARDS FROM THE PROFESSION

The "Model Statement of Objectives for Academic Bibliographic Instruction" published by the Association of College and Research Libraries in 1989 fills a formidable five pages, single-spaced. Its specifics invite us to compare ourselves with our colleagues in the disciplines. I suggest that we regard it as our "content area" since it enumerates the things we are supposed to be teaching. But it is overwhelming in its detail. How can we reconcile this reality—the overwhelming number of skills that are involved in library research—with what has been said about "less is more"?

I suggest that we approach the model statement as a wonderful resource, but that we use it judiciously. We should consider it as a grand inspirational scheme, a platform from which to create an infinite number of classroom activities that incorporate all the good teaching elements mentioned earlier.

Take one element of the "Model Statement of Objectives" and play with it. Take, for example, item 2.T1.b., "the user understands how the timeliness of the date of publication may determine the value of the source." This suggests several classroom activities, such as discussion of books versus periodicals, primary sources versus secondary sources, and historical sources versus contemporary sources. Compare and contrast exercises suggest themselves. Item 1.T3.a., "the user recognizes that information sources can be recorded or unrecorded sources which may appear in different physical formats" suggests a lesson about the media and microforms, oral histories, and so forth. However, the emphasis continues to be content rather than format. The possibilities are endless, but the temptation to pontificate, to demonstrate everything one learned in the pursuit of the MLS, must be sublimated and replaced by interactive learning experiences for the students.

It may seem awkward—and some may even feel that it is inappropriate—to incorporate short writing tasks and small group work into bibliographic instruction, especially during the characteristic "cold call," to use a business term, but these learning exercises actually "warm up" a class and make students more receptive. The librarian/instructor can suggest to the classroom instructor that some of these tasks be graded, an additional incentive for students. Without a doubt, less material is going to be delivered, but there are myriad ways to provide road maps for the big stuff—handbooks, bibliographies, pathfinders. Open, ongoing workshops, as was suggested earlier, may be the best way to teach the use of electronic formats.

Ever so long ago, Miriam Dudley (1983) urged the profession to stand tall and librarians to be passionate about their work. Librarians "don't need to justify what they are doing, . . . they don't need to prove that students are better off for having been in the library, for having been exposed to a lesson in how to approach the catalog" (p. 62), she said, pointing out that our colleagues in other departments do not worry about the value of their work. She urged librarians to teach what we know, to celebrate ourselves in the teaching of it, and to be confident in the value of what we do.

We need to keep her words in mind, to tape them to our morning mirrors as a daily affirmation, so to speak, reminding ourselves at the same time that we need to envision ourselves anew. To that end we must continue to reflect with humility on the nature of our relationship with those we serve (Bunge, 1984; Schoen, 1983), for we are concerned with service. More than that, in bibliographic instruction we are teachers. Let us then teach and be fully engaged with our students, faculty colleagues, writing program administrators, and other librarians, in the effort to liberate through learning.

REFERENCES

Anthes, S. H., & Crowe, L. (1987). Teaching "library literacy." *College Teaching, 35*(3), 92–94.

Association of College and Research Libraries/Bibliographic Instruction Section Task Force. (1989). Model statement of objectives for academic bibliographic instruction. *College and Research Libraries News, 48*(5), 256–260.

Bunge, C. A. (1984). Potential and reality at the reference desk: Reflections on a "Return to the Field." *Journal of Academic Librarianship, 10*(3), 128–132.

Dudley, M. (1983). A philosophy of library instruction. *Research Strategies, 1*(2), 58–63.

Fister, B. (1992). Common ground: The composition/bibliographic instruction connection. In T. Kirk (Ed.), *Proceedings of the Sixth National Conference of the Association of College and Research Libraries* (pp. 154–158). Chicago: Association of College and Research Libraries.

Jacobson, T. E. (1993). Module 2: Selecting a teaching technique. In *Learning to teach: Workshops on instruction, a project of the learning to teach task force* (pp. 13–17). Chicago: Bibliographic Instruction Section, Association of College and Research Libraries, American Library Association.

Kaplowitz, J. (1993). Module 8: Contributions from the psychology of learning—practical implications for learning. In *Learning to teach: Workshops on instruction, a project of the learning task force* (pp. 57–67). Chicago: Bibliographic Instruction Section, Association of College and Research Libraries, American Library Association.

Kirk, T. G. (1984). Concluding comments. In T. G. Kirk (Ed.), *Increasing the teaching role of academic libraries: New directions for teaching and learning,* June, No. 18 (pp. 95–97). San Francisco: Jossey-Bass.

Lutzker, M. (1986). A good teacher: What to look for, how to find it. In A. S. Clark & K. F. Jones (Eds.), *Teaching librarians how to teach: On-the-job training for bibliographic instruction librarians* (pp. 13–19). Metuchen, NJ: Scarecrow.

Michaels, C. (1986). Library literacy: Some practicalities. *RQ, 25*(3), 319–321.

Reichel, M. (1986). Preparing to teach: Bruner's theory of instruction and bibliographic education. In A. S. Clark & K. F. Jones (Eds.), *Teaching librarians how to teach: On-the-job training for bibliographic instruction librarians* (pp. 20–31). Metuchen, NJ: Scarecrow.

Roberts, A. F., & Blandy, S. G. (1989). *Library instruction for librarians* (2nd rev. ed.). Englewood, CO: Libraries Unlimited.

Schoen, D. A. (1983). *The reflective practitioner.* New York: Basic Books.

Sheridan, J. (1990). The reflective librarian: Some observations on bibliographic instruction in the academic library. *Journal of Academic Librarianship, 16*(1), 22–26.

Chapter 9

Happy Endings: Creating Collaborative Relationships

Jean Sheridan

This chapter presents a scenario in which librarians share equally with writing program administrators and faculty in the content areas a commitment to promote intensive writing throughout the curriculum. Together librarians, administrators, and faculty promote writing as a means to a lofty end, namely so that when students leave college or university they will be better prepared to function competently in their professional lives.

In this scenario, collaborative and team approaches are preferred over solitary efforts. Administrators, writing program staff, English departments, content-area faculty, and librarians, all with unique gifts, engage in group efforts. They are confident that the literature of the past serves as a springboard for the newly written word created by student writers. They believe that truly effective mature writing is as dependent on content as it is on enthusiasm. Together they take a hard look at unnecessary reliance on textbooks and their hold on classroom teaching, and turn instead to the primary and secondary sources housed in libraries. The case studies found in Part IV of this book attest to the existence of such collaborations today.

THE LIBRARIAN AS AN AGENT OF CHANGE

Supported by an awareness of these successful programs, an understanding of writing-across-the-curriculum which I hope this book provides, the supreme confidence in their mission so well articulated by Dudley (1983), and the assertion of Kirk (1994) that we are "independent individuals who have responsibilities for addressing . . . issues" (p. 8), librarians can assume the role of agents of change at their institutions.

In order to be successful at this, however, it is essential that they operate out of a knowledge of the stages involved in effecting change. None of these should be ignored or neglected (Mellon, 1983). In order to effect change, one should: (1) build strong relationships in strategic areas; (2) assess the situation which needs change; (3) acquire sufficient information about it; (4) test possible solutions and then select one; (5) convince others to accept this solution; and (6) institutionalize the solution and gain wide acceptance for it (p. 7). Since much of this activity is dependent on personality and skill, librarians need to apply group dynamics principles to their efforts, learn how to work in teams, and recognize each other's strengths and gifts.

Acting as agents of change in the larger campus community, they will find seats on committees that manage the promotion of intensive course-based writing. (In larger institutions, where access through the hierarchy can be complicated, library administrators may need to exert influence at higher levels.) If these efforts are not successful, or if no writing-across-the-curriculum program exists, the library will sponsor or cosponsor conferences, workshops, or panel discussions to which composition teachers, content-area instructors, and appropriate administrators will be invited. Other library-sponsored workshops will follow.

Information will be transferred and shared through an electronic mail bulletin board. It will be used to suggest library-based writing assignments, to promote bibliographic instruction classes, and to expedite communication between librarians and other faculty. Alliances will be formed with composition teachers and writing program administrators. If student portfolios are part of the evaluation structure of the WAC program, librarians will strongly suggest that a library skills/research component be included.

In all of this, to use the words of Thomas G. Kirk (1994), "we must recognize the interdependent relationships which are involved, [for] the failure to acknowledge that interdependence is a fundamental weakness in developing strategies to achieve our goals" (p. 8). In all of these efforts, librarians should also be aware of inherent difficulties.

The incorporation of library instruction with writing programs requires planning above all. Too often, librarians have launched programs without defining their objectives clearly and without consulting faculty outside the library. Such efforts have frequently resulted in disappointments because librarians did not understand the needs and objectives of students and faculty, who, in turn, continued to struggle with library research because they could not see the relevance of the instruction to their endeavors. (Peroni, 1981, p. 7)

THE LIBRARIAN AS TEACHER

In our ideal scenario, librarians will, above all, teach. This is their most powerful and sustaining contribution. It is a labor that deepens relationships as it is a common effort shared with others in the academic community. To be effective here, librarians will revitalize their classroom presentations by using some of the methods employed in writing-across-the-curriculum and collaborative learning. Numerous possibilities have been described in Chapter 5. Chapter 8, "What Bibliographic Instruction Librarians Can Learn from Writing-Across-the-Curriculum Instructors," directly addresses the teaching issue.

In Chapter 6 a library-centered, librarian-taught course was described. Its broad appeal makes it attractive for inclusion in a core writing-intensive curriculum. Another possibility, a term paper writing and research class similar to what Caryl K. Sills (1991) has called a "paired composition course" has been described by Janet Streepy, Nancy Totten, Gabrielle Carr, and Teresa Reynolds (1987). In their model, two classes are taken in conjunction with each other, one a regular academic class in a content area and the other a writing/research class made up of students who are taking different courses. The writing/research class begins in the library with both the writing instructor and the librarian present. In succeeding classes, the writing instructor continues to teach about the protocols and procedures of preparing a term paper and the librarian acts as a consultant, setting up a conference schedule with each student. In these examples, the librarian is either the primary educator or takes equal responsibility with content-area instructors.

THE LIBRARIAN AS CONSULTANT

Librarians in our utopia are equally responsive to faculty and students and use e-mail and other avenues of communication to maintain strong connections. Realizing that libraries are complex systems which can cause discomfort to even the most sophisticated researcher, they keep all users informed of new technologies and research tools. To assist instructors in writing-intensive courses, especially courses grounded in content, they analyze course syllabi and respond with suggestions for library-based writing assignments. (The lists found in the appendixes of this book will be helpful here.) As guest lecturers, they demonstrate quietly and authoritatively both their expertise and the resources of the library. Taking a tip from the business world, they supplement their presentations with well-written reports, including bibliographies, pathfinders, and e-mail messages.

THE STUDENT WRITER'S PERSPECTIVE

One aspect neglected in this study, and perhaps a fit topic for further research, is the student's own story. Others have taken a stand, have been vocal about their positions, and have hotly debated the issue. Notable among these are writing program instructors and faculty in English departments. Content-area instructors question the effectiveness of their own teaching and devise ways to improve student learning. Those who advocate collaborative learning champion the democratic classroom and campus. Librarians hope for happy, satisfied, competent student "customers." Although all are sincere in their intentions, they generally talk among themselves; seldom are the students asked to voice their opinions. (For one student perspective, see McCarthy's 1987 study, "A Stranger in Strange Lands.")

It is time we listened to what students have to say to us and to what they say among themselves. They might give us a clue about what the future holds, a clue that may in fact be hidden in the present. A chance encounter at the University of Massachusetts at Amherst when I was visiting there to conduct research may illustrate what I mean. While walking across campus to keep an appointment, I fell into stride with a tall, fast-walking young woman who agreed to lead me to my destination. On a whim, I asked her about her experience with writing. She seemed to appreciate the question and spoke enthusiastically about learning to write under the guidance of Peter Elbow. Her experience in his class had been exciting and inspiring and had opened her up to writing. "In that class," she said with some emotion, "I found my voice." Then I asked her how she felt about research writing. Her mood changed, and she looked somber. "I don't know what's wrong," she confided. "Somehow when I start to write a term paper, it all changes. I stop having fun. I have to write in the third person. I can't seem to find my voice."

I believe that writing-across-the-curriculum is about helping students like this young woman find their voices. In our previous discussions, we have considered changes in the ways we teach writing and have challenged old assumptions about how students learn. We have considered changing the ways we teach students to conduct research, implementing the concept of process, and incorporating new pedagogies into our presentations. But perhaps more needs to change. Perhaps even the nature of academic writing needs to be transformed so that true voices can be heard.

These are the voices that are connected to learning in the sense illustrated by Belenky et al. (1986) in *Woman's Ways of Knowing,* in the way advocated by Limerick (1993) in her *New York Times* piece, and in the example in this very book by Ross LaBaugh (Chapter 2), whose treatment of his subject combines real scholarship with a pleasing and personable writing style. Perhaps our students, like the young woman I met at the University of Massachusetts, having learned from us, will themselves be the ones to move us away from the dominance of restrictive conventions and toward a happier, though no less demanding, place where information is exchanged in natural ways. This writer hopes so. And with that hope, I wish those students who will reap the benefits of this revisioning, instructors, librarians, and all writers everywhere a heartfelt "Happy Endings."

REFERENCES

Belenky, M. F., Clinchy, B. M., Goldberger, N. R. & Taruler, J. M. (1986). *Woman's ways of knowing: The development of self, voice, and mind.* New York: Basic Books.

Dudley, M. (1983). A philosophy of library instruction. *Research Strategies, 1*(2), 58–63.

Kirk, T. G. (1994). Guest editorial: The spirit of networking, beyond information resources. *College and Research Libraries, 55*(1), 7–8.

Limerick, P. N. (1993, October 31). Dancing with professors: The trouble with academic prose. *The New York Times Book Review,* pp. 3, 23–24.

McCarthy, L. P. (1987). A stranger in strange lands: A college student writing across the curriculum. *Research in the Teaching of English, 21*(3), 233–265.

Mellon, C. A. (1983). Instruction librarian as change agent. *Research Strategies, 1*(1), 4–13.

Peroni, P. A. (1981 July). *The second kind of knowledge: The role of library instruction in writing across the curriculum* (Report No. CS21 7 050). Glenside, PA: Paper presented at the Meeting of the National Endowment for the Humanities/Beaver College Summer Institute for Writing in the Humanities. (ERIC Document Reproduction Service No. ED 217 487)

Sills, C. K. (1991). Paired composition courses: Everything relates. *College Teaching, 39*(2), 61–64.

Streepy, J., Totten, N., Carr, G., & Reynolds, T. (1987). *Writing and research across the curriculum: A proposal for a new course* (Report No. CS-211-537). New Albany: Indiana University, Southeast. (ERIC Document Reproduction Service No. ED 300 807)

Part IV

Writing-Across-the-Curriculum: Real Life Collaborations (Case Studies)

Case Study: Oregon State University

Loretta Rielly, *Coordinator*
Sarah Beasley, Vicki Collins, Danielle Fagan,
Christopher Langdon, Loretta Rielly, and Janet
Webster, *Contributors*

Oregon State University

Number of FTE (Full Time Equivalent) students: 13,500

Number of FTE (Full Time Employed) faculty (including nonteaching faculty): 2,000

Student/faculty ratio (including nonteaching faculty): 7:1

Highest degree granted: Ph.D.

Type of institution: Public

MISSION OF OREGON STATE UNIVERSITY

Oregon State University serves the people of Oregon, the nation, and the world through education, research, and service.

Oregon State extends its programs throughout the world and is committed to providing access and educational opportunities to minorities and to disabled and disadvantaged persons.

Oregon State has an inherent commitment to provide a comprehensive array of high-quality educational programs in the sciences, the liberal arts, and selected professions. The university encourages students, both on and off campus, to develop an enriched awareness of themselves and their global environment.

Through research, Oregon State extends the frontiers of knowledge in the sciences, the liberal arts, and all aspects of natural, human, and economic resources. Oregon State contributes to the intellectual development and the economic and technological advancement of humankind.

As a Land, Sea, and Space Grant university, Oregon State has a special responsibility for education and research that enables the people of Oregon and the world to develop and utilize human, land, atmospheric, and oceanic resources. Unique programs of public service throughout Oregon supplement campus-based university teaching and research.

Oregon State University Libraries

Number of volumes: 1.2 million

Number of serial titles: 18,800

CD-ROM titles, including US government publications; OCLC FirstSearch on CD-ROM Network: 212

Total number of librarians: 35
  Public Services/Reference: 23
  Technical Services: 8
  Administration: 4

THE MISSION OF OSU LIBRARIES

As a unit of Oregon State University, the OSU Libraries share the university's overall goals and objectives. The primary mission of the libraries is to provide a comprehensive program of services that support the university's instructional, research, and public service programs. Within the context of these guidelines, the mission of the libraries is to:

Provide access to information and services that support the processes for learning and enhance the development of independent lifelong learners;

Acquire, preserve, and conserve collections that support OSU scholarship worldwide;

Work closely with persons in business and industry to provide essential resources and services that assist in the economic development of the state of Oregon; and

Satisfy a broad range of information needs of Oregonians through cooperation with other libraries in sharing resources.

Through user education programs and information services, the university libraries acquaint thousands of users each year with the wealth of information available within its collections and through the application of information technology.

LIBRARY INSTRUCTION PROGRAM

The Library Instruction (LI) Program at OSU is typical of many mid- to large-sized public universities and consists of an aggregate of components developed and modified over the years in response to an identified need. The LI "department" consists of a coordinator and an assistant, who are responsible for scheduling courses, rooms, and instructors, collecting and producing instruction statistics, producing general instructional materials, monitoring and coordinating materials produced by subject librarians, and maintaining a networked classroom and the audio-visual equipment. Seventeen librarians have subject assignments and are responsible for LI in their subject areas; eleven of them and the LI Coordinator rotate general, non-subject-based instruction. Paraprofessionals from all divisions of the library and selected student assistants help with general tours of Kerr Library. (The OSU Libraries consist of Kerr Library, the main library on the OSU campus in Corvallis, and Guin Library at the Hatfield Marine Science Center [HMSC] in Newport, fifty-five miles from Corvallis. Janet Webster, Director of Guin Library, describes library instruction at HMSC later in this case study.)

TOURS

Thirty-minute guided tours of Kerr Library are offered at the beginning of each term on a drop-in basis. OSU students, faculty, staff, and resident borrowers can also check out thirty-minute self-guided audio tape tours. The tours provide a general orientation to the library and focus on its services and resources. A computer-assisted instruction program, "Student Tutorial: Access & Resources (STAR)," complements the tours and provides instruction in the principles of library research.

COMPUTER-ASSISTED INSTRUCTION

STAR is a hypercard program developed by a team composed of a member of the art faculty, a student graphic designer, a student programmer, and two librarians, one of whom has a degree in instructional design. It consists of five modules, each covering a different information need and the type of source most likely to meet that need: Quick Overview (encyclopedias), The Big Picture (books), What's Happening Then and Now (magazines and newspapers), What the Experts Say (journals), and Brief Facts (reference sources). Within these modules, students learn about using the on-line catalog, interpreting and locating call numbers, selecting and using print and electronic indexes, and distinguishing between magazines and journals. STAR is networked and available in a student computer lab located in Kerr. Between 3,000 and 5,000 students a year complete STAR, most to meet the requirements for Speech Communications 111. Although it is intended for freshmen and other students who have not used an academic library, faculty often require upper-division students to take it in order to review research principles. Interestingly, these "experienced" students seem to get more from STAR than the freshmen, probably because it answers questions they have—the new student does not know the questions yet.

ELECTRONIC LIBRARY SEMINARS

Each term, in an ''Electronic Library'' seminar series, we provide instruction in specific electronic resources. Topics vary from term to term and have included the on-line catalog (offered every term), the Internet, gophers, personal bibliographic software, FirstSearch, specific CD-ROM data bases, and CARL-Uncover. Attendance at these is uneven, the most popular seminars being those that deal with the Internet and personal bibliographic software.

CREDIT COURSES

Several of the science and technology librarians teach one-hour credit courses in agriculture, engineering, fisheries and wildlife, and beginning in the spring of 1995, chemistry. Library Research in Agriculture (AG 199) is a required course for horticulture majors. Engineering Research Communication (ENG 485/585) and Retrieving and Using Scientific Literature (FW 507) are electives; Chemical Information (CH 407/507) will be an elective.

COURSE-RELATED INSTRUCTION

At OSU, course-related or course-integrated instruction is very much ad hoc and has been dependent upon contacts between individual librarians and teaching faculty. We meet with a number of classes in the English Language Institute, a program for undergraduate and graduate students who will be attending OSU or another university in the United States, and in the Educational Opportunities Program for provisionally admitted students. Subject librarians teach classes in their subject areas, and some actively promote their services by contacting individual faculty, speaking at department meetings, publishing newsletters, and so forth. The librarian teaching a particular class customizes the instruction to suit the needs of that class or assignment.

CONCLUSION

The LI Program has undergone a number of changes over the years in response to changes on the OSU campus. The most profound change has been the increasing use of networked electronic information: our on-line catalog, over thirty of our CD-ROM data bases, and OCLC FirstSearch can be accessed via telnet or modem. Consequently, faculty, staff, and many graduate students do much of their research from their offices or homes and come to the library only to get the materials. This past summer all the residence halls were networked, and we anticipate increasing numbers of undergraduates will work from remote locations. This, of course, presents interesting instructional challenges since we have relied heavily on one-on-one instruction at the reference desk in Kerr Library. As we move even further into a networked environment, we will be exploring new ways to reach students (and faculty). These will include increasing our efforts to encourage faculty to include library research components in their courses via programs such as the Writing-Intensive-Curriculum (WIC). For further information about the LI Program at OSU, please contact:

Loretta Rielly, Coordinator of Library Instruction
Kerr Library 121
Oregon State University
Corvallis, OR 97331-4501
E-mail: RIELLYL@ccmail.orst.edu
Phone: 503-737-7288
Fax: 503-737-3453

WAC and The Academic Library

Vicki Collins, Assistant Professor and Director of the Writing-
Intensive-Curriculum Program

THE HISTORY AND SUPPORT OF WAC AT OREGON STATE UNIVERSITY: WAC AND THE BACCALAUREATE CORE

In 1989, the Oregon State University faculty senate, as part of the revision of the general education requirements, mandated an upper division writing-intensive requirement in the major for every student. The resulting new curriculum model, called the Baccalaureate Core (Bac Core), sets course requirements in the areas of skills, perspectives, and synthesis. Writing courses are included in the skills area, and students are required to complete three courses in writing/communication at the lower division and one writing-intensive course in the major at the upper division.

The inclusion of the Writing-Intensive-Curriculum (WIC) requirement in the Bac Core was the result of a consensus among key administrators, rhetoric and composition faculty, and faculty in other disciplines, many of whom had come to believe that training and experience in writing in the disciplines could best be taught within the majors. Faculty from various colleges had expressed concern about the writing skills of the students in their departments. Graham Spanier, who was then provost, had recently come to OSU from SUNY-Stony Brook, where Peter Elbow had convinced him of the value of Writing-Across-the-Curriculum (WAC). And within the English department, rhetoric and composition specialists—particularly Chris Anderson, Director of Freshman Composition; Lisa Ede, Director of the Center for Writing and Learning; Simon

Johnson, Director of Technical Writing; and Lex Runciman, Writing Center Director—began to envision an upper division writing-intensive program which would locate the teaching of writing in the disciplines and at the same time take advantage of cutting-edge research and pedagogy in the field of composition.

From faculty across the disciplines came the willingness to take responsibility for teaching their students to write. From the writing faculty came vision and expertise in curriculum design and faculty development. And from the administration came the budgetary commitment necessary to fund not only a director and office space for the Writing-Intensive-Curriculum, but also modest honoraria for faculty development and fees for outside speakers.

IMPLEMENTATION AND ADMINISTRATIVE STRUCTURE OF THE WRITING-INTENSIVE PROGRAM

After significant faculty development during the 1990–1991 school year, the WIC course approval process began in 1991–1992. By the spring of 1994, when the first students graduated under the new Bac Core requirements, all departments with undergraduate majors had at least one WIC course in place, and a total of 117 WIC courses were offered at the university. The WIC program has been directed by Lex Runciman 1990–1992, Jon Olson (who served as acting director) 1992–1993, and Vicki Tolar Collins 1993 to the present.

The WIC program is funded at the university level. It is housed in the Center for Writing and Learning (in a different building from the English department) and is administered by a tenure-track assistant professor in the English department whose appointment is split, with half of his or her time devoted to serving as Director of WIC, and half to teaching undergraduate and graduate courses in English. For administrative purposes, the program is included in the College of Liberal Arts. The WIC director sits on the Dean's Council of the College of Liberal Arts, along with department chairs and other program directors. Nevertheless, the WIC program is a university-wide program and a function of the faculty senate. A writing advisory board appointed by the faculty senate serves as a resource for the WIC director.

Faculty who wish to institute a WIC course submit a proposal, along with a syllabus and writing assignments, to the director of undergraduate studies. The WIC director reviews the proposal, works with the faculty member on needed revisions, and sends a recommendation for approval to the Bac Core committee of the faculty senate.

Departments have chosen to structure their WIC courses in a variety of ways. Many departments have revised capstone courses in the major to include significant writing. For example, in the Department of Animal Science, all production systems courses are writing-intensive, including Equine Production, which meets only in the barn. The College of Business offers multiple sections of one 400-level course, Strategic Management and Business Policy, as its WIC course. Because departments such as English and Speech Communication each offer more than ten upper-level WIC courses, their students are likely to take several writing-intensive courses rather than the one required by the Bac Core. After pilot courses in the Department of Art such as the one described in Danielle Fagan's section of this article, the department decided that art majors would satisfy the WIC requirement by taking a small seminar with a professor in their main area of concentration. Students enrolled in the International Degree Program satisfy the WIC requirement by engaging in informal and formal writing related to a capstone project under the guidance of a major professor.

FACULTY DEVELOPMENT FOR WRITING-INTENSIVE COURSES

One key to the success of the WIC program at Oregon State is university funding and support for faculty development. Initially, the WIC program brought to campus well-known experts in the teaching of writing such as Peter Elbow and Andrea Lunsford, who conducted workshops for all faculty interested in writing in the disciplines. Since 1990, the WIC director has regularly offered faculty seminars. Seminar participants, who meet once a week for five weeks, explore ways to develop the Writing-Intensive-Curriculum, either by restructuring old courses to include formal and informal writing or by designing new courses. Through seminar discussion and outside reading assignments, seminar participants become familiar with current theory and practice in the teaching of writing, with particular emphasis on writing-to-learn and writing as a process. Discussions center on ways to use writing even in large classes, ways to use minimally graded writing to stimulate learning, ways to design effective formal assignments and grade them efficiently, ways to help students revise, and ways to conference with students on their writing. Seminar participants are enthusiastic about the opportunity to meet colleagues from other departments and disciplines. For participating in the seminar, they receive a modest honorarium in support of their continued professional development.

Beyond the initial seminar, support for faculty who teach writing-intensive courses includes individual conferences, periodic small-group lunches to discuss successes and problems, and the quarterly publication of *Teaching with Writing,* a newsletter for all faculty, which promotes the use of writing in all university courses. At the request of faculty teaching WIC courses, the WIC director has added an advanced faculty seminar focusing on issues such as effective use of collaborative writing assignments and the special needs of ESL (English-as-a-second-language) students in writing-intensive courses.

BAC CORE WRITING REQUIREMENTS, LOWER DIVISION

The faculty senate's decision to require twelve course hours of writing, including the WIC course in the major, signifies a solid commitment by the university to the teaching of writing. Writing I is satisfied by Writing 121, which focuses on writing and reading as processes, invention strategies, drafting and revision techniques, and the forms and conventions of writing. While encouraging the appreciation and understanding of language, form, and style, Writing 121 also emphasizes critical thinking, including the ability to analyze content and reader response, and it requires a significant amount of student writing.

When the Bac Core was instituted, the Writing 121 curriculum was structured around five essays that were written and revised in a ten-week term. The essays were sequenced from personal reflective writing and critical analysis of reading to informative and deliberative writing. The Writing 121 curriculum has now shifted toward writing-across-the-curriculum and is based on the premise that student writers need to know how to read and how to write about reading. With Chris Anderson and Lex Runciman's rhetoric reader, *Forest of Voices: Reading and Writing the Environment* (1995) as the textbook, writing assignments move from informal reading response journals to summaries of readings, and finally to arguments composed in response to readings. In most sections of Writing 121, students compile a portfolio of their informal and formal writing. There is no research component in Writing 121, and students do not receive instruction in library skills or in the effective use of borrowed information. Writing 121 is taught primarily by first-year teaching assistants working on a Master of Arts in English.

To fulfill the Writing II and Writing III/Speech requirements, students typically choose from among approved courses in business writing, technical writing, creative writing, and speech communication. While business and technical writing courses generally require a documented report (written and oral), and while some teachers of writing and speech involve librarians in preparing students to conduct research, there is no standardized practice in the Writing II and Writing III/Speech courses of library instruction or of instruction in the correct use of borrowed information.

BAC CORE WRITING-INTENSIVE REQUIREMENT, UPPER DIVISION

After completing nine hours of course work in Writing I, Writing II, and Writing III/Speech, Oregon State students take an upper-division Writing-Intensive-Curriculum (WIC) course in their major, taught by a professor in the department. The Curricular Procedures Handbook expresses the faculty senate's rationale for this requirement:

To be accepted in a profession or a group, individuals must be able to communicate with colleagues in a manner considered acceptable within that field. Courses in a student's major provide students with writing practice as members of their particular community. Writing-intensive courses serve to further acquaint students with writing as practiced in their respective disciplines. These courses are not intended as courses in writing instruction; they are capstone courses within the student's major field, in which writing is emphasized. The WIC will encourage students to integrate major concepts and important facts about their disciplines and to communicate such information in a professional manner. (Fall, 1994, p. 50)

GUIDELINES FOR WIC COURSES

The following criteria for WIC courses were adopted by the OSU faculty senate as part of the Baccalaureate Core:

Criteria 1: Writing-intensive courses shall use student writing as a significant approach to learning.

Criteria 2: Writing-intensive courses shall base a significant part of the grade on evaluation of writing.

Criteria 3: Writing-intensive courses shall discuss writing issues pertinent to that discipline, as such issues apply both academically and professionally.

Criteria 4: Writing-intensive courses shall be upper division.

SO WHAT?

So far this description of the WIC program at OSU may sound like the kind of curricular mandate that makes teachers' and students' lives more complicated. Faculty lives are definitely more complicated when professors across the curriculum begin to take responsibility for the writing instruction of their students and when that instruction includes the informality of writing-to-learn, the messiness of helping students with the whole writing process, the challenge of peer review of drafts, and the mandate to prepare students to write as professionals in the discipline. Students' lives are definitely affected when they must abandon the passive role of note-taker/memorizer and become critical thinkers and writers.

Despite these complications, many WIC teachers report new energy in their classrooms: students learn more as they actively engage the subject matter through writing, and faculty become better teachers because student writing gives them steady feedback on student learning, understanding, and misunderstanding. Often faculty members find teaching with writing so effective that they begin using writing-intensive approaches in non-WIC classes. Influenced by WIC-trained faculty members, several departments have redesigned their curricula to include writing instruction and development from introductory courses on through the entire major.

PROBLEMS AND PROMISES

Implementation of a far-reaching writing-intensive program is not without problems and resistance. A primary concern among faculty is the question of "coverage," when teachers who are used to nonstop, content-laden lectures are asked to allow class time for writing-to-learn exercises and conversation about student writing. In the seminar, I try to allay fears by citing research that shows student attention to and retention of lecture material decreases dramatically as the class hour progresses and by bringing in experienced WIC teachers from across the curriculum to share their own views of the content coverage question.

Another area of resistance is the extent to which faculty from all disciplines obsess about correctness as the primary signal of good student writing. My original intention was to deal with mechanics and error in the final seminar as a part of the whole question of evaluating student writing. But I quickly came to see grammar as the hairy monster under the seminar table, which would disturb every conversation until we invited it to join us. Faculty are relieved to learn that composition research indicates that marking every error does not improve correctness. Rather, as Richard Haswell (1993) shows, if the teacher simply puts a check in the margin where there is an error, students can, if given the opportunity, identify and eliminate most of their own errors. Students need more than one chance to get it right.

While teachers are alarmed and concerned about the poor writing of their students, seminar discussions and journal entries reveal that many faculty are also anxious about their own writing, fearing that teaching a WIC course will reveal their own inadequacies. The seminar is intentionally structured to foster reflections on one's own history as a writer and one's own writing process and to encourage faculty to become part of a community of writers in the seminar and in their larger lives as scholars and writers.

As Loretta Rielly discusses in her section of this article, a university-wide writing-intensive requirement puts new demands on libraries and librarians. Budget cuts affect journal access for advanced students in some disciplines and limit the library's ability to acquire reference material and journals in emerging areas of research, such as African literature. Students on the quarter system can hardly count on acquiring necessary reference material through interlibrary loans in time to produce and revise a WIC project. Because many professional accreditation bodies require departments to train students in collaborative projects, a number of WIC courses include such projects. However, the traditional design of library space can be an impediment to students conducting collaborative research. And with the advent of on-line research on the Internet, WIC faculty and librarians alike face the challenge of teaching students to discriminate among sources they find while "surfing the net." Students may give equal value to the views of a loose cannon on a topical bulletin board and a United Nations document on world hunger. And the truth is that students, despite their lack of critical knowledge of Internet sources, may be far ahead of their professors in ability to use electronic search sources. So library support for writing-intensive courses may necessitate education of faculty, as well as students, in using electronic resources.

At Oregon State, the willingness of librarians to meet with the WIC faculty seminar, to come to WIC classes, and to design presentations and resources for particular curricula has encouraged teachers, librarians, and students to see themselves as a community of writers, readers, and researchers.

The following accounts by faculty and librarians present WIC research projects that depend on and grow out of friendly collaboration between teaching faculty and library staff. Art professor Danielle Fagan and librarian Sarah Beasley describe their collaboration on a project for graphic design students in a course that piloted WIC teaching techniques in the art department and led to the departmental decision to spread writing instruction across the department in small seminar-like sections. Christopher Langdon, professor of fisheries and wildlife, and Janet Webster, librarian for the Guin Library at the Hatfield Marine Science Center, describe the challenges of supporting students in a WIC course taught on the Oregon coast, fifty miles from main campus resources.

REFERENCE

Haswell, R. H. (1993). Minimal marking. *College English, 45,* 600–604.

The Writing-Intensive-Curriculum: The Library Perspective

Loretta Rielly, Assistant Professor and Coordinator of Library Instruction

My first year as coordinator of library instruction coincided with the first year that the Writing-Intensive-Curriculum was included in the Baccalaureate Core and, also, the first year that the five-week seminar for faculty teaching WIC courses was offered. Since students in WIC would be required to include documented sources in their writing, WIC offered a great opportunity to connect program-wide with upper division classes in which students would be using the library. I took the seminar that first year in order to better understand the purpose and content of WIC classes and to identify ways the library could support them. Subsequently, I have met with the seminar each term to discuss library services, but more importantly, to hear from the faculty what they and their students need from the library and to share observations from the library's point of view. We have a symbiotic relationship in many ways, and communication between the library and teaching faculty is critical if students are to develop effective library research skills and get the most from the burgeoning amount of information available to them at OSU and elsewhere.

DISCIPLINE-SPECIFIC RESEARCH

Many, if not most, faculty assume that students are "taught" library-use skills in their freshmen or sophomore years. At OSU, the only program to include a library component in all classes is Public Speaking (Speech Communications 111), in which students complete STAR, the library's hypercard program. Although Speech Communications 111 reaches many undergraduate students, it certainly does not reach all of them. Even those students who complete STAR, however, have only been taught *general* principles of library use, and like writing, research is discipline specific. This is not something students necessarily understand. If students are not directed to use, or made aware of, subject-based resources, they will use the resource that is most familiar, easiest, and closest at hand to complete their work.

Librarians believe that identifying, accessing, and evaluating information in their discipline is a skill that students need in order to succeed both academically and professionally. Coming from librarians, however, this sounds like a "library thing." If information-retrieval skills are important to professional work in their discipline, students need to be given the opportunity to make them part of their professional repertoire. Librarians can teach the bibliographic skills, but they cannot teach the professional application of those skills. That is best and most appropriately done by the professionals, the teaching faculty. Both of the OSU classes described in this case study illustrate discipline-specific uses of information and the value of collaboration between librarians and teaching faculty in helping students understand both the hows and the whys. In the aquaculture class, Christopher Langdon and Janet Webster introduce students to the gray literature important to the sciences; in Graphic Design II, Danielle Fagan and Sarah Beasley offer solutions for identifying and using text-based information to students who are more accustomed to, and comfortable with, visual communication.

THE RESEARCH PROCESS

Librarians can also be of value to faculty because of their understanding of the research process, which is based on their knowledge of bibliographic tools and, perhaps more importantly, their observations of and interaction with students at the reference desk. WIC courses emphasize process in a way that other, traditional upper division classes do not. Librarians observe the research process daily, and their observations could be useful to faculty developing process-based formal assignments. At a recent WIC seminar, one faculty member was surprised to learn that "is this a journal?" is one of the most frequently asked questions at the reference desk. He had assumed this was a distinction that students understood by their junior or senior year; perhaps it should be, but it is not. Similarly, students are puzzled when told to look for primary, secondary, or tertiary sources. These are common stumbling blocks for students that can be addressed at early stages in the research process. Students will approach library research more seriously and more confidently when the assignment acknowledges the process as well as the product, as Professor Fagan did by requiring her design students to submit preliminary stages of their work.

LIBRARY INSTRUCTION IN WIC COURSES

Faculty who teach WIC courses are committed teachers. They are also very busy teachers, learning a new way of teaching. Many are not prepared to incorporate another new component into their courses. Time is also a critical factor, especially when there are only ten weeks in a term. Although the librarians at OSU are advocates for the library and for information literacy as a goal for all OSU students, they try to be sensitive to the many demands placed on the teaching faculty. When I meet with the WIC seminars, I stress the librarian's role as a consultant who can customize the instruction to meet the needs of a particular class. Librarians will review library assignments to ensure that the library's resources will support them. They will notify the reference desk about library assignments so that librarians and staff are prepared to help students in a way that reinforces the instructor's objectives. They will provide "information bulletins" or specialized research guides in print or electronic form on the library's gopher. They will meet with a class in order to demonstrate techniques for searching a particular data base or for locating Internet resources. They will develop short instructional modules in print or electronic form that students can complete outside of class. The fifty-minute library lecture is only one way to teach information-retrieval skills.

CONCLUSION

The most critical element in the relationship between the library and the WIC program is communication between librarians and teaching faculty. The more librarians know about the assignments being made and the expectations of the instructors, the more they can do to ensure that students have a successful library experience. Similarly, the more the faculty know about our collections and our services, the more they can contribute toward that goal. Vicki Collins, WIC Coordinator, notes that the WIC program has placed new demands on the library. It has, but they are welcome demands, for they are giving students the opportunity to develop the library-research and information-retrieval skills important in their discipline.

WIC and the Visual Arts: Graphic Design II

Instructor's Statement
Danielle Fagan, Assistant Professor, Art

[Note: Danielle Fagan is now at Miami University, Oxford, Ohio.]

I had long wanted to include a writing component in my upper-division graphic design class, but I was familiar only with graded, formal writing, such as research papers. I did not feel I could require students to submit both a research paper and a design project, nor would a research paper help them learn the kinds of writing they would need to do as professional designers. Thus, I enrolled in the Writing-Intensive-Curriculum Seminar for OSU faculty the first year it was offered, although the art department had not yet identified a WIC class. The "time line" project described here was the result of my having taken the seminar.

THE PROBLEM

As the instructor of junior graphic design students, I encountered many bright students who were frequently, if not universally, hard working, but who had real difficulties in any aspect of design that required writing and research. In some part, this may be due to the belief that artists speak in a visual language and are not necessarily required to communicate as effectively in a verbal language. In fact, I suspect that some art students gravitate to the visual arts so that they will not have to write. However, my professional graphic design experience made me realize just how important writing, research, and verbal articulation skills would be to these students. Graphic design is primarily a means of communication, and designers are frequently required to write copy, to write proposals to clients, to make both written and spoken presentations to clients and prospective clients, and to do an amazing amount of background research for almost every professional assignment. Without these skills, students would be unprepared for the "real world" that awaited them.

Given this setting, I needed a project for my junior class students that would provide a complex and challenging communications problem in which they could develop research skills for their specific discipline, apply writing skills to the design context, and have the opportunity to explore in depth the interrelationship between visual and verbal communication.

THE VISUAL TIME LINE

The assignment I developed was a "visual time line." Before the course started, I identified a specific interval of time from 1925 back, until I had enough periods to cover the anticipated number of students. The 1925 date was somewhat arbitrary, but was intended to be far enough back to avoid bursts of nostalgia or "retro" styles and to insure that at least some real "digging" had to be done even for relatively recent history. To compensate for the smaller amounts of information that are available for the earliest periods of history, the period assigned to each individual varied. Intervals ranged from twenty-five years to as long as several centuries.

The project required each student to research and design several components. The primary piece was to be an 11" × 17" sheet containing visual and verbal information on eight to ten significant events of the period, including at least one event from each of the following categories: science and technology, the arts, social and political developments, and a non-European, non-U.S. culture. Each student was to write all the copy for this and could use as many or as few visual images as he or she felt was needed. No exact length was required for the copy. Each student's design had to coordinate with the other students' work since at the end of the project, all the pieces were to be assembled in order and displayed together.

In addition to the "base" piece, each student was required to research and design two additional "amplifications." One of these was to be a further explanation of the background, relevance, or little-known details of one of the events used on their main time line. There was a minimum copy length of at least three paragraphs for this, and it was up to the student to determine what combination of text and images to use. The second required amplification was an original map, chart, graph, or diagram to clarify something from the base. There were additional limitations and specifications relating to the visual aspects of the problem that were based on the tools, materials, and techniques available.

THE LIBRARY COMPONENT

Another faculty member in the art department had taken one of his classes to the library and enthusiastically endorsed the short seminar given by Sarah Beasley, the art librarian. I gave her the acid test and contacted her about three weeks before the assignment. I asked if she thought it was a workable idea and if she could help the students learn to find information for such a project. Sarah not only said that she could and would, but also that she would do some sample research using their assignment as the basis of her presentation. Sarah actually sounded enthusiastic about the project's potential for developing research skills.

As juniors, the students were familiar with the library and the location of the main stacks, but their research skills consisted primarily of using the computer to look up books on their topic. If the library did not have a book under the heading or title of "Viking ships," for example, the students would come back and tell me that our library did not have any information on Viking ships, which I always found difficult to believe given four floors of books, magazines, journals, encyclopedias, reference handbooks and CD-ROM disks. I will admit, however, that digging visual material out of a system set up to access verbal information can be frustrating and requires some creative research. I know there are pictures of black and white spotted cows in the library, especially in a school with a veterinary program, but trying to find one can involve a long and frustrating search. The design students needed to relate their writing to the visuals and had to be able to find information about both.

Sarah's presentation introduced the students to the various types of sources in the library and the kind of information they might find in each. She used examples from their assignment, pointing out that if they needed information on China in 1557, they might have to look under something other than "China," or that information on Arabic writing might be accessed from a variety of beginning points. She helped them think of alternatives if the first idea for a keyword search did not yield results. She introduced them to the concept that different information resources may use different words for subject categories and helped them determine where to go when they hit an apparent dead end. In addition to opening up many new possibilities for searching, Sarah also shared tips on how to keep track of where and what they had searched. Perhaps of equal importance was the idea that verbal and visual information was to be found in a variety of places and that they were doing research for the writing at the same time that they were conducting research for the visual portion of the project. The writing was not a separate thing that students had to do, but was a natural part of telling the story.

CONCLUSION

By the end of the project, the students had so much information that the biggest problem became editing. They were editing from a solid base and were able to make some very good decisions on just what might be expressed visually and what might be best related in written copy. Most of the students commented that they really enjoyed the project, and I was certainly happy with the outcome. The complete time line, along with an explanation of the project, was displayed in a student gallery. The students were so enthusiastic about their work that during the weekend of the Easter break, they painted the gallery walls so their work would look its best. In addition to the final project, each student made a packet of the preliminary work and project development stages. These packets helped me trace the development of the project and, more importantly, gave the students something that could be put in their portfolios so they could show prospective employers their skills at concept development, research, and writing. These are skills that prospective employers almost always emphasize, but that are difficult to assess based only on a final, finished product.

Almost every student commented to me on the importance of the research seminar. Most echoed one student's comment: "Why didn't someone tell us this two years ago? It would have made things so much easier." As a result of integrating writing and research skills into the design course, students gained more flexibility in solving communications problems. They had a great deal more confidence in their writing and research skills and did not tend to use solutions that seemed easy but were in fact an avoidance of the problem. One assignment did not turn a poor writer into a good one, but it did seem to give all of them a bit more confidence and experience and help each see how visual and verbal information can relate to tell a better, more interesting story.

WIC and the Visual Arts: Graphic Design II

Librarian's Statement
Sarah Beasley, Instructor, OSU Libraries

INITIAL CONSIDERATIONS

From the perspective of an academic reference librarian, I thought the time line assignment proposed by Professor Fagan for Graphic Design II was brilliant. It required investigation of a wide variety of information resources (including the on-line catalog, periodical indexes, old and current newspapers, books, and reference works) and critical evaluation of the information found. This forced students to analyze with each resource whether they needed to focus or expand their query. In terms of making library research a process filled with tangible rewards, while reinforcing the strategy of finding and evaluating information and then focusing the question as needed, I am not sure I have encountered its peer.

Beyond meeting the library instruction demands of the assignment itself, I came to the time line project with an agenda. Because many students, perhaps especially art students, think that the library is not relevant to their needs, I looked forward to opportunities to dispel this perception. However, the organization of information in libraries is not intuitive to anyone, and as a system it can engender instant animosity. In the delivery of this instruction, in addition to teaching the basics of how information is organized in libraries (by formal subject headings, classification, and access tools), I wanted to demonstrate how someone who knows how to use the system can readily pursue varying avenues of inquiry and not be bound by its formality.

My second concern was for students studying for professions in which they will work with clients who will come from a wide variety of disciplines. How can, in this case, graphic designers become familiar with their clients' fields? How can they do this quickly? If the characteristics of information are understood, figuring out the appropriate information resources for a field is not difficult.

There was a third, perhaps more reality-based, issue involved in devising the content of this instruction. Because I had only one class period, and this would likely be the one opportunity for formal library instruction available to these students, the presentation included general information about types of information sources, their characteristics, and their access tools.

OBJECTIVES

The objectives for the class session were:

- To provide the students with a strategy for doing the time line assignment.

- To acquaint students with the variety of information resources available to them and to give a context for using some of them.

- To demonstrate some of the main features of searching in on-line catalogs (controlled versus free text vocabulary and the information contained in a bibliographic record and what is useful about it).

- To profile reference works that were good starting points for the assignment and also to acquaint students with the fact that there *are* reference works.

THE CLASS SESSION

The class was taught as a lecture/demonstration in the library's networked classroom, which also has projection capabilities, so in the discussion of searching the on-line catalog, students could see the screen and follow the search logic. The session included a statement of learning objectives, a list of suggested habits for library research, a description of the characteristics of standard information sources with pointers to the appropriate accessing tools, and presentation of reference works that would be of particular use in getting started. (These were more fully described in the handout which is not included here.)

The description of information sources and their characteristics included discussion of how the students might incorporate the information found in each type of source into either their final project or into further developing their understanding of an era or a historical development. For example, an ancient monument that was an engineering marvel in its day might still be photographed for newspapers, discussed in a technical encyclopedia, or given significant treatment in a book about the antiquities of its home country.

I underscored the principle that for each kind of resource there is a particular finding tool and that the tool has a particular arrangement and often a controlled vocabulary. Because of the time limitation and because books would be one of the better sources of information for this assignment, the focus was on the on-line catalog as a finding tool. I discussed subject headings and taught the concept of controlled vocabulary versus natural language by using my favorite example in OSU's catalog. "Beekeeping" is not a Library of Congress Subject Heading (LCSH). When "beekeeping" is searched as a subject heading, there are no hits (which makes no sense in the library of a land grant institution with strong programs in agriculture), but if it is searched as a title keyword, there are eighty-seven titles. Examination of the record shows that "bee culture" is the appropriate Library of Congress Subject Heading.

The OSU catalog has a feature that allows extending from a particular bibliographic record on any of the title, author, series, subject heading, or call number fields. Extending on the subject heading field leads to a dictionary listing of subject headings. From this listing, I pointed out the form subheadings, such as handbooks, manuals, dictionaries and encyclopedias, and—the boon to art students—pictorial works. By examining the records cataloged with pictorial works, students saw that the bibliographic record would tell them whether a work was illustrated or whether it included a bibliography—a lead to more sources if they needed them.

Throughout the demonstration, students were encouraged to develop a list of search terms by thinking in two dimensions: the specific thing (Chinese characters) and the more general area of which the thing is a part (writing systems, alphabets, or China, and within the area of China, antiquities, culture, or language).

REFLECTIONS

This lecture/demonstration was quite successful, in large part because the students knew that they needed to understand how to navigate through a library and identify material more efficiently than they could through serendipitous browsing or by hearing about a resource from a friend, their more familiar methods. The fact that their final product, as well as the intermediate steps, required a written synthesis of the information they gathered raised their level of motivation, and the material presented gave them a starting point for their research.

One small drawback was the lack of time. If there had been more time, or a second session, the instruction could have been strengthened by giving the students time to write their search terms and make lists of alternatives, evaluating them for interconnections and different approaches. For example, a search for information about Chinese characters could easily, depending upon the information found, lead to a new topic: early printing systems in China. Providing a workshop setting to do this kind of exploration would have reinforced the thinking and research skills presented in the lecture/demonstration.

In conclusion, I will return to my enthusiasm for the assignment's design. The nature of it forced students to think critically and creatively about the information they encountered, and not surprisingly, they were excited about using the library.

WIC and the Sciences: Aquaculture

Instructor's Statement
Christopher Langdon, Associate Professor, Fisheries and Wildlife

CONCERNS ABOUT THE MODERN UNIVERSITY STUDENT

When I first arrived in the States about thirteen years ago from Britain, I asked some students to write me an essay. One student indignantly replied, "We don't write essays in this country.'' At that point, I knew I was in for a long hard slog. As the years have gone by, I have come to realize that in the States sound bites make meals of the literate.

In the midst of all this chatter, the ability to think conceptually and logically is essential to the work of a scientist and many other professionals. It takes concentration over a period of time to develop or evaluate a concept by oneself. It's not surprising that students, continually exposed to strong and rapidly changing stimuli, find it more and more difficult to concentrate and think. Writing has always been a discipline that forces me to slow down and methodically sort through my thoughts. It's a familiar process or meditation that momentarily frees me from the various demands of everyday life. I have often wondered during my teaching career whether the scattered thoughts of my students could be focused by greater emphasis on writing, but have not experimented with course structure to answer this question.

The written word has always been important in academic circles where the axiom "publish or perish" is still held. Papers, proposals, reviews, correspondence, reports, and evaluations are just some of the forms of writing that occupy an ever-increasing portion of the academic's life. Both inside and outside of academia, e-mail and the computer revolution are revitalizing the importance of the written word. Electronic communication is cheaper, more convenient, and more efficient than the telephone, meetings, or conferences. How can we prepare the student for writing in an age where electronic communication has opened the classroom and office to a world of information and potential interactions?

CONCERNS ABOUT WIC

I attended the WIC seminar series for faculty in the fall of 1993. Part of the reason was to find out if I could do anything about the poor writing abilities of students taking the aquaculture course at OSU. The seminar series was made up of about twenty faculty from many different departments and was organized by Dr. Vicki Collins, director of the WIC program at Oregon State University.

The overall goal of the seminar series was simply to help faculty design courses to encourage students to write. The seminars were very helpful, but some of us wondered if class writing exercises could be included without significant loss of essential course material. I had to remind myself that the purpose of my course was not to cram students with facts but to teach them to evaluate and understand concepts. Writing is a very good method to achieve this goal as it can help the student slow down and think.

Was I going to turn into an overworked grammar dictator spilling red ink over pages of corrections late into the night? The WIC seminars reminded me that most dictators are bullies who do not encourage free thought and criticism in their subjects. Less red ink and more encouragement and light-handed guidance would be my response to symptoms of the dictator syndrome; so I threw away the red pen, sharpened the erasable pencil, and put grammar into the background.

PUTTING THEORY INTO PRACTICE

The WIC seminars provided me with a fat folder of ideas on how to construct a WIC course. I decided that the best strategy was to expose students to three different kinds of writing exercises to widen their experience. Short impromptu writing exercises, an in-depth scientific evaluation of a potential aquaculture species, and a management report based on a computer model of a commercial fish farm were the three writing components of my WIC course. Thankfully, the WIC program provided me with funds to hire a graduate student to help students with their writing. This was particularly valuable for foreign students who initially were not able to read and write in English as proficiently as American students.

Short impromptu writing exercises were carried out in class on a range of subjects, from general evaluations of videos shown in class to specific questions on aquaculture techniques. I asked students to write responses on 3×5 cards within three-minute time intervals, encouraging them to write concisely and rapidly. About twelve impromptus were scattered throughout the term, and about half of them were graded using a simple scale: +3 for clear, concise, and correct; +2 for satisfactory; +1 for inaccurate (but at least you tried); and +0 for no response (you were either asleep or absent). The accumulated scores at the end of term constituted 10 percent of the final grade. The students were kept on their toes by these impromptu exercises, resulting in greater participation, attendance, and assimilation of course material than I had previously noticed using the traditional lecture format.

The second writing exercise was quite different from the impromptus and involved the students selecting a species and then writing a series of components over the term that together made up a profile of the species' aquaculture potential. Components of the profile included taxonomy, geographic distribution, life history, existing aquaculture status, species requirements for growth and reproduction, extensive and intensive aquaculture practices, and future aquaculture potential. Each week the student submitted a component 250–1000 words in length that was reviewed, edited, and returned to the student ungraded. Over the term, each component would be revised at least once, and the student could make suggested improvements. Near the end of term, the student submitted a polished complete profile for evaluation; it constituted 50 percent of the final grade.

Learning to use the resources of the Hatfield Marine Science Center library was an essential part of preparing the species' profile. The librarian, Janet Webster, introduced the students to the library both in class and on an individual basis. The aquaculture literature is very mixed in composition and consists of books, international journals, and a great deal of "gray" literature, i.e., literature that is not widely distributed or referenced. The students had to find and sort through this literature and decide on what to include in their profiles. For some students working on rather esoteric species, a great deal of digging and sifting was required in order to find gems of information. It was important for students to be able to identify gaps in the scientific literature because it is the unknown that poses both the greatest problems for aquaculturists and the greatest opportunities for researchers.

Although I had to work harder in the first term of the WIC aquaculture course than I had in previous years, I feel that the students' positive response was worth the extra effort. By the end of the term, the students had been exposed to several different forms of writing. I was anxious to find out in the final exam how much they had learned of the subject matter. I was pleasantly surprised to find that the students had understood the main concepts of the course and were able to apply these concepts in answering exam questions. The students found the course worthwhile and gave it high marks in their end-of-term evaluations.

WIC and the Sciences: Aquaculture

Librarian's Statement
Janet Webster, Assistant Professor, OSU Libraries

THE SETTING

The Hatfield Marine Science Center (HMSC) rests on the edge of the Pacific coast, far away from the resources of the main campus. It is home to a varied collection of researchers, resource managers, educators, and students. In the winter, fifteen to twenty-five upper division students majoring in fisheries spend a quarter in residence at HMSC and take a full complement of classes. This unique setting allows students to experience life at a research station.

Students soon realize that the remote setting challenges their *modus operandi*. They are thrust into a new living and learning environment, much as any new researcher at the HMSC faces upon relocating there, and must quickly learn where to go for help and advice. The library is one of those places and becomes more than a physical collection of books and journals; it provides Internet links to information throughout the world, houses the computer lab, and evolves into a social center on long rainy winter nights.

The small staff (one professional librarian and one full-time and one half-time support staff) have the opportunity to become key players in the students' experience at HMSC. We try to create a relaxed, service environment, which most students welcome. For the first time in many of their educational lives, the students work with, or at least see, a librarian on a daily basis for the entire quarter. I am the computer trouble-shooter, information resource, confidante on struggles with course work and instructors, and calming presence during the dervish of finals.

Just as the students are challenged to adapt to a new environment, I am challenged to develop new methods of working with the faculty and the students to constantly improve the experience. One of the winter classes, a three-credit lecture class exploring the principles and practices of aquaculture, is taught by Dr. Christopher Langdon as a WIC course with substantial library research. We work cooperatively to help students improve their research and writing skills through quarter-long projects. We agree that research and writing provide means to develop critical thinking and encourage the transformation of information into knowledge. My role is not limited to presenting a single class or assisting on one assignment, but extends to guiding the students through their quest to fathom the intricacies of aquaculture information resources.

PLANNING FOR THE ONSLAUGHT

Before students arrive at HMSC in January and jump into research and writing, I lay the groundwork. Traditional library services, electronic access, and coordination with main campus services are planned, and responsibilities delegated. Over the past few years, Dr. Langdon has developed an extensive list of reserve materials ranging from monographs to trade literature. With the addition of the writing-intensive component, several basic writing books were added to the reserve list. In December, Dr. Langdon finalizes the syllabus and we schedule one class session for the general library orientation.

Access to electronic resources is essential. The HMSC library has several CD-ROM indexes that are searchable locally and remote access to the main campus's extensive CD-ROM network. There are challenges to searching any system remotely, the major obstacle being retrieving search results. The best local method is to mark records, download them to file on the campus computer, and then have the downloaded file mailed to an electronic mailbox. As part of the course preparation, I set up a general e-mail account for the class and negotiate with computing services on the main campus for those students wishing a mainframe account.

The WIC director, Dr. Langdon, and I share a concern over the lack of access to the writing center on the main campus. One option tried was hiring a graduate student working at HMSC to serve as a writing consultant. This had mixed results, due to availability, personality, and differences in writing styles. Future options include setting up and staffing a mini writing center, hiring a graduate student with experience in writing and communication, and setting up a link to the campus writing center using the video conferencing capabilities available in the library.

All of this prepares the library as the service center for students. They arrive from the main campus not knowing what to expect and immediately have to settle into new housing and start classes. Laying the groundwork for a useful reserve collection, functional electronic access, and writing assistance establishes the library as a central service point and the librarian as a key resource in the WIC program.

GENERAL ORIENTATION: WHERE DO WE START?

Orientation takes place in two sessions: a whirlwind library tour on the first day of classes, and a class session later in the week. The objectives of the tour are to introduce students to the library, describe the collection, explain services (especially how to request materials from the main campus), introduce library staff, and check out keys and photocopy cards. It is my first opportunity to impress on them that they should ask me and my staff for any assistance that is needed during the term.

During the one-hour class session, I focus on the resources students will need to use for their major writing project, a species profile. The profile consists of eight sections researched and written sequentially, and then compiled at the end of the quarter to give a thorough description and discussion of the biology and culture of an aquatic animal. My major dilemma in introducing the resources is balancing explanation of the mechanics of searching with explanation of the substance of the resources. Blending in discussion of the mechanics without losing focus on the tools themselves, I start the session with a description of the library collection and the nature of aquaculture information. This includes discussing the hierarchy of information, such as monographs, journals, proceedings, and trade literature, using examples to describe the strengths and weaknesses of each. My objectives in this section are to introduce the students to the array of information and emphasize the importance of ''gray'' literature in aquaculture.

Describing the literature leads to explaining how to locate specific information. I discuss the differences between catalogs and indexes using OASIS (OSU's on-line catalog) and the primary fisheries index, *Aquatic Sciences and Fisheries Abstracts*. The training room is equipped with a computer and projector, and though the connections usually work, I do not rely solely on electronic connections. I explain any glitches as part of the process of doing science; you do what you can and always have alternative approaches to the problem. I demonstrate keyword and browsing strategies and explain Boolean logic by searching for specific organisms, such as abalone and salmon, and relevant concepts, such as life history or production. I also cover any special search features that are particularly relevant, including geographic limitations, descriptors, and publication type. The limitations of the catalogs and indexes are emphasized; limitations can be due to the depth of the backfiles, inconsistent coverage, problematic retrieval, and availability of items.

After describing the tools, I identify basic resources for the species profiles, using the eight sections outlined by Dr. Langdon in his syllabus. I encourage students to build a core of information and use cross-references to expand it. If I give them a starting point such as a government report or a classic text, they tend to progress quickly to other resources. Some species are more difficult to research than others, so I suggest methods for finding problematic information, for example, using trade literature and contacting industry associations. I conclude by emphasizing the importance of documenting the information and by giving practical tips on citations.

The primary objective of the session is to give students a concrete starting point for the writing project. Even if they are familiar with using the main campus library, all of the students must adapt to the new collection, new layout, and new tools. Those students who miss the orientation session take longer to get started and often suffer from the lack of the ''insider'' information I provide. The session is also an opportunity for me to develop a rapport with the students and demonstrate that I am accessible rather than formidable.

CONTINUING THE QUEST

I manage a specialized research collection and provide individualized service. For the WIC students, that translates into having access to an expert on the information needed for their writing projects. As the quarter progresses, the students learn that they can count on me and my staff to provide information in a timely manner and direct them toward new and often obscure references. I enjoy working one-on-one as I learn the students' interests and the depth of their curiosity. It also helps me track how well the library fills their needs and how well the class assignment is understood. I use my observations to build the collection, learn new approaches to teaching, and provide feedback to Dr. Langdon.

Consultation continues as the quarter progresses. In the first week, students get familiar with the lay of the land—what word processing programs are available, that the library is really open to them twenty-four hours a day, how they can communicate with the campus, and where the coffee pot is. The new environment is both freeing and intimidating; gone is the familiar structure of the main campus where the dominant presence is the students. At this point, it helps to have the library as a consistent reference in their experience.

In the second week, the students select the species they will research. I am familiar with most of the ones they select and can direct students to materials. Those that select more obscure species often ask for help to identify whether there is adequate information and where the gaps will be. These students need immediate assistance as the first written section is due at the end of the second week.

Once started, students need help in locating resources peculiar to aquaculture. I help them identify species-specific trade journals, gray literature on aquaculture practices, and market information. I spend quite a bit of time explaining the problems with production statistics and encourage them to relate to Dr. Langdon any problems they have finding accurate information. The message is not to make it up, but to document the gaps in knowledge.

FINAL OBSERVATIONS

The library's interaction with this WIC class is unusual for several reasons:

1. The interaction lasts for the entire term rather than being limited to a single session. The librarian becomes an accessible and obvious resource for the writing process.
2. The writing project's success is directly linked to the students' library research skills: they cannot fake the information and expect to succeed by just writing well. The instructor knows the resources and expects that they will be used.
3. The library is the center for more than just information—it is a social center and the computer lab. The students' constant presence makes it easy for the librarian to interact with them on an informal basis.
4. The class is offered every year, so the instructor and the librarian can work together continually to identify and use new resources. Each brings new ideas to the course, most recently those ideas included use of Internet resources available through the library and multimedia lab notes in the classroom. Continuity strengthens the cooperation.

Case Study: Richard Stockton College of New Jersey

Mary Ann Trail, *Coordinator*
Pamela Kennedy-Cross, Mary Ann Trail,
and Jack Connor, *Contributors*

DESCRIPTION OF THE INSTITUTION

Richard Stockton College is a state-supported, undergraduate college of arts, sciences, and professional studies. In 1991, there were 4,384 full-time and 1,266 part-time students. There are 188 full-time faculty positions and 60 part-time or adjunct jobs. The college awards Bachelor of Arts and Bachelor of Science degrees.

The mission of the college is as follows:

Stockton is dedicated to the liberal arts education for its students, an education which develops their capacity for continuous learning and their ability to adapt to a multicultural and interdependent world, centered in a curriculum with both breadth and depth. As one of its essential elements, the curriculum has an interdisciplinary approach designed to prepare students for career changes as well as to enrich their lives. Consequently, the guiding principles of Stockton's mission are two: first Stockton insists on excellence in teaching and dedication to learning; second, since the college recognizes a responsibility to participate in the development of new ideas as well as to transmit knowledge, it requires continuous research, learning, and professional development on the part of its faculty and staff. (Mission Statement, Richard Stockton College, 1982)

THE COLLEGE LIBRARY

Description of the Library

The library is an integral part of the students' work and development at the college. The library consists of more than 265,000 books, periodicals, and documents. The library's 52,000 square feet will be increased by 40 percent by 1996. The library subscribes to a dozen CD-ROM services. The reference desk is staffed by four full-time librarians and three part-timers. Each reference desk librarian also has other areas of responsibility, such as government documents, serials, on-line services, or interlibrary loans. There is also one cataloger in technical services, and there are three administrators.

Mission of the Library

The goal of the library is to support the undergraduate educational mission of the college by providing sources of information that will satisfy virtually all the academic needs of the students, a high percentage of the faculty's needs for course preparation, and a reasonable percentage of the faculty's research needs.

The library assists its patrons in their search for specific information. However, it also assists them in developing the capacity for continuous learning. Through its instructional program, it fosters versatility by teaching students how to identify, locate, and use the sources through which knowledge is communicated.

Description of Bibliographic Instruction Program

Since all entering freshman are required to take a freshman seminar, the focal point of the BI program is to introduce students to the library through the BI classes. In about 90 percent of the freshman seminars, students receive some kind of introduction to the library. Our next goal is to reach students when they are beginning studies in their major, by guest lecturing in a variety of introductory courses. Generally the lectures consist of one-hour classes that introduce research tools in a specific discipline. We are now attempting a pilot program through the senior seminars in which we are introducing some students to end-user searching.

The program has not been as successful in reaching transfer students, who are not required to take a freshman seminar. We have tried term paper workshops and tours, but few students show up. This semester, we are trying individual appointments for students who want more help than is available at the reference desk.

In 1989, we ran a survey which showed that over half of the students had received some kind of bibliographic instruction. Their attitudes were generally favorable, and BI was recognized as being useful in their academic careers.

Bibliographic instruction has been part of library services since the founding of the college in the early 1970s. Never a stand-alone program, from its inception it depended on faculty involvement for access to students. In fact, it was not terribly consistent in its effectiveness or ability to reach students. Therefore, in 1989, when Stockton adopted a program requiring a freshman seminar for all freshman, the coordinator for bibliographic instruction realized the potential for the library with such a program. The freshman seminar would provide consistent access to all entering students. Although she participated in the planning stages of the freshman seminars and the Dean of General Studies was very supportive, it was the successful marketing by the coordinator that made the BI program effective.

Instructors in the BI program and the writing program (through the freshman seminars) found early on that their efforts on behalf of the students were closely joined. "The (Freshman) seminars are designed to help students get their college career off to a good start by emphasizing individualized attention, active discussion and development of important skills" including writing (College Catalog, p. 63). The writing faculty wanted their students to write essays supporting their ideas with facts. Through the BI program, the library faculty could furnish the students with information that showed them how to find the facts that would make their writing better. The librarians also emphasized critical analysis and evaluation of sources. Many of the faculty tied the two together and used library research in their writing assignments.

The bibliographic instruction program uses several different methods to introduce library and research skills into freshman seminar classes. The first and most popular is a generic workbook based on the Earlham model. The workbook is a self-paced project covering different areas of the library and search techniques. The workbook and some basic research methods are introduced by a librarian in a twenty- to thirty-minute in-class lecture. Faculty do not feel they have to give up too much class time since most of the work is done outside of class. The workbooks are collected and graded by the librarian, but are used by faculty in computing the final grade. Because faculty place a grade on the workbooks, there is a high rate of completion. Only one or two students per class do not complete the workbooks. About 75 percent of the freshman seminar classes use this method of library instruction.

Some freshman seminar faculty choose to write their own assignments but invite library faculty to introduce the library sources needed. This allows the assignment to be specifically written for the class. For example, the faculty member teaching Experience of Literature required his students to find several book reviews for comparison purposes. Pamela Kennedy-Cross, a faculty member who teaches a freshman seminar in critical thinking, requires her students to interview people who have some knowledge of a historical event. The students must then use the library to find primary and secondary sources. The librarians introduce students to a variety of reference books, including dictionaries, chronologies, and indexes. The presentations also give much needed visibility to the librarians. Students have a face to look for when they need help.

The program is not 100 percent successful. Some faculty do not include librarians either in the writing of the assignment or in a library introduction. One faculty member decided that his students should read about the college experience of famous people. This assignment could have been combined with learning a research skill and been very effective, but the faculty member simply put a list of possible biographies on reserve for the students to choose from. Although he feels this introduces students to the library, the opinions of the librarians obviously differ.

Stockton has two kinds of writing courses. There are courses labeled writing intensive, or W–1, in which writing is the subject of the course. Examples of this type are *Journalism: Practices and Perspectives* or *Writer/Editor Workshop.* Courses that require a lot of writing but in which the subject matter is in a particular discipline are labeled W–2. In a W–2 course, writing does constitute a major component in the evaluation of the student. Many of these courses are also courses that introduce students to their majors, i.e., *Introduction to Criminal Justice Research, Psychological Research Methods,* or *Aspects of Aging.* This ties in nicely with the library's attempt to reach students as they enter their chosen disciplines. Therefore, besides the freshman seminar, most of the efforts of the bibliographic instruction program are aimed at W–2 courses.

Request for instruction in the typical W–2 class is made by the individual instructor, although the librarians have reached out to faculty when identifiable members of a class appear to be having trouble doing research. The librarian, in a one- to one-and-a-half-hour lecture, will present basic reference materials, use of the on-line catalog, and periodical indexes, either in print or in CD-ROM format, where applicable. The presentation now includes presentation of computer-formatted materials and requires the use of a computer, an overhead display unit, and a CD-ROM player. To complete the library experience, the librarian includes an assignment that makes use of the materials covered. For incentive, most faculty count it as a quiz grade. Besides the material listed above, recent classes have included lectures on research materials for *Women's Studies, Environmental Issues,* and *Soils Research.*

The BI program and its effectiveness seems to pivot on an effective marketing program. This means it is necessary to take an aggressive approach with new faculty members and reaffirm personal contacts with tenured faculty. These relationships need to be built up over the years and constantly nurtured. The librarians need to be perceived as partners. When this happens, faculty will approach librarians for ideas. At Stockton, we intentionally strive for more visibility for the librarians, through campus committees, union participation, and personal contacts. Many classes are scheduled over lunch. Faculty seem to require constant reminding that we are here and offer a valuable service. It takes time, but it works to our benefit because these contacts promote the BI program. This is especially true of the W–2 introductory classes as faculty think of us as active colleagues not archivists.

Stockton is moving rapidly into the use of technology in the classroom. Several faculty have designed classes to teach writing skills using computers rather than paper. The library is proceeding in this direction. The current BI program will be expanded to incorporate the teaching of new technologies. In order to provide a locus for instruction and electronic research, the college plans to construct an information laboratory in the library where the librarians and faculty will instruct students in the use of information resources in a variety of electronic formats. W–2 courses will be the primary focus for this expansion.

It is imperative in this age of information proliferation that faculty and librarians continue to work together. Today's college students are confronted with a confusing array of information resources that they must master in order to be successful in college and in their future careers. There was never a time when bibliographic instruction was more necessary. We look forward to keeping apace with these new developments and to enhancing our professional relationship with the faculty and the writing program.

For further information about bibliographic instruction at Richard Stockton College, please contact Mary Ann Trail, Public Services Librarian, at 609–652–4266.

The Writing Program at Stockton

Jack Connor, Associate Professor of Writing

Stockton's Writing Program developed out of the Basic Studies Program and General Studies Division in the late 1970s, when the college was half a dozen years old. The Writing Program was formally recognized as a separate entity, within the General Studies Division, in 1981, and a college-wide writing requirement was instituted for all entering freshmen in the fall of 1983. All students were required to take a minimum of three writing-designated courses, two before the junior year and one after it. We used two tests for placement: the New Jersey College Basic Skills Placement Test (designed and required by the state) for entering freshmen, and a Junior Writing Test (our own test) for first-semester juniors. Students with low scores on the NJCBSPT were required to take *College Writing* in their first semester; students with average scores were required to take a W–1 (Writing-Intensive) course of their choosing in the first semester; all other freshmen were advised to take a W–1 or W–2 course in their first year. Students who scored "Not Proficient" on the Junior Writing Test were required to take a W–1 course in their next active semester (ordinarily their second junior semester or first senior semester).

W–1 courses, also called writing-intensive courses, are those in which writing is the primary focus of the course ("Writing is the Number 1 thing"). In W–2 courses, also called Writing-Across-The-Curriculum courses, subject content is the primary focus of the course, but writing is an important component of the course ("Writing is the Number 2 thing").

The college's writing requirement was modified and strengthened in 1993. A fourth course, a "C or better" standard, and an upper-division requirement were added, and the Junior Writing Test was eliminated. Students who begin here as freshmen are now required to take a W–1 course in their first year, no matter what their score on the NJCBSPT, and a minimum of three other writing-designated (W–1 or W–2) courses before they graduate. At least one of those four courses must be an upper-division (junior or senior level) course, and the student must earn a C or better in all four courses.

Six full-time faculty members and the writing center coordinator are the core members of the writing program; however, all faculty at Stockton are considered members of the writing program. The core faculty and adjuncts teach most of the W–1 courses offered at the college, but each semester other faculty teach more than fifty W–2 courses. When we voted to modify the writing requirement last semester, the discussion was held at the faculty assembly meeting and all faculty were eligible to debate and to vote.

The library and librarians are crucial to the success of both W–1 and W–2 courses. Research papers are standard components of our most frequently offered W–1 courses—*College Writing, Rhetoric and Composition, Argument and Persuasion, and Writing for Many Roles*—and they are far and away the most common shared component of W–2 courses. We count on the librarians to help us guide our students to the literature—some of us depend on the librarians more than others, and some of us probably ask too much of them. The electronic highway confronts us now, and we will be depending on our librarians even more than before. Many faculty have organized their classes so that CD-ROM data-base searching and/or Internet explorations are mandatory. Some of us have begun teaching writing on the computer network, and these and other complexities opening before us are exciting and a little frightening too. We move forward into this new world of research following our librarians' lead.

"Readings: American Lives"—A Freshman Seminar

Pamela Kennedy-Cross, Coordinator of the Skills Writing Lab

DESCRIPTION OF THE COURSE

The course entitled *Readings: American Lives* is a freshman seminar which looks at life in America from a variety of perspectives. We explore the experience of childhood in America and the interplay between social class and ethnicity in determining one's sense of entitlement or alienation. We discuss how environment and family life play major roles in all our lives. We try to examine a cross section of American life, and read texts ranging from John Edgar Wideman's *Brothers and Keepers* to the *Maus* books by Art Spiegelman to biographical material on the Kennedy family and Dan Quayle. Last year we added Marian Wright Edelman's *The Measure of Our Success* to encourage discussion on parenting and the materialization of youth culture.

Since the course is a freshman seminar, our goal is to get students to think critically about the issues presented, to debate with more logic than emotion, and to improve their academic reading and writing skills. The students enrolled in this particular freshman seminar have been identified as academically at risk due to low scores in reading comprehension, as measured by the New Jersey College Basic Skills Placement Test. The class is smaller than other freshman seminars (it consists of fifteen to twenty students, compared with twenty-five in other classes), and it is linked to twice-weekly tutorial modules in the writing center. In the tutorial modules, the students meet with a tutor in groups of eight to ten to discuss the readings and go over material for quizzes, tests, and writing assignments.

THE WRITING COMPONENT

Writing plays a critical role in advancing the goals of the course. All tests and quizzes are in essay form, and students write an average of six short essays (around 750 words each) plus a structured research project. Most of the essay assignments ask the students to interact personally with course readings and to take a defendable position. Grading is based largely on effort and level of analysis, but editing and proofreading skills are also important. Students are strongly encouraged to work with their tutor throughout the writing process, to discover their strengths and weaknesses as writers, and to take action accordingly. Some students may need little help with organization or development of ideas, but struggle with rules for punctuation or grammatical correctness. Some students present the opposite set of needs. We preach that self-knowledge is essential to the growth and improvement of all writers, and we push students to take personal responsibility for the overall quality of the written work they submit.

One short essay assignment springs out of our discussion of Art Spiegelman's *Maus* books, which tell the story of the Holocaust using the author's medium of the comic book. The books contain interviews with Spiegelman's father, an Auschwitz survivor, who relates his story of survival against all odds. The students discuss the concept of history as "his (or her) story," which paves the way for their next project: to interview someone who has a story to tell about a moment in history. Choice of interview subjects has varied widely. One student interviewed her grandmother about her work at the Philadelphia Naval Yard during WW II; another talked to his mother about the death of Elvis Presley (she was a big fan); several students interviewed family members about the assassination of John F. Kennedy or Martin Luther King, Jr.; still others chose sports stories—one interviewed our athletics director about the 1968 Summer Olympic Games, where he earned a gold medal.

The students are reminded many times that the interview should serve as a preliminary step in their research. The interview sets the stage and perks the student's interest in the subject matter. To drum this idea into their heads, I insist the students conclude their interviews with a postscript in which the students reflect on what they learned from their interviews, and I ask them to include a statement about where they want to go next with their research. One student who talked with her mother about the Newark riots of 1968 concluded her interview by wondering how the newspaper accounts of the riots would differ from the perspective her mother had shared with her. The student who interviewed his former high school basketball coach about the 1983 NBA champion Philadelphia Seventy-Sixers wanted to learn what the Philadelphia and national sports writers thought about the team's success.

INTEGRATING THE LIBRARY

When the students all have an idea of where they want to go after their interviews, we schedule a class meeting in the library. I meet in advance with the reference librarian, Mary Ann Trail, and provide her with the students' topics. She looks over the list of topics and tailors her presentation directly to the students' needs. Most of the students have had limited exposure to library work and are often apprehensive about their capabilities as researchers. By offering such a personalized approach, we are able to keep their attention and maintain their confidence level. Mary Ann usually begins her presentation by asking a few students to identify their topics and research questions. Her responses show that she is aware of the assignment, their individual topics, and sees the students as individuals. The students see her not just as the librarian but as "their librarian," someone who is uniquely qualified to serve their needs. The distinction is more than a label; inexperienced researchers, especially freshmen identified as weak readers, are often very intimidated by libraries and nervous that their questions will reveal their ignorance. By establishing a rapport with the students connected to their choice of research topic, Mary Ann facilitates the students' perceptions of themselves as researchers.

Some of the students have selected recent moments in history and are told they will need to start their searches on the computerized indexes. Other students are directed to the reader's guide and the *New York Times* index in book form. If students are unsure of the exact date of their topics, Mary Ann demonstrates how to use a time line. Within the first ten minutes, all the students know where to begin. Both the instructor and the librarian stay close at hand as the students begin to look up information about their topics. We look over shoulders, ask questions, and make specific recommendations. When one student is using a computerized index, we encourage the other students who are waiting for the computer to become involved. What has Student A found on his or her topic? Where else could he or she look? Which articles seem most useful to him or her?

Our goal is that by the end of this first library class students will have gained experience using indexes, evaluating types of sources, and locating articles on microfilm or microfiche in the periodicals room. The students are then instructed to write a research progress report for our next class.

In our next class, we discuss our first day of library research, and the students share their experiences and frustrations. Some students have lower thresholds of frustration than others and may conclude, "I need to change my topic—there were only three articles listed in the Reader's Guide." It is always gratifying when another student quickly suggests that the student look in the *New York Times* index or ask the librarian. The discussion in this follow-up class reveals the value of the librarian in the research process. The students who worked directly with Mary Ann encourage the others to do the same. We also talk about how to ask good questions of librarians, to be specific rather than general, concrete rather than abstract. By the end of this class, we always conclude that we need to go back to the library. If our schedule permits, we will go again as a class.

The second class session in the library feels very different from the first. We are a collection of individual researchers. The students seem more focused and less nervous, more likely to get down to work quickly. Again, Mary Ann makes herself available to the students and gives individual attention to students most in need of help. As with the first library session, I ask the students to submit another progress report, in order to get feedback and become alerted to any problems that they are experiencing.

This assignment has produced many fine essays. The key to the students' success is the personal attention given them by Mary Ann and other library personnel. Over and over again the students give sincere testament to the help they received in our library. I ask the students to include an acknowledgements page with their essays, following a tradition set by scholars and other published writers. Besides thanking roommates, tutors, and MTV, Mary Ann Trail (or some variation on her name) always gets singled out for credit—deservedly.

Case Study: University of Massachusetts at Amherst

Helen Schneider, *Coordinator*
Annaliese Bischoff, Anne Herrington, Paula
Mark, and Helen M. Schneider, *Contributors*

DESCRIPTION OF INSTITUTION

Number of FTE (Full Time Equivalent) students: 21,063
Number of FTE (Full Time Equivalent) faculty: 1,183.3
Student/faculty ratio: 17.8:1
Highest degree granted: Ph.D.
Type of institution: Public

INSTITUTIONAL MISSION

The University of Massachusetts is dedicated to providing Massachusetts citizens with a world-class institution that will prepare them to take their place in the international economy of the next century. The special character of the university stems from that aspect of its mission that focuses on the creation of new knowledge. This research component is not only critical to providing the highest level of support to Massachusetts business and industry, but it also contributes significantly to the high quality of undergraduate education. Through its educational programs at all levels, the university strives for broad preparation of individuals who will be able to adapt successfully to the changing needs of a changing world. The university is responsible for the upper tier of the educational curriculum that includes all the public education efforts throughout the commonwealth. This special responsibility affects the university's approach to every subject, be it the preparation of elementary and secondary school teachers or the education of future health care professionals. The university strives to provide a multicultural environment and demonstrated recognition of the importance of a global perspective.

THE LIBRARY

Description of the Library

Number of volumes: 2,651,649

Number of microforms: 2,068,004

Number of serial titles: 15,265

Number of maps: 126,796

Number of librarians (total): 47

Number of public services/reference/BI librarians at the main library: 10

Number of public service/reference BI librarians at all branches (including the main library): 18

Administration
  Director of Libraries: 1
  Associate Directors: 3
  Staff Assistants/Associates: 9

Library Mission

The mission of the library is to provide appropriate support for the instructional, research, and public services of the University of Massachusetts at Amherst.

The primary objective of the university library is to make materials and information available to the library user when needed. In order to achieve this objective, the library will:

1. select and acquire as much recorded knowledge, in whatever form, as is consistent with the current and developing educational and research needs and goals of the university community;

2. organize and bring under bibliographic control the materials acquired;

3. actively promote the library as a resource, interpret its collection to users, and assist them in utilizing the library and in obtaining access to needed information located elsewhere;

4. maintain the collection in good order and good physical condition;

5. promote the effective utilization of resources by cooperating with other libraries and information centers;

6. develop and utilize better ways of providing library resources and services, based upon the analysis of user needs and the economical application of new technologies; and

7. recruit, develop, and support the staff needed to provide the appropriate services.

Description of Bibliographic Instruction Program

Paula Mark, Instructional Services Librarian

The library instruction program at the University of Massachusetts at Amherst provides instruction in library use for classes which range from the introductory level to the graduate seminar. When it is fully staffed, the program is proactive, advertising the willingness of librarians to meet with classes whose instructors require the independent discovery and use of library materials by their students. When the reference department, which provides most of the instruction, is not fully staffed, the program generally becomes reactive, responding to faculty requests but not seeking out new classes.

In the 1993–1994 academic year, the reference department of the main university library was somewhat understaffed and met with 4,473 students in 218 classes. Of those classes, 117 were connected with the writing program, with the greater number being first year classes, involving 1,939 students. Junior year writing course library sessions have varied in number over the decade during which that part of the writing program has been in place; in 1993–1994, we met with 432 students in 27 classes, the lowest number in several years.

Since students in the first year writing program are writing on a wide range of individually chosen topics, generally of current interest, we do not provide them with special written materials other than those which will orient them to the location of books and periodicals to which they have developed citations. At the level of the junior year program, we may distribute brief guides to a limited range of materials, or we may prepare an extensive and detailed guide if a faculty member requires the students to write a substantive paper. What the librarians will provide and whether the students will spend some of the class period beginning to use some of the resources that have been described to them is negotiated between librarian and instructor.

We have adopted a minimalist approach to library instruction. At the first year level, we believe that it is important to provide as many students as possible with a brief introduction to library resources and an opportunity to meet with a professional librarian. At the junior year level, we have generally resisted the temptation to offer a detailed overview of the literature of each major, preferring instead to tailor our presentations to the needs of a particular course, a principle we follow throughout the library instruction program.

For more information on the bibliographic instruction program described here contact:

Jill E. Ausel
Instructional Services Librarian
(413) 545-0150

Background and Administrative Structure of the Writing Program

Anne Herrington, Professor of English and Director of the
Writing Program

The present university writing program, created in 1982 by an act of the faculty senate, includes two formal curricular requirements as part of the university's general education program.[1] The first is completion of a one-semester prose-writing course, *College Writing*, in the first year. This course is overseen by English faculty who also teach the course along with trained graduate teaching associates. The primary aim of College Writing is for students to become more independent writers, able to adapt to the ways of writing of various specific contexts.

The second requirement is completion of the Junior Year Writing Program (JYWP) course, overseen and taught by faculty in each major at the university. This formal writing-across-the-curriculum component of the curriculum aims to introduce students to some of the ways of writing valued for learning and professional work in areas associated with each major.

This university-wide curriculum reflects the belief that as part of their education, students should know how to use writing for personal and public purposes—for self-reflection, for learning and presentation of their ideas, for civic participation, and for professional life. It follows from this assumption that teaching writing is a collective, university-wide responsibility of the academic community. The writing program's links with the university library arise out of a related collective belief that writing and inquiry in academic and professional life often entail knowing how to use a variety of research resources.

The administrative structure of the program is consistent with its university-wide scope and mission. Most significantly, the writing committee, a standing committee of the faculty senate, has oversight responsibility for the writing program. To fulfill its charge, the writing committee conducts periodic formal reviews of each component of the writing program, at the first year level and the junior year level. The writing committee also has important advocacy functions, both within the writing program and with other campus constituencies (e.g., other faculty and administrators).

While it is stipulated that the director of the program be a member of the English department, the program and its budget are overseen by the provost's office.[2] The director, who is released from three of the five courses expected of English department faculty, has general administrative and budgetary responsibility for the full program and day-to-day administrative responsibility for the first year program. Further, there is an associate director for the junior year program who is a faculty member from another department. The associate director, who receives the equivalent of one course released time, advises the various departments on developing and revising their JYWP courses, proposes budget distributions for JYWP courses, and acts as general troubleshooter for the program. The other full-time writing program staff include a deputy director, who oversees and teaches the basic writing course, handles course scheduling and budget matters, and advises the director; two assistant directors who each teach one course, one also serving as grievance officer and the other as director of teacher training and development; one secretary; and one bookkeeper.

Seven faculty from the English department, along with professional staff, serve as course directors for the first year program. They each teach a section of *College Writing* or *Basic Writing*, convene teaching meetings, and supervise approximately ten graduate teaching associates.

CURRICULUM AND LIBRARY LINKS

First-Year Writing Program

The primary aim of *College Writing* is for students to become more knowledgeable of and able to manage their composing process, which includes generating ideas, revising to organize and shape those ideas for specific purposes, and styling and editing their prose. Two secondary aims are that they have some experience in such kinds of thinking as questioning, interpreting, and considering multiple perspectives and that they be able to compose essays in which they not only narrate and explain, but also interpret particulars and develop a line of thinking. The course is run more like a writing workshop than a lecture or reading class. A good deal of writing is done in class; students' own writings constitute the primary text of the class; and students are expected to be active in their learning. For example, they are encouraged to take responsibility for defining some of their writing projects, to conduct inquiries for those projects (e.g., library research, interviewing), and to work collaboratively with their classmates so that they exchange feedback on drafts of their writings.

The course's link with the library comes by way of the documented essay, a research essay required in all sections of *College Writing*. We purposely call it an essay to stress to students that the aim is for them to develop *their* view on a topic, using the research sources to assist them in that aim. To try to avoid its becoming a term paper exercise of demonstrating knowledge, we encourage students to begin with something they are already knowledgeable about—preferably something that they have already written on and want to investigate further. That provides the impetus for learning to use the resources of the university library, another purpose of the course unit.

To serve this purpose, we work with the instructional services staff of the library to inform faculty of the resources available to them and their students for learning to do library research, and we encourage them to make use of these resources. To this end, each semester one of the librarians speaks at the writing program's opening general meeting for all teachers. What they have to offer is an instructional session tailor-made for any section of *College Writing* that requests it. So, for instance, last semester in advance of a session I had scheduled for my class, I let the librarian know some of the research questions my students were pursuing. She worked through a few of these during the session, using them as a way to introduce various reference sources, indexes, and on-line bibliographic search programs. The session concluded with time for students to begin their own searches with me and the librarian available for consultation. Typically, one-third of our teachers make use of this service; others do their own library orientation.

Junior Year Program

The curriculum for the junior year program courses in each major is determined by each department. Initial program designs and curricula have to be approved by the writing committee. The committee's approval is also needed for any proposed revisions. The basic guidelines are that each course must link writing activities to learning and/or professional work in the major, must require frequent writing—not just one long paper—with peer and teacher feedback on drafts, must present writing as a process, and must address principles of writing. The course descriptions of Annaliese Bischoff and Helen M. Schneider offer examples of these principles in practice. (For other descriptions, see Forman et al., 1990; Mullin, 1989; Herrington, 1992; and Herrington & Cadman, 1991.)

As in the first year program, in the junior year program the connection with the library is made through the outreach efforts of the instructional services librarians. At the beginning of each semester, one of them explains their services at a workshop for teachers of junior year program courses. As in the first year program, the librarians will offer instructional sessions and prepare resource guides tailored to the specific interests of a given discipline and course.

Those of us in leadership positions in the writing program value our instructional connections with the library because we believe that learning to use the research resources of the library is an important part of our students' education. We also feel that those learning ends are best achieved when students and teachers make the connection with the library out of their own needs and interests. For such connections to remain viable, however, we need to sustain continuing personal collaboration across our programs and to articulate and enact our shared values regarding writing and research.

NOTES

1. This new program replaced the rhetoric requirement, a two-semester, entry-level sequence of courses. (See Forman, Harding, Herrington, Moran, & Mullin, 1990.)

2. When the two-semester rhetoric program was replaced by the current program, the instructional budget was, in principle, divided in half to fund the one-semester first year

College Writing course and the one-semester junior year writing course. Each year, the allocations for each half of the program are determined by the number of students in the first and junior years. For the junior year program, each department receives an allotment based on a per capita figure for the number of junior majors in the department.

REFERENCES

Forman, S., Harding, J., Herrington, A., Moran, C., & Mullin, W. (1990). University of Massachusetts junior year writing program. In T. Fulwiler & A. Young (Eds.), *Programs that work: Models and methods for writing across the curriculum* (pp. 199–219). Portsmouth, NH: Boynton/Cook.

Herrington, A. (1992). Composing one's self in a discipline: Students' and teachers' negotiations. In M. Secor & D. Charney (Eds.), *Constructing rhetorical education* (pp. 91–115). Carbondale: Southern Illinois University Press.

Herrington, A., & Cadman D. (1991). Peer review and revising in an anthropology course. *College Composition and Communication, 42,* 184–99.

Herrington, A., & Moran, C. (Eds.). (1992). *Writing, teaching, and learning in the disciplines.* New York: Modern Language Association.

Moran, C. (1986). University of Massachusetts, Amherst, university writing program. In P. Connolly & T. Vilardi (Eds.), *New methods in college writing programs* (pp. 111–116). New York: MLA.

Mullin, W. (1989, May). Writing in Physics. *The Physics Teacher, 27*(5), 442–47.

The Junior-Year Writing Course in Environmental Design and Landscape Architecture

Annaliese Bischoff, Associate Professor of Landscape
Architecture and Regional Planning

Environmental Design 394A, the junior year writing course, is a three-credit course offered in the fall semester for majors in both environmental design and landscape architecture. This year in this course, which meets twice a week from 9:30 A.M. to 10:45 A.M., there are forty-two undergraduate students, two teaching assistants from the Master of Landscape Architecture graduate program, and one associate professor from the Department of Landscape Architecture and Regional Planning.

For one of the weekly class meetings, the faculty member directs the class as a whole group. Time is divided among lectures, in-class writing exercises, and discussion. For the second meeting in the week, the students are divided into three smaller sections, each led by either a teaching assistant or the professor. Each section meets in a separate room to allow more focused discussions and individualized attention to the process of revising writing assignments. Multiple drafts are required of each assignment; peer review is sometimes utilized during class time.

The course content includes seven major writing assignments. The objectives of the course are twofold: (1) to help the students define their own interests in the broad field of environmental design and landscape architecture; and (2) to help students develop effective writing skills for use within the context of the discipline. All assignments are graded on a point basis. Points are then converted to letter grades. Additionally, feedback is provided with both written and verbal comments in class. At midsemester, individual student conferences are scheduled so feedback can be directly exchanged.

For the first piece, students must write an environmental autobiography in which they reflect upon the influences of three to five significant places throughout their lives. No library use is expected for this first, personal subject. Students are encouraged to develop their ideas, organization, and style from their own sense of experience. Attention is given to the voice created in the writing throughout the three required revisions.

For the second assignment, an environmental biography, students must select a noted author whose work has been influenced by the New England landscape in some way. To help students with the research and required format for a documented essay, a reference librarian has designed a specific session with prepared handouts in the library. Topics covered include finding works about authors, works by authors, and also works on literary genres, themes, and forms. The librarian acquaints the students with both on-line catalog use and basic information sources in literary criticism. The organizational structure within these resources can be helpful to students in conceiving an approach to the topic. For example, after studying secondary sources, one student chose to focus on the element water played in Poe's writing. Students are also welcome to reflect back to their own environmental autobiographies for ideas and organizational structure. All students are required to include citations and references from both secondary and primary sources in MLA style. Using the library is a central part of this assignment.

In the third assignment, students work on writing job application letters and an optional resume. Students are directed to several items permanently shelved in the reserve department of the library. The materials provide tips on writing cover letters and preparing resumes. Students must select real-world job opportunities for which they are currently qualified. Personal style and skill inventories constitute in-class exercises to help students prepare their self-presentations. Most students respond to summer employment possibilities.

Next, students develop a proposal summary for a project that they are particularly keen on undertaking. Sample project ideas might range from developing interpretive walking guides to designing curriculum packets on environmental issues for high school students to studying abroad. Two guides from the library, "Finding Out About Grants," and "Financial Aid for Students," are helpful in directing students to supportive sources of information in the area. How much students utilize these resources depends upon their degree of motivation to find actual funding sources. Some students do submit their proposals to actual sponsors; some students have been successful in gaining financial support to execute their plans.

The final three assignments include a creative writing piece, journal-based writing, and a critical analysis of a planning or design proposal. Continued use of the library could offer a rich source of models, ideas, information, and inspiration for each of these assignments. However, the reality of time seems to preempt library use at this point. Students seem busy finishing drafts and other course work. In this course, students are required to organize all of their work into a writing portfolio. This year, students will be required to submit two copies of the portfolio. One set will then be placed upon permanent reserve in the library to serve as a model for future students.

Library use is currently most vital in the early and middle parts of this writing course, which covers a broad range of writing types. The structured library session to support the second assignment provides the students with a user-friendly and critical orientation to the needed information sources. In subsequent assignments, students are self-motivated to seek out library resources. In part, the early session with the reference librarian encourages students to take more initiative in solving whatever problems they investigate later. Students do learn to ask for the help they need in exploring resources. Students in the writing class also learn to appreciate the patience, perseverance, and expertise available to them, particularly through the reference librarians in the library.

The School of Education Junior Year Writing Program

Helen M. Schneider, Lecturer in Education

The school of education junior year writing program was established as part of the reform of the general education curriculum in 1982. The course has six major writing assignments which go through multiple drafts, and students are required to keep a journal and organize a writing portfolio, as well as to do numerous in-class writing assignments.

From the beginning, the school of education faculty who designed the junior writing program saw the library as an integral part of the writing course. We were concerned that our students, as future teachers, not only learn to write well but also feel comfortable with the library as a source for research materials. We hoped that they in turn would pass on this sense of enthusiasm to their future students in public schools.

Initially we focussed on our students' becoming proficient in the use of print materials, but in the past few semesters, urged on by the new state regulations including educational technology competence as a component in teacher certification, we have become more and more involved in electronic information retrieval systems and have begun to focus more on the technological resources of the library.

Students in the school of education junior writing program begin the semester by interviewing a person practicing in the field to find out what kinds of writing they will need to do well in order to be successful educators. Many quickly discover that in addition to writing reports and communicating with parents they may need to be able to apply for grant money to enhance their future school programs, or to write to public officials, such as legislators, on complex educational issues. A report on their interview findings becomes the first formal writing assignment in the course. As with all other assignments in the course, students produce multiple drafts which are shared first with a peer group and then with the instructor.

The source for the issues that will become the basis for several writing assignments, culminating in a research project involving library research, is a casebook that sets out opposing views on several critical issues in the field of public education. Students are asked to choose an issue presented in the text which interests them. They then respond to the material from the text in an essay presenting a balanced viewpoint on the issue of their choice. The sequence of writing this essay, receiving peer feedback on the essay, and discussing the essay with the instructor is designed to help the student not only clarify the topic for the research project, but also identify what resources will be needed to complete the project.

After these preliminary steps, during the fifth week of the course, students visit the library as a class for instruction on finding and accessing the sources they will need in order to complete the project. To facilitate the best use of the librarian's expertise and time, the course instructor forwards the proposed topics to the educational research librarian prior to the library class period. We are fortunate to have a research librarian who has designated education as one of her areas of special interest, and she is able to introduce students quickly and efficiently to the resources most pertinent to the topics they are working on. In spite of the demands on her time, she has been willing and able to set aside a two-hour class period to meet with every section of the course.

To further aid in the research process, our librarians have put together an excellent written library guide for education majors, a series of listings for print sources such as indexes (including *Resources in Education* [RIE], *Current Index to Journals in Education* [CIJE], and the *Education Index*) and abstracts. This handout is thoroughly explained during the library class. In addition, the librarians have recently added considerable material on the use of ERIC and other electronic sources such as INFOTRAC and FUNDFINDER. Since we are now encouraging all students to become familiar, and comfortable, with electronic mail, the reference librarian has begun to include advice on using the Internet system in her presentation. She also demonstrates how the system can be used to find materials other than traditional journal sources for research projects. Such materials often include sample lesson plans that will be useful for future teachers.

After the librarian has introduced the various sourcing methods, students are asked to find at least five references from different sources on their topics during the library class period. We believe that having students try to use print and electronic sources when library staff and their instructor are present greatly enhances the probability that they will successfully use the library's resource materials on their own and thus write better projects. (Students have a choice for the format of their project: a traditional research paper, a documented proposal for a funded project, or a documented letter to a government official on an issue in public education. We have found that more and more students are choosing the grant proposal option as they recognize the need teachers increasingly have to supplement funding from state and municipal governments.)

After completion of the three sequenced writing assignments that make up the research project, students complete their writing portfolios for the course in two final assignments: a career unit including a letter and resume, and an essay on multiculturalism and diversity. Both of these assignments invite further use of the library's resources.

When they present their portfolios at the end of the course, many students cite the importance of their becoming literate in the use of the library's resources, both print and electronic.

An important feature to note about the course is that it is taught largely by graduate teaching assistants. These instructors, all of whom are graduate students in education, attend a weekly seminar that I conduct on issues in teaching writing. A key feature of the seminar is that the teaching staff also spend seminar class time upgrading their knowledge of the library, both print and electronic sources, in order to be more helpful to their students. Several members of the library research staff, including the education specialist, have cooperated in instructing the teaching staff.

The library classes for instructors have had two positive results: first and most important, instructors are better able to assist their students and convey a sense of competence in research; and second, they are better able to conduct research for their own graduate studies. The seminar sessions with the librarians have resulted in our instructors all acquiring e-mail addresses and all learning to use the on-line catalogue and electronic data bases with relative ease.

The result of this collaboration in staff development has been the creation of a cadre of people who can be a better resource to the undergraduate students in the course and who can reinforce what the librarians have taught in the library classroom. We consider the library staff to be an integral part of the instruction of both our students and teaching staff, not an add-on. Our hope is that our graduates, in their careers in education, will draw on their positive experiences with the library staff and resources.

Case Study: University of Rhode Island

Jean Sheridan, *Coordinator*
Margaret J. Keefe, Linda Shamoon, William Lynn McKinney, and Karen F. Stein, *Contributors*

The University of Rhode Island is a medium-size state university. The main campus is in southern Rhode Island. There are branch libraries at the College of Continuing Education in Providence and at the Graduate School of Oceanography on the Narragansett Bay Campus.

Number of FTE (Full Time Equivalent) students: 11,879

Number of FTE (Full Time Employed) faculty: 706.8

Student/faculty ratio: 17:1

Student/librarian ratio: 642:1

Highest degree granted: Ph.D.

Type of institution: Public

Source: Fall 1993 data. 1992–93 Fact Book. University of Rhode Island, Office of Institutional Research.

INSTITUTIONAL MISSION

The University of Rhode Island is rooted firmly in the tradition of land-grant education, and it is one of the original sea-grant institutions. Its three major responsibilities are to provide traditional as well as innovative opportunities for education at both the undergraduate and the graduate level; to pursue research and other scholarly and creative activities; and to serve the needs of the people of Rhode Island by making knowledge and information readily available to individual citizens, community programs, schools and educational agencies, businesses, industry, labor, and government. Fifty-nine percent of the students are from Rhode Island, and the remaining students are from fifty states and territories and seventy-four foreign countries.

The University Libraries

Number of volumes: 1,038,721

Number of serial subscriptions: 8,859

Total number of librarians (FTE): 18.65
  Public service/reference/instruction librarians: 8
  Technical services librarians: 5.25
  Library administration personnel: 5.40

Source: June 30, 1994 data. Collection development update No. 40. URI Library. 10 November 1994.

THE MISSION OF THE UNIVERSITY LIBRARIES

The university libraries have a mandate to serve all segments of the campus— students, faculty, and staff—as well as the general public. They must be responsive to students and their instructional needs, to faculty and their teaching and research requirements, and to administrative personnel and their informational needs. Beyond these activities is the commitment to safeguard intellectual freedom, to preserve and organize the institution's records, to acquire a special collection of a scholarly nature, to provide sophisticated reference service, and to engage in bibliographic exchange and resource sharing on both regional and national scales.

THE BIBLIOGRAPHIC INSTRUCTION PROGRAM

The bibliographic instruction program is continuing to evolve and adapt to changes in the methods of education. In the 1950s, there was a one-credit bibliography course taught in the English department by the head librarian. That course lapsed during the early 1960s while the library's efforts were consumed by the crisis of overcrowding and the institution's transition from a college to a university. By 1965, there was a library tour for each section of the required freshman English course; it included a brief introduction to the organization of the catalog and the use of periodical indexes. This was quickly transformed into group instruction in term paper research and writing. The arrival of the Graduate School of Library Science on the Kingston campus provided the opportunity to hire graduate research assistants and graduate interns, who were incorporated into the instructional program.

Over the years, a number of programs have been developed. Some have been dropped and others suspended because of staffing restrictions. Among the programs have been group and individualized instruction; "term-paper clinics," in which students meet with subject specialists for personalized help; credit-bearing courses; team-teaching writing-intensive courses in the sciences; seminars for incoming graduate students; workshops on specific reference tools and on CD-ROM searching; workshops in the Learning Assistance Center on how to do library research; literature guides that outline steps for research on particular issues or introduce basic sources on popular topics; class research teams in which librarians serve as project leaders; and panels on which librarians serve that review student presentations.

There has been a formal association with the writing program for several years, through which each section is offered a library session that introduces students to the library and provides minimal instruction in identifying and locating serial sources. An exercise is completed in class and graded by the writing instructor.

The amount and type of collaboration with the teaching faculty varies with the individuals involved. In some cases, librarians have helped to design the class assignments, and at one point, they had the responsibility of final approval of all student topics. In others, they have been responsible for part of an assignment and have graded at least part of the final report.

The university is currently reviewing the organization and method of delivering the curriculum to undergraduates. The president's proposal would change the first two years of a student's program to a series of seminars taught by tenure-track faculty in small group settings. Each class would be either writing-intensive, communication-intensive, or mathematics-intensive. Librarians have already worked on the pilot project and are continuing to work with appropriate committees to involve the library instruction program. Upper division classes would be organized in interdisciplinary research centers rather than collegial departments, and each student would be involved in collaborative research teams with graduate students and faculty. This part of the proposal is less developed, but library faculty continue to participate in the exploration of these potential changes.

At present, the majority of students are met in group instruction. Over 5,000 students were reached in 1992–1993, a figure that may be lower than expected because the library was undergoing a very disruptive expansion and renovation. Classes may include an introduction to the physical layout of the library, research strategy, resources appropriate to the assignment, and access to off-campus resources. Some are lecture classes, but others involve exercises or actual collaborative research. Classes are usually one hour long, but in many cases may be followed up with a class to review a particular source or problem. Some instructors allow a second session devoted to CD-ROM searching. Many classes are divided into research teams, and the librarian will meet with separate groups after the initial lecture to the entire class.

Many upper division undergraduate or graduate classes have seminars that last two or three hours or even two days. These seminars are an intensive introduction to the literature of a particular field.

Both undergraduate and graduate students may make appointments with reference librarians for individualized instruction. Such appointments frequently lead to regular consultation throughout the student's university career or even to formal classroom instruction for classes the student may be taking or teaching.

There is only one course that is currently being taught for credit. It is ZOO 508: Seminar in Zoological Literature, which is taught by the biological sciences reference bibliographer. It is a "survey of zoological literature including traditional methods of bibliographical control, contemporary information retrieval services, and the development of a personalized information system" (Bulletin, 1994–95, The Graduate School, University of Rhode Island).

The program currently has a single classroom. The classroom has the capability for demonstrations of on-line and CD-ROM searching, as well as instruction in Internet use. An electronic classroom that will permit hands-on experience with these services will be available in the spring semester of 1995.

For more information on the bibliographic instruction program described here, contact:

Margaret J. Keefe
Reference/Bibliographer in the Social Sciences
University of Rhode Island
Kingston, RI 02881
MJKEEFE@URIACC.URIEDU

An Introduction to Writing-Across-the-Curriculum at the University of Rhode Island

Linda Shamoon, Associate Professor of English and Director of the Writing Program

In 1989, URI's faculty senate endorsed the findings of its ad hoc committee on writing, asserting that "a problem with the quality of student writing exists at URI." It defined the problem as one "... of improving a low skills level and of maintaining improvement." The faculty senate also endorsed the committee's proposals, declaring:

1. Students must write more in courses across the campus, but additional credit hours should not be added to degree requirements.

2. Students should take courses across the curriculum that are writing-intensive versions of already existing courses.

3. Writing-across-the-curriculum, which enriches subject area courses with a variety of writing experiences, offers direction for URI.

With these endorsements, URI joined the more than four hundred colleges and universities around the country that have active WAC programs.

Today, we promote WAC through presemester workshops for faculty, led by faculty from the college writing program and other disciplines. Through these workshops, faculty from all disciplines discuss the similarities and differences in student writing, and together they design assignments that increase the amount of writing in classes in order to improve the quality of both the students' writing and the students' learning. As of January 1994, ninety-five faculty will have attended WAC workshops, two colleges (the College of Arts and Sciences and the College of Continuing Education) will have sponsored workshop participation for all interested faculty, and one college (the College of Nursing) will have sponsored a workshop for its entire faculty.

URI's WAC effort differs from the University of Vermont's or the University of Michigan's or the University of California's, but the assumptions underlying all of these programs are surprisingly similar. They, too, were framed in the original committee's report:

1. Writing ability develops slowly over time.
2. To maintain or improve good writing, students must write throughout their school years in all of their courses.
3. Good writing must be demanded and valued by faculty.

These assumptions have led faculty at the various institutions to conclude that writing is appropriate to all classes, but that the types of writing assignments vary widely from class to class. In some classes, formal papers or lab reports are appropriate, but in other classes, short informal writing is beneficial. Similarly, faculty have concluded that good writing evolves throughout a semester and that students need time and help in developing, drafting, and revising their papers. Finally, many faculty have decided to change from using writing to test students' learning to using writing as a means of promoting and improving learning. Working from these commonalties, faculty at URI have developed a dazzling array of assignments and materials for their classes, many of which are available to other faculty through *URI's WAC Handbook: Teaching Tips and Writing Assignments from the WAC Demonstration Faculty.*

This year, 1994, URI's WAC effort is heading in new directions. WAC workshops will now include the designing of formal "writing-intensive" (WI) courses, and the general education program will probably have a strong WAC component, comprised of WI courses that will provide materials for student writing portfolios; students will be required to complete their writing portfolios as part of their general education requirements. These developments will help to institutionalize WAC for all students in all colleges at URI. Nevertheless, the faculty senate remains the guiding body for WAC, and the WAC effort at URI will continue to reflect faculty concerns about how best to promote good writing in academia.

How the Library Helped Me Teach "Women and the Natural Sciences"

Karen F. Stein, Professor of English and Women's Studies

How does one develop and teach a course in a newly emerging subject, a subject that has no available textbooks? One uses the library, of course.

The course entitled *Women and the Natural Sciences* would not exist at all if it were not for the library. When I served as acting coordinator of the women's studies program, I found that the program offered many courses in the humanities, the social sciences, and the arts, but none in the natural sciences. What might such a course look like? I drew up an outline of possible topics: women scientists, ways that science studies women, and how science is taught and its implications for women students. Did a feminist critique of science exist? I felt it ought to, but what had been done? Sandra Harding's intriguingly titled study *The Science Question in Feminism* rounded out the course outline. From this beginning, I conducted a library search, using a wonderful tool, a bibliography compiled by Bernice Lott of texts relating to women's studies available in the collection of the URI library. Cooperating faculty in the sciences, mathematics, speech communications, counseling and career development, and psychology helped develop a new course, *Women and the Natural Sciences*.

When the course is taught, from five to ten faculty deliver guest lectures on topics such as "Women and Engineering Careers," "Rachel Carson and the Environmental Movement," and "Women Primatologists." Students write short papers, which may require library research, to answer questions the guests lectures pose.

The library was crucial to the course at its inception, and it has continued to play a large role. No single book covers the topics examined in the course. Several texts are relevant, but library use is an important component. With the syllabus, students receive a bibliography of women and science books in the URI collection. Students write both individual papers and a group paper and prepare a round-table presentation. Some assignments, such as a journal of experiences related to the course, are experiential, and some necessitate library research. Some of the research topics for individual papers are:

1. Research a little-known woman scientist. Answer a series of questions about her life and career and her contribution to science. (Why did she decide to become a scientist? What was her education like? Who encouraged/discouraged her? Did she face discrimination? What did she accomplish? What recognition did she receive?)

2. Read and review one of the books listed in the bibliography.

For the group paper, students are asked to research a particular topic, hand in a paper, and present a round-table discussion about it. At the round-table presentation, students explore different points of view about an issue. Each group member (groups consist of from two to four members) takes one aspect of the topic to research and present to the class. We avoid a debate format, which assumes that every question has only two sides and that there will be a winning and a losing side. Questions have included:

1. Is the SAT test biased? Does it discriminate against women and minorities? How might it be modified to be more fair?
2. How does science education in Japan compare with science education in United States?
3. What images of women do science textbooks present, both historically and currently?
4. Should surrogate motherhood be legal? Should it be regulated?
5. What are the new reproductive technologies? How do they impact women?

For the group assignment, students often use the library group study rooms as meeting places.

When I first taught the course, the book review paper was especially important and useful for me. Students answered questions that provided useful feedback about the books. How appropriate were they for course assignment? What topics did they address? How difficult were they for students?

The course has been highly successful. As reported on anonymous questionnaires, students not only develop greater interest in women and in science, they become more confident of their own academic abilities as a result of taking the course.

Using the Library to Develop Positions on Current Issues

William Lynn McKinney, Professor of Education

Important goals in my introductory human service class are for students (1) to get to know one another, (2) to work with people whom they might not choose to work with (all human service jobs are likely to require this), and (3) to begin to debate and take positions on policy issues in the broad human service field. Structured writing assignments that include library research allow me to work toward the achievement of all three goals.

Introduction to Human Services ordinarily enrolls about fifty students, nearly all of whom are sophomores with, at best, modest writing and library research skills. The class meets twice weekly for seventy-five minutes. I use one standard text and two or three works of fiction about poor people and/or others who are either in the human service system or eligible for it. Grading is based on four short papers, two exams, a journal on the student's twenty hours of required community service work, and class participation.

During the first class, I assign individuals randomly to groups of four or five, which I refer to as pods, and in the first and second classes, I give them discussion questions which they must discuss in twenty minutes. We then talk about how to state a clear thesis, garner strong evidence/support, and argue passionately in support of positions. In the second class, I introduce the first writing assignment—a two- to three-page paper in which they are to argue either for or against giving to beggars in the streets. Most of my students are not prepared to engage in the issue and bring, at best, the sociopolitical thinking of their families and their limited personal experience to it. Many, because of their development stage, attempt to argue both sides of the issue. They need some background before beginning to write, so the first step in completing this assignment is for each student to find one article about begging, in either a scholarly journal, a magazine, or a newspaper.

For the third class, each student must bring a photocopy of the article he or she has found for every other member of his or her pod. Appropriate articles are surprisingly easy to find since issues of the sort we discuss in this class regularly confront both policy makers and people concerned about our welfare system. A recent example is a lengthy article entitled "To Give or Not to Give" published in *The New York Times Magazine* on April 24, 1994. Students will find an array of articles, some sympathetic to beggars and some not, and each student will begin to understand that those who beg are as heterogeneous as the general population. I hope they will then begin to understand why the problems of poverty do not lend themselves to easy solutions. Most students wanting to major in human services are rather soft-hearted and liberal. In most classes, I must work hard to find the conservative students and to insure that their voices are heard. In this class, there is nothing worse than everyone agreeing with everyone else on the issues I raise.

During the third class, students work in their pods, discussing what their library research has yielded. Surprisingly, there is usually little duplication of articles. At the end of the third class, each pod must turn in to me a bibliography in an acceptable style (by this time I will have introduced them to both APA and MLA bibliographic styles). I will then prepare one large bibliography for the entire class and distribute it during the fourth class. By this time, each student has both a long bibliography and copies of as many as five articles about the topic of begging and is ready to begin drafting the paper. For this first paper, each student must cite at least two articles.

The first draft of the paper on giving to beggars is due during the fifth class. Each student must bring two copies, one for me and one for a peer editor. I distribute a structured peer-editing form for student use. Both that form and my editing stress clarity of thesis, adequacy of support, and overall organization. At this point, we ignore spelling and other grammatical errors.

It is challenging for me to read up to fifty draft papers, even short ones, over a weekend, but I find most students unable to declare a position and support it without considerable feedback from me. I find that the extra work at the beginning of the semester pays off in superior student writing by the end of the term. Both my comments and the peer editing forms are due back to the authors in the sixth class. Students then have until the eighth class to turn in final drafts of their papers.

The rules change slowly as we proceed through the next three writing assignments. Each paper focuses on an issue and is two to three pages long, but for the remaining assignments, each pod must find nonduplicated articles and distribute copies within their pods. I continue to prepare full bibliographies for distribution to the entire class. I do not read drafts after the first paper, although I allow students to rewrite their second and third assignments if they are D or F papers. The highest possible score on a rewritten paper is B–minus. I continue to require peer editing of the second and third assignments. I then grade the peer edits.

The second and third writing assignments require students to cite at least four articles. Beginning with the second paper, I announce that I will not accept papers that have any misspellings or grammatical errors. I am regularly rewarded with papers that are nearly error free. Any exceptions are returned without a grade for proofreading and resubmission. The final assignment is like the others, except that students must cite at least five articles and I do not accept rewrites.

The library aspect of the assignments changes slowly through the semester. By the third paper, I require that each pod find five different kinds of sources, for example, one government publication, one dissertation abstract, one book, one scholarly article, and one newspaper article.

By the end of the semester, most students are much better able to use the library. They are better writers. They know that current issues in the field of human services are complex, and they can persuasively argue a position.

Case Study: University of Vermont

Nancy Crane, *Coordinator*
Nancy Crane, Janet Reit, Toby Fulwiler, and
Jean Kiedaisch, *Contributors*

University of Vermont

Number of FTE (Full Time Equivalent) students: 9,341[1]

Number of FTE (Full Time Employed) faculty: 864[2]

Student/faculty Ratio: 11:1

Highest degree granted: Ph.D.

Type of institution: Public

[1] Degree students, fall 1993.

[2] Data for FTE faculty, academic year 1992–1993.

INSTITUTIONAL MISSION

The University of Vermont and State Agricultural College (UVM), Vermont's only university-level institution of higher education, blends the academic heritage of a private university with service missions in the land-grant tradition. UVM directs its resources toward the provision of excellence in instruction, innovation in research and scholarship, and public service. The curricula in UVM's undergraduate, graduate, and professional programs integrate the principles of liberal education to enhance the personal, professional, and intellectual growth of its students. Enrollment is selective; about 50 percent of the students are from Vermont, and the remaining 50 percent are from more than forty states and approximately forty foreign countries.

THE UNIVERSITY LIBRARIES AND MEDIA SERVICES

Number of volumes: 1,105,649

Number of serial subscriptions: 17,229

Number of CD-ROMs, including government documents: 20

Number of librarians (total): 29
  Public services/reference/library instruction: 19
  Technical services: 5
  Administration: 5

Library Mission

The mission of the libraries and media services is to further the creation, application, and dissemination of knowledge by providing access to information resources and education in their use. The libraries are a vital component of the university's commitment to excellence in instruction, innovation in research and scholarship, and dedication to public service, and are a unique resource for the state of Vermont and its people.

Description of the Bailey/Howe Library Bibliographic Instruction Program

Group instruction. The majority of UVM students (approximately 4,000 students per year) receive library instruction through special classes taught by library faculty and staff. These classes are scheduled at the request of teaching faculty and are designed to meet the requirements of a particular research assignment and/or field of study. In the past, the primary modes of delivery were lecture and demonstration. Upon completion of the library's electronic classroom in the summer of 1994, students will be receiving hands-on training as well.

Individual instruction. The Bailey/Howe Library Reference-by-Appointment service is designed for the approximately 230 students per year who want to consult a reference librarian about difficulties they are having with their research. Each appointment is planned in advance, lasts about half an hour, and is scheduled at a time the librarian is not expected to be at the reference desk. Students who avail themselves of this service receive the full attention of a librarian who has expertise or interest in the topic at hand.

SAGE Advice. SAGE Advice (for dial-in users of SAGE, the library's electronic gateway) is an on-line help program for navigators and searchers of the SAGE information gateway. This program was developed by a member of the library faculty to help remote users of SAGE. SAGE Advice is accessible to anyone searching the SAGE from terminals inside or outside the library.

For more information, contact:

Janet Reit
Library Instruction Coordinator
Bailey/Howe Library, Reference Department
University of Vermont
Burlington, VT 05405
(802) 656-8132
JReit@moose.uvm.edu

The Writing Program at the University of Vermont

Toby Fulwiler, Professor of English and Writing Program
Director

The faculty writing project originated in 1984. The objective of the program is to introduce faculty from all disciplines across campus to a variety of new pedagogical ideas involving a more active use of language—both oral and written—by students in all subject areas and levels. The primary vehicle for introducing these ideas is the writing workshop—a two-day experiential workshop introducing faculty to ideas such as writing-to-learn, multiple-draft assignments, and collaborative learning. In addition, these off-campus workshops promote among the faculty a sense of community, encourage interdisciplinary publication and research projects, and, along the way, help faculty with their own writing skills. As of the spring of 1994, approximately six hundred UVM faculty had taken part in twenty-three writing workshops.

During the past ten years, a number of UVM faculty from several disciplines have participated in leadership roles within the faculty writing project. The faculty writing project has offered a variety of follow-up and advanced workshops, ranging from two-hour Thursday afternoon meetings that from three to twenty-three faculty have attended to a two-day overnight "veterans" workshop at which seventy-five UVM faculty conducted workshops for each other. Beginning in 1988, we have offered two- and three-day "writing retreats," inviting workshop veterans to bring their own manuscripts to the Bishop Booth Conference Center ("We will feed you and leave you alone"). Retreat attendance each time has ranged from eighteen to thirty faculty, who have revised dissertations, cowritten articles, developed grant proposals, and even worked on next year's syllabi. A full report of the Vermont program was published in *Programs that Work* (Dickerson, Fulwiler, & Steffens, 1990).

The status of the program right now would best be described as steady, due to lack of funding for new programs or faculty. At present, UVM has no curricular requirements connected with the program. However, the main objectives of the program already seem to have been met; anecdotal evidence suggests that faculty writing assignments are currently more frequent and varied throughout virtually all departments and programs in the university.

A two-tier, cross-curricular writing proposal has been developed for the College of Arts and Sciences; however, action on it has been delayed for several years now due to lack of funds. The proposal, if passed by the college, calls for first-year writing-intensive seminars for all incoming students to the college, and senior writing-intensive seminars in the major for all graduating arts and sciences students. The first-year course would focus on general writing strategies and be taught by tenured instructors across the curriculum; the major seminar would focus on disciplinary writing conventions and be taught by instructors within the major discipline. Both courses would include writing-to-learn strategies, such as free writing, short response papers, and journals, and learning-to-write strategies, such as revision and editing.

As writing-intensive courses are developed at first-year or advanced levels, it becomes apparent that students will require outside resources to complete their projects satisfactorily. Faculty have worked with librarians to develop quite an array of research or library assignments that go beyond the traditional research paper. These include "speeches, debates, argumentative or persuasive essays, newspaper articles, annotated bibliographies, collaborative writing projects and in-class presentations, and even course journals" (Dickerson *et al.,* 1990, p. 57). Resources relevant to a particular writing/research assignment are introduced to the students, along with discussions of research strategies and the research process in general.

REFERENCE

Dickerson, M. J., Fulwiler, T., & Steffens, H. (1990). The University of Vermont. In T. Fulwiler & A. Young (Eds.), *Programs that work* (pp. 45–63). Portsmouth, NH: Boynton/Cook.

The Writing-Intensive Course

Jean Kiedaisch, Director, Writing Center; Codirector, FOCUS
Program

One first-year writing-intensive seminar that arts and sciences students can elect to take is FOCUS (Focus on Creating Undergraduate Success). The FOCUS program, begun in 1993–1994 with 120 students, aims to develop students' oral and written communication, critical thinking, and research abilities in two-semester, interdisciplinary seminars team taught by three faculty.

The overall FOCUS theme for 1993–1994 was "Power." Our particular seminar, in keeping with the theme, was titled "The Power of Power Hydro-Quebec in James Bay." It was taught by faculty from the departments of geology, English, and communication science and disorders. We were interested in power as a natural resource, power struggles between native Canadians and Quebecois, and the power of communication in affecting political and economic issues.

We anticipated that students would come to our course knowing little about the issue we were studying and that they would be somewhat intimidated by the size of our library and by the need to use computers to access information. Although they could electronically access the on-line catalog from their rooms, we expected that, without instruction, they would resist this option. We therefore worked with Laurie Kutner of the reference staff at Bailey/Howe Library to plan a series of activities that would make students more knowledgeable and more comfortable using library resources.

The first activity, run by faculty during the first week of classes, was devoted to assessing and improving students' comfort with computers and word processing, introducing them to e-mail, and getting them set up with an e-mail account. Next we asked Laurie and two other reference librarians to design and conduct a workshop on using SAGE, the library's information gateway to a variety of information resources, including UVM's catalog and a number of on-line indexes. They were willing to do this workshop in the computer lab that is part of the Living/Learning program. In the year 1993–1994, most of the students enrolled in the FOCUS program were housed in the Living/Learning complex. The Living/Learning program is an academic program with a residency component specifically set up for the program. From this complex students could access information directly from their dorm rooms. To go along with the workshop, Laurie designed an exercise tailored to the course subject matter that would familiarize students with library resources and let us see where they needed more work.

At the end of the first semester, we hoped students would be close to choosing their subjects for the independent research projects that would take up most of their time in the second semester. To help them find a subject while learning more about Hydro-Quebec in James Bay, we asked them to prepare a twenty-item annotated bibliography. In order to help them with this task, we arranged for a second workshop, this time on using Lexis/Nexis, a full-text search system that gives access to current news and business information.

During the second semester, just as we ourselves worked with students on their projects through one-on-one conferences, reference librarians worked with them individually through a reference-by-appointment service. Students could set up appointments to get help finding resources on their particular subjects (for example, the changing role of women in Cree society, future power sources for Vermont, or Hydro-Quebec International's work on the Three Gorges project in China). Students worked weekly with a writing tutor, who also encouraged students to use the reference-by-appointment service. About half of the students in my seminar took advantage of this option. Students made use of library materials such as a one-page handout on APA style and another on how to cite Lexis/Nexis sources.

How effective were the various components of the library work for students? In final evaluations, when asked to respond to the statement "The FOCUS program was better, about the same, or worse than your other courses in terms of developing your research skills," over 70 percent of my students responded "better." Still, since this program is in its very first year, there is much room for refining every aspect of it, including how we familiarize the students with the library.

Next year, when we teach the same course, we hope to do a better job of getting our students to communicate with us, with each other, and with Laurie, via e-mail. If we are successful, they will be asking more questions about library resources as they go along. This will be very helpful for those students who tend not to be thorough enough in ferreting out research materials. We also would like to involve all students in the individualized reference-by-appointment service.

Collaborative Efforts in Library Instruction

Janet Reit, Library Instruction Coordinator

The success of the faculty writing project, which was begun in 1984, has increased the number of writing-intensive courses offered at UVM. With each new introductory or upper-level writing course that has required a research paper, an increased demand for library instruction has followed. This important connection was officially acknowledged by the College of Arts and Sciences in its 1992 writing requirement proposal, which featured a library instruction component. Although the requirement was not adopted for lack of funding, most instructors of writing-intensive courses still build library instruction into their syllabi.

The decentralized nature of the UVM writing program has engendered an informal approach to collaborative efforts between library and teaching faculty. Discussions about library assignments usually commence after problems arise. However, librarians have made contributions at earlier stages; the exercise designed by Laurie Kutner for her group of FOCUS students is one example. The library's involvement in FOCUS actually dates from the program's inception in 1993. Librarians supported a request for grant moneys to launch the program and contributed material to the "Success Packet," a selection of brochures designed to guide and inform first year students in the FOCUS program.

During the early days of program development, librarians consulted with FOCUS faculty to explore mutually acceptable levels of support and collaboration. Librarians offered to lead special electronic resources workshops for faculty and to establish a FOCUS listserv, a computer list for a certain kind of topic discussion group. They also expressed an interest in training FOCUS students how to tutor each other in library skills. In addition, each librarian agreed to serve as a liaison to one of the five smaller study groups or seminars into which FOCUS faculty and students were organized. Collaborative efforts between FOCUS faculty and their library liaison were generally quite successful. Workshops, listservs and peer tutoring are still possibilities, but they were too ambitious for the first year of a program piloting a number of other innovations.

Four of the five library liaisons met with their FOCUS groups in instructional sessions during the 1993–1994 academic year. The interdisciplinary makeup of the faculty teams leading each FOCUS group determined the nature of student exploration, which in turn influenced the content and method of library instruction delivered by each liaison. All first sessions were designed as introductions tailored to meet the needs of the first-year students and the particulars of their various research assignments. Two of the liaisons met with their seminars more than once throughout the year. They each devoted their second session to teaching about Lexis/Nexis and to strategies for searching.

Jean Kiedaisch, the director of the writing center, was very enthusiastic about the two sessions her students attended, but next year she recommends that we wait until her students have become acquainted with their faculty and peers before scheduling the first session. She will continue to promote the library's reference-by-appointment service for students who want help with their research on an individual appointment basis. Through regular contact with Laurie Kutner in individual and group meetings, Jean's students gained the access they needed to library resources and were insured against falling through the library research cracks. Jean hopes to build upon these experiences by teaching next year's students to search the library's electronic resources directly from their dorm rooms, a project that will offer us another opportunity to work collaboratively with FOCUS faculty.

In looking ahead, we see that FOCUS students and their peers will have information needs that go beyond the research requirements of their writing projects. We know they will be entering a more highly automated library environment than the one they experienced in high school, and we are sure they will need specialized training to make effective use of the library's electronic resources. In anticipation, we have designed an electronic classroom for hands-on learning in a realistic library setting. We hear from our colleagues at other institutions that librarians and teaching faculty who work collaboratively as a team create the most successful electronic classroom learning experiences for their students. Now that we have such a facility, we can look forward to expanding our collaborative efforts with faculty who teach writing-intensive courses on our campus.

Case Study: Whatcom Community College

Iva Sue Grover, *Coordinator*
Barbara Dahl, Iva Sue Grover, and Luanne Lampshire, *Contributors*

INSTITUTIONAL MISSION

Whatcom Community College (WCC) is a two-year college which is part of the Washington State Community and Technical College system. It offers the Associate in Science and Associate in Arts and Sciences degrees and certificates in several allied health and business vocational programs. In 1992–1993, the college served 2,072 FTE (Full Time Equivalent) and 4,606 individual (part-time) students. WCC is located in Bellingham, Washington, in the northwest corner of Washington State. It began as a "college without walls" in 1969 and has evolved into a small central campus with three permanent buildings and three smaller facilities located in the rural areas and communities of Whatcom County. Its mission includes providing comprehensive two-year degree and certificate programs at the main campus and at the two community facilities in Lynden and Blaine, Washington. The Northwest Road facility is home to several community-based programs and the student-sponsored child care center. Service to adult students through alternative modes of instruction, an individualized degree program, learning contracts, and credit for prior experiential learning, as well as serving diverse populations has always been a major part of the college's mission. That diversity now includes many more students of traditional college age and an increasing number of high school age "running start" students, as well as a growing number of international students, dropping the average student age from 32 in 1980–1981 to 24 in 1993–1994.

THE LEARNING RESOURCES CENTER (LIBRARY)

Number of volumes: 13,000

Number of serials: 595
  Paper and microfiche: 145
  Full text and image CD-ROM: 450

Number of CD-ROMs: 8

Number of librarians (FTE): 1.89
  Full-time faculty librarian/administrator: 1
  Part-time faculty librarians: 2

The Learning Resources Center (LRC) at WCC has evolved from a small in-hospitable room three miles from both the population center and the instructional center to a 15,000 square foot integrated facility on the centrally located Cordata Campus in Bellingham. The campus is located six blocks from Bellis Fair Mall and about half a mile north of Interstate 5.

The mission of the LRC is to provide access to and instruction in the use of information resources in all formats located anywhere. Our collection is intended to support the basic curriculum needs of the WCC programs and course offerings. The on-site collection is small by most standards (13,000 print and nonprint items), but is carefully selected and constantly weeded out to provide an up-to-date and actively evolving base of information to serve the daily needs of students. It is not intended to be a repository or major research collection. WCC students have full undergraduate access to the resources of Western Washington University's Wilson Library, which is a large research and repository collection. This agreement between the two institutions has been in place since 1973 and has been an effective collaborative effort. The LRC collection is open to any community resident of Whatcom County including WWU faculty and students. About 90 percent of WCC students who go on to four-year colleges and universities transfer to Western Washington University.

In 1979, WCC began its electronic connection to information as a participant in the then Washington Library Network, now called WLN. The WCC catalog has been either on-line public access through a direct line to WLN, electronically based CD-ROM using WLN LaserPAC, or as it is currently, an in-house OPAC using Follett SearchPlus with WLN LaserCat on CD-ROM as our window to the world beyond Bellingham. Dial-up access to the Bellingham Public and Whatcom County Library System OPACs is also provided. The LRC reference tools are increasingly electronic, and currently, besides LaserCat and SearchPlus, they include ProQuest/Periodical Abstracts Research II, NewsBank, ERIC annual service, CINAHL, and a few other CD-ROM reference titles. In order to provide access to resources worldwide, DIALOG on-line searching for students and faculty was implemented in 1984. Dial-up access to the Internet for reference activities is also available to librarians.

To support the effective use of highly sophisticated materials available through these electronic avenues, a bibliographic instruction program was begun in 1981. It includes instructional orientations to classes, covering basic research skills and resources and techniques germane to the specific discipline of each course. Of the some two hundred classes offered each quarter, orientations are given to twenty-five to thirty classes at the request of the content instructors. They are scheduled on a first come, first served basis. Among the historically earliest and most consistent users of this service are the instructors of sociology, psychology, anthropology, and college study skills. Many others entered the fold through the emphasis on writing-across-the-curriculum. In addition to these sessions, each quarter the LRC provides for Whatcom students general orientations to the facilities of the LRC and to Wilson Library at WWU. In addition, a Library Use and Research Skills course is offered two quarters each year. Students may enroll in this self-paced modular course for one to three credits. Library faculty are contracted separately from their LRC assignments to teach this course.

The Writing-Across-the-Curriculum Program at Whatcom Community College

Iva Sue Grover, Coordinator, Learning Resource Center

HISTORY

At a forum on May 13, 1983, associated student representatives offered suggestions for motivating students to write better. Several of their suggestions provided strong impetus for implementing a writing-across-the-curriculum (WAC) program. One said, "I think I learned some things in English last year, but in my other classes no one seemed to care until this quarter. Now I've got two classes where I have to pay attention to my writing, and I'm having a terrible time." Another remarked that "All faculty should give feedback on written assignments not just a grade." And a third commented, "All faculty should be willing to explain why writing is important—particularly to someone in their discipline." Still others commented that instructors frequently offered editorial notations about grammar and spelling errors, but only occasionally provided helpful suggestions for improving the presentation of content, organization, or reasoning, yet assumed students knew how to write thesis statements and how to use research tools. So in the fall of 1983, writing-across-the-curriculum got underway.

Jean Carmean, English instructor, and then coordinator of the communications, arts, and humanities areas, took up the challenge of leadership. With support from the college president, William Laidlaw, a WAC steering committee of interested faculty representing instructional areas was formed. The coordinator of learning resources/librarian was a member. Three days of faculty seminars emphasizing practical implementation of suggestions launched the project. A small budget allowed the committee to provide stipends ranging from $100 to $600 to part-time faculty whose proposals for projects were accepted and completed. Full-time faculty received professional development units toward salary increases for the completion of their projects. The committee reviewed the proposals and also determined the rate of the stipend to be awarded. Most projects undertaken were completed, and the results in almost every case seemed to be positive.

A rationale and goals statement for the WAC program was written. Guidelines for the participant proposal process and a curriculum activity/project proposal form were prepared. A workshop for all interested faculty was held to introduce the program and provide faculty with a variety of assistance tools. Jean Carmean developed a bibliography of related readings, and selected reading handouts were provided. Response from faculty was enthusiastic.

Several years into the project, increased enrollment created a need to limit the size of writing-intensive classes. At this time the steering committee developed a statement of "Writing-Intensive Courses Criteria" and a statement of "Expectations for Student Writing." According to the statements, writing-intensive courses at WCC were to include:

• graded writing totaling a minimum of 2,000 words distributed among at least three different papers

• evaluation by the instructor on both form and content

• writings that may be of a wide variety but that should reflect the research which "shows that student writing improves when structured in a number of different ways and improves most when students write frequent short papers with instructor feedback geared to improving the next draft or the next paper" (Whatcom Community College, ca. 1983).

Once a quarter, a brown-bag lunch was held, at which faculty could share what was happening with their projects, and annually in the spring, a half-day retreat was held in a pleasant location off campus so that faculty could share project information and camaraderie. Enthusiasm and involvement grew through the continued efforts of the program leader, Jean Carmean, and the support of the steering committee. The president and the dean for instruction also provided verbal and budgetary support to keep the activity level high.

In 1984 and 1985, Carmean conducted two writing sample studies of recent graduates. Study A (1984) was made when the WAC program had just begun; Study B (1985) when it was well established. Of the writing samples in study

A, 65% were rated as competent or better while 80% of the samples in Study B were so rated. Twenty students wrote samples for both studies; thirteen of the twenty showed significant improvement over their earlier writing samples.

IMPLICATIONS OF WAC FOR THE LEARNING RESOURCES CENTER BIBLIOGRAPHIC INSTRUCTION SERVICES

For bibliographic instruction, the implications of the WAC program included increased requests by instructors for class orientations to research; increased awareness and use of the reserve collection; increased demand to improve and develop both the reference and the general collections, especially in the disciplines where instructors were including WAC activities in their curriculum; increased use of DIALOG and other electronic resources; and increased demand for reference assistance.

Increased Class Research Skills Orientations

With the addition of more electronic tools, the emphasis in the BI presentations shifted gradually from emphasizing search strategies applicable for print tools to emphasizing search strategies specifically pertinent to electronic tools. For example, the use of Boolean operators became a basic element of all research orientations. We also discovered that many students were still having difficulty understanding how to write a thesis statement and the benefit which that provided them in developing effective research strategies. This was especially true in the content-discipline courses where instructors either assumed students had that knowledge or were reluctant to take content time to teach basic skills. So teaching the thesis statement became the opening element of BI orientations. It provided a good starting place and led directly into the formulation of research strategies, especially when using electronic reference tools.

Increased Awareness and Use of the Reference Collection

Students and faculty alike were often reluctant to utilize the LRC reference collection. Since it was small, it was often assumed that it was not useful. As electronic resources and finding tools were added, they expanded the access to resources exponentially for the amount of dollars invested. ERIC on CD-ROM was one of the first electronic indexes added. Since WWU subscribes to 90 percent of the journals in ERIC and to all of the microfiche documents, WCC students have immediate access to these resources through this finding tool, and they do not have to stand in line to use ERIC as students at WWU often do. WAC has definitely had a large impact on the expansion of reference finding tools in the LRC.

Increased Demand to Expand and Develop the Reference and General Collections

The increase in writing activities in the discipline courses immediately increased the demand for books and nonprint resources in the general collection. For example, when the science instructors began including writing activities in their assignments, the increased demand for up-to-date books in those disciplines was noticeable. We began to get suggestions from these instructors for both general areas of interest and specific titles. The involvement of the two medical assisting instructors in WAC resulted in both of them bringing their students to the LRC for research introductions and in the expansion of both the general and the reference collections. Many of these students were returning adults and were hesitant to use electronic tools without considerable direction, so the group activity provided a basis for peer support among themselves. This interest and the introduction of a professional nursing program brought CINAHL on CD-ROM to the LRC. This tool was then available to all students and is heavily used by human services and psychology students as well as the health sciences students.

Increased Use of DIALOG On-line Services

Since the nature of student research activities was becoming more sophisticated, the need for more complex information increased. Almost concurrent with the beginning of WAC, the LRC began providing DIALOG searches for students as part of its reference service. The cost of use grew from $630 during the first year of WAC to $954 during the second year and $1,510 during the third year. Sociology, psychology, human services, health sciences, and anthropology questions were the most common and needed information beyond the scope of the tools available in the LRC. As the availability of quality CD-ROM tools increased and tools like UMI Periodical Abstracts were added, the demand for DIALOG searches has waned, but it is still an important part of our reference service for very difficult or highly technical questions.

Increased Demand for Reference Assistance

The most significant impact of WAC on the LRC has been the increased demand for professional reference staff. Except for the Library Use and Research Skills course, all bibliographic instruction is done by the reference librarian assigned to the reference desk. There is not sufficient funding to provide a second librarian during these times. While we view teaching thirty-five students at once instead of one at a time as a good investment of time, it still leaves the individual researcher without assistance during class presentations. Since we teach twenty to twenty-five of these class sessions each quarter, there are a significant number of hours of reference desk service time that is unstaffed, even though it is advertised. Also, the increase in writing and research continues to create the need to provide additional reference service hours. Since the reference desk is staffed only thirty-seven of the fifty-seven hours each week that the

LRC is open, additional demands of programs like WAC can exacerbate an already difficult situation. On the other hand, it means students have to apply the skills they are taught in the class presentations and become more independent in their research activities. The Library Use and Research Skills course was developed in 1984 and is offered two quarters a year. This self-paced, modular, lab-based course has evolved over the years into an important option for students who want to expand their knowledge of and skills in locating, selecting, and evaluating information resources. The three modules encompass learning how to use the four major libraries in Whatcom County effectively. They include the Whatcom Community College LRC, the Bellingham Public Library, the Whatcom County Library System, and the Wilson Library at Western Washington University. This is a hands-on course. The WAC program increased the need to improve its design and effectiveness.

BENEFITS

With the interaction of the library and the content instructors, there have been a number of benefits. At the Student Success Strategies Conference, held in Portland, Oregon, in February, 1988, and again at the National Seminar on Successful College Teaching, held in Orlando, Florida, in March, 1988, Robert Winters, English composition and literature instructor, summarized the benefits of this library-classroom collaboration and its effect on students as follows:

- Better and clearer development of thesis statements
- Earlier arrival at the LRC or library to start research
- Increased willingness to venture into other, larger libraries for resources
- Increased use of academic, specialized, and original source materials
- Increased interest in topic and in research process, due to ease of use
- Increased energy on creative use of materials rather than on burdensome searching
- Increased preparation to undertake future research projects and to pursue deeper research questions and more sophisticated research projects
- Enhanced learning of both library/research skills and course content

Writing-across-the-curriculum at Whatcom Community College has been an ongoing success for ten years. With the leadership provided by Jean Carmean and her continued resolution to keep it alive and moving forward, the enthusiastic involvement of many full- and part-time faculty over the years, and the involved commitment of the LRC librarians to be full partners in bringing writing and research skills together, this program has produced measurable results in improving student writing. It has also succeeded in bringing faculty together into dialogue, which has paved the way for other effective programs—such as the FIPSE drug and alcohol curriculum infusion projects—to be supported and successful. It has also provided a model for implementing an exciting outcomes assessment program, and it has challenged students to appreciate the need to be competent writers in all fields. Although WAC activity has slowed in recent years because of lack of coordinator released time, a renewed administrative commitment has provided support for revitalizing WAC with faculty workshops and sharing sessions. These activities will once again introduce new faculty to the purpose of the writing-across-the-curriculum program at WCC.

REFERENCE

(ca. 1983). Writing-Intensive Courses Criteria. Whatcom Community College. Bellingham, WA.

Early Childhood Education Courses

Luanne Lampshire, Contributing Instructor

Writing is an important component in early childhood education courses at Whatcom Community College. Students are expected to reflect on their learning, demonstrate their mastery of the subject through writing, and through use of the college library, locate and write on current literature in the field. It is critical for an early childhood professional to be aware of the current issues and trends and to be able to develop good writing skills in order to communicate clearly and effectively with other professionals and with parents.

In student writing assignments that involve research, the expectation is that students will be able independently to locate the applicable information, evaluate and analyze what is relevant, integrate this information with their existing knowledge of the subject, and write a clear, organized report. In other assignments, such as annotated bibliographies, students need to locate a variety of professional education journals and write a summary and reaction to selected articles.

The college library plays a major role in these writing assignments, since it is the repository of the information needed by students. The first step is for students to feel comfortable in the library setting. They need to learn how to use the computer system to access the information they need, and they need to feel at ease in asking the library personnel for assistance. Students are encouraged to participate in a library tour or orientation at the beginning of the term to help in this process.

Faculty and librarians need to communicate about the resources in the library. Librarians assist faculty by informing them of available materials and resources in their given field. Faculty recommendations to the library on appropriate and current professional literature keep the collection relevant. This communication system is vital in providing the best possible resources to students.

Medical Assisting: TAP I and II (Terminology, Anatomy, and Pathophysiology)

Barbara Dahl, Contributing Instructor

In medical assisting, there are two courses, TAP I and II (six credits each), which in two quarters cover the twenty-two units into which the body systems are divided. There are lecture and lab components in each unit. The presentation of information for the pathology section of each unit differs from typical courses.

We first cover *generic* symptoms, diagnostic evaluations, and treatments for each body system, using a very general approach. For instance, digestive system disorders will often manifest themselves in fairly predictable and consistent ways that one might expect if the organs responsible for digestion are traumatized or diseased. We might also diagnose those disorders using generic techniques, such as x-rays with radiopaque dyes, endoscopy, laboratory testing, and subjective information and clinical assessment. Even some of the treatments are generic.

After the students are familiar with the general, we deal with the specific, which is when they use the library most. Students receive a list of diseases and disorders common to the body system being studied, and they each choose one which is of particular interest to them. It may be that they have a friend or relative with a particular disorder, or the disease or disorder they choose may be of personal interest or concern. The assignment includes library research, a written report, and an oral presentation to the class which includes answering audience-generated questions. The research needs to come from sources other than the course text and can include a variety of materials, such as books, periodical articles, and personal and professional interviews or videos. Students are expected to use at least three different sources. For the oral presentation, the student presenter is responsible for sharing accurate and complete information, but the class audience needs to be sure that their questions are answered adequately, since they will be tested on the information presented. And since these research-based presentations and guided discussions are the only source of the test information, this approach makes for interesting group interactions and accountability.

Afterword

Elaine P. Maimon

The writing-across-the-curriculum movement encompasses three interrelated goals: (1) improved teamwork among faculty members, stimulated by interesting conversations across disciplinary boundaries; (2) stronger coherence in the curriculum, so that students will more clearly understand connections and contrasts in their studies; and (3) more student involvement in their own learning, through process writing, collaborative learning, acknowledgment, journal writing, letter writing, and in short, whatever fixes students' attention on the intellectual life. The library is the logical center wherein these goals can be enacted. Faculty members from all parts of the campus naturally gather in the library. At study carrels and reading tables, students work on assignments from all classes. And it is in the library that students are most ready, often because they are under pressure, to give attention to matters intellectual—although the library on many campuses is also the social meeting place of choice.

Librarians who have read this book are ready to assume their natural role as faculty team-builder, curricular bridge-builder, and intellectual coach for students. In this sense, librarians are uniquely situated to become agents of change on their campuses.

As Barbara Fister says, the library is now being reimagined as "a laboratory for learning . . . in which we engage in knowledge construction" (see Chapter 3, p. 42). Librarians who have moved beyond the old, static image of the library, what Fister calls "a peculiarly organized storehouse of ready-made and infinitely reusable knowledge" (see Chapter 3, p. 42), can engage students in the excitement of talking back to books. Writing-across-the-curriculum also promotes that conversation in which students are not looking things up and copying them down, but are instead agreeing, protesting, offering counterarguments, questioning, thinking logically, thinking associationally, and, in the most important sense, thinking actively. Such students are never alone in the library, even when their classmates are working on other projects.

Let me offer a few specific suggestions on ways that librarians can become leaders of writing-across-the-curriculum on their campuses or, if a program already exists, how they can participate most valuably. First, in terms of encouraging teamwork among faculty members, librarians can reach out by offering to catalog and provide space for assignments and papers from courses across the campus. Many faculty members know that such resources are useful to students and would prefer availability in a publicly documented way, rather than as contraband in the fraternity houses. If the campus does not yet have a writing center where peer tutors are available to help students with work-in-progress, a room in the library can be an ideal place. Librarians can assist in the training of peer tutors in library research techniques, which the tutors can then integrate with other advice on students' drafts. If a library writing center can be equipped with computers, allowing for word processing, e-mail, and use of the Internet, then all the better. The library is also an ideal place for faculty writing workshops—the sine qua non for faculty cooperation in writing-across-the-curriculum.

Participation by librarians in WAC workshops is essential to their role as curricular bridge-builder. In fact, most writing program administrators would appreciate the active cooperation of a librarian in organizing workshops. The librarian is exactly the right person to lead discussions about types of assignments that are useful in a variety of disciplines.

Here are a few examples of assignments that I have suggested in workshops that would benefit from a librarian's special expertise:

1. Students use the Oxford English Dictionary (OED) to write a lively history of a favorite word. Or students use the OED to understand the history of words in a short poem (stopping their histories, of course, at the date that the poem was written).

2. Students research the history of their names.

3. Students find a newspaper published on their birthday and write about that day from the vantage point of history, popular culture, meteorology, business opportunities, real estate, film, and so forth.

4. Students read an assigned classic article in a field, for example, Miller's article on short-term memory, "The Magic Number Seven, Plus or Minus Two," and then check *Citation Index* for the number and types of references to the article since publication. Students might then select key citations and write an update of the article.

5. Students read an important, recent article in a field and then check all the sources cited in the article. Students write a paper critiquing the writer's use of sources.

Librarians presenting such assignments in faculty writing workshops will provide the occasion for stimulating discussions of disciplinary differences and similarities in conducting research. Faculty members will see librarians as scholars who understand research in a variety of contexts and can help professors and students to move across disciplinary boundaries.

Librarians have recognized for a long time that the best way to teach is to coach. WAC did not discover this. Students come to the library in a heightened state of readiness for instruction. Usually, they are trying to complete an assignment that causes them some degree of anxiety. They are openly grateful when a reference librarian provides guidance. Since an emphasis on work-in-progress and collaborative learning necessitate, in my view, the writing of an acknowledgments page, I have read many lavish, moving thank-yous from students for the help of librarians. The library is also a treasure trove of gracious acknowledgments written by published authors. When students read these testimonies, they understand that writing and reading in all disciplines are parts of an ongoing conversation. Librarians are the friendly hosts who invite readers and writers to join this conversation that we call civilization.

Appendixes

Appendix A

Article Analysis

On one typewritten page, present only the following information, in the order specified, and attach it to a copy of the article.

1. The name of the paper index or electronic (CD-ROM) data base used to identify the article.
2. A correct bibliographic citation (APA, MLA, CBE) for the article.
3. An abstract, in one hundred words or less, of the article.
4. One or two sentences which paraphrase or quote from the article. Include proper in-text referencing.
5. A brief assessment of the author's target audience, with supporting evidence of vocabulary, writing style, level of sophistication, and so forth.

Appendix B

Types of Library Resources

Bibliographies
Biographical sources
CD-ROM/electronic data bases (other than indexes)
Circulating books
Conference papers
Directories
Electronic catalogs
ERIC documents
Films and videos
Government publications
Guides to the literature
Indexes (paper or CD-ROM/electronic)
Legal sources
Library of Congress Subject Heading List
Manuals of style
Newspapers
Professional and scholarly journals
Reference books
Statistical sources
Thesauri

Appendix C

Discourse Forms for Content Writing

The following list of forms represents types of writing that can incorporate library use. Using Appendix B and their own ideas, librarians will be able to suggest sources that will link these writing tasks with content material.

Biographies

Letters:
  personal
  informational
  travel

Requests

Applications

Resumés

Historical stories

Dialogues and conversations between historical figures

Editorials/responses to editorials

Letters to the editor:
  school
  local
  national

Case studies:
  school
  local

national
scientific

Reviews:
books
films
television
performances

Science notes

Technical reports

Marketing proposals

Company intelligence reports

Industry analysis

Booklets

Radio, TV, drama scripts

Reading reports

Abstracts and summaries

Written debates

Newsletter items

Project/grant proposals

Annotated bibliographies

Position papers

Political opinion pieces

Financial reports

Fact sheets

Interviews:
real
imaginary

Essays

Microthemes (brief essays)

Subject outlines/webs/maps

Statistical summary

REFERENCES

Kloss, R. J., Feeley, J., Hanks, S., O'Connor, M., Parker, H., & Perry, D. (1985). *On writing well* (p. 2). Wayne, NJ: William Paterson College.

Tchudi, S. N. (1986). *Teaching writing in the content areas* (p. 26, 32). Washington, DC: National Education Association of the United States.

Appendix D

Guidelines for Peer Evaluation of Drafts

1. If the length allows, the author reads the paper out loud.
2. The group reacts:

   What is the main point of the paper? Its audience? Its purpose?

   What are the topics and subtopics?

   What confused you about the focus of the paper?

   Is each section fully developed?

   Is the sequence clear?

   Was any material or information omitted?

   Do the opening and closing sections reflect the focus?

   Where is the language clumsy? Where is it most clear?
3. The writer responds:

   Is silent.

   Accepts the readers responses without argument.

   Takes notes.

   Asks for clarification.

   Shares ideas for improving the paper based on the group's comments.

   Rephrases what the group has said (feedback).

REFERENCE

Walvoord, B. E. (1986). *Helping students write well* (p. 113). New York: Modern Language Association.

Appendix E

Guidelines for Effective Group Behavior

CHARACTERISTICS OF EFFECTIVE GROUP FORMATION

Participation. Everyone should have an opportunity. Efforts should be made to encourage participation. No one should dominate.

Leadership. Does a leader emerge? Is leadership shared? Is the group structured?

Roles. Who is the initiator? Who supports? Who blocks? Who moves for closure?

Decision Making. Are a lot of ideas presented, or only one? Does everyone agree with the decisions? Does one person influence the others?

Communication. Do people feel free to talk? Does anyone interrupt or cut others off? Do people listen? Are points clarified?

Sensitivity. Is everyone sensitive to the needs of others?

DESIRABLE GROUP ROLES

Initiator. Suggests change.

Information Giver. Contributes authority or information.

Information Seeker. Asks for additional clarification or facts.

Opinion Giver. States belief based on feelings.

Opinion Seeker. Asks for the opinions of others.

Summarizer-Integrator. Summarizes points of discussion.

Group Builder. Supports the group as a whole.

UNDESIRABLE GROUP ROLES

Aggressor. Attacks or disapproves of the opinions of others.

Blocker. Maintains a stubborn, negative position.

Recognition Seeker. Calls attention to self.

Self Confessor. Uses group setting to deal with personal issues.

Playboy. Cavalier, "who cares?" attitude, uncooperative.

Dominator. Controls discussion in an overpowering, manipulative manner.

Help Seeker. Refuses to assume responsibility pleading insecurity, and so forth.

Special Interest Pleader. Brings the interests of another group to the meeting.

DESIRABLE FUNCTIONS OF GROUP MEMBERS

Encourager. Supports other individuals in the group.

Harmonizer. Mediates the group interactions or discussion.

Compromiser. Effects consensus within the group.

Expediter. Ensures that all participate.

Standard Setter. Reminds the group of its mission.

Observer-Recorder. Keeps a record of the proceedings.

Follower. Receives and executes the decisions of the group.

Appendix F

Guidelines for Journal Keeping

1. Journals are written in the first person and are about the experiences and content of the course.
2. Looseleaf notebooks are preferred as they can expand and allow students to eliminate any pages that may contain personal material.
3. Journals should be divided into several sections, some for the current course, some for other courses, and others for personal entries.
4. Some journal entries should be done in class; the instructor also writes and shares entries with the students.
5. Journal material should be used to create course-related activities and experiences; this encourages the sharing of ideas and also validates journal writing.
6. Although journal entries are not graded, they should be counted in some way toward the overall class grade.
7. Instructors should respond only to entries that have unique value or interest.
8. At the end of the semester, students should be asked to number the pages, title the entries, prepare a table of contents, and write a summarizing statement. This review helps them reflect on their experience in the course.

REFERENCE

Fulwiler, T. (Ed.). (1987). *The journal book.* Portsmouth, NH: Heinemann.

Appendix G

Guidelines for Writing Groups

1. Create group projects around enjoyable, real-world situations.
2. Parcel out the tasks—brainstorming, library research, peer review—rather than assigning an entire project without guidelines.
3. Develop mechanisms for monitoring projects in progress.
4. Designate the roles and tasks for each individual involved in the group activity, carefully and with full discussion. (See Appendix E.)
5. Allow groups to do their own problem solving and rule keeping; the instructor should take great pains to avoid interfering.
6. Follow these four guidelines: (1) write out clear instructions, goals, and expected outcomes; (2) preview the tasks involved by doing them yourself first; (3) keep students on task by requiring written proof of progress; (4) grade how the group functions as a whole, as well as their output.

REFERENCE

Shamoon, L. K. (1993). *URI's writing across the curriculum handbook: Writing assignments and teaching tips from the WAC demonstration faculty.* Kingston: University of Rhode Island.

Selected Bibliography

(*Note*: For additional bibliography, see References and Additional Readings for each chapter.)

Abercrombie, M.L.J. (1960). *The anatomy of judgement: An investigation into the processes of perception and reasoning.* New York: Basic Books.

Abercrombie, M.L.J. (1979). *Aims and techniques of group teaching* (4th ed.). Guilford, UK: Society for Research into Higher Education.

Anson, C. M. (1988). Toward a multidimensional model of writing in the academic disciplines. In D. A. Jolliffe (Ed.), *Advances in writing research, Vol. 2: Writing in academic disciplines* (pp. 1–19). Norwood, NJ: Ablex.

Anson, C. M., Schwiebert, J. E., & Williamson, M. M. (1994). *Writing across the curriculum: An annotated bibliography.* Westport, CT: Greenwood.

Barr, M. A., & Healy, M. K. (1988). School and university articulation: Different contexts for writing across the curriculum. In S. H. McLeod (Ed.), *Strengthening programs for writing across the curriculum: New directions for teaching and learning* (pp. 43–53). San Francisco: Jossey-Bass.

Bartholomae, D. (1986). Released into language: Errors, expectations, and the legacy of Mina Shaughnessy. In D. A. McQuade (Ed.), *The territory of language: Linguistics, sylistics, and the teaching of composition* (pp. 65–88). Carbondale: Southern Illinois University Press.

Belenky, M. F., Clinchy, B. M., Goldberger, N. R. & Taruler, J. M. (1986). *Woman's ways of knowing: The development of self, voice, and mind.* New York: Basic Books.

Benderson, A. (Ed.). (1989). The student writer, an endangered species? *Focus 23.* Princeton: Educational Testing Service.

Berlin, J. A. (1987). *Rhetoric and reality: Writing instruction in American colleges, 1900–1985.* Carbondale: Southern Illinois University Press.

Bernhardt, S. A. (1985). Writing across the curriculum at one university: A survey of faculty members and students. *ADE Bulletin, 82,* 55–59.

Biddle, A. W., & Bean, D. J. (1987). *Writer's guide: Life science.* Lexington, MA: D.C. Heath.

Biddle, A. W., & Holland, K. M. (1987). *Writer's guide: Political science.* Lexington, MA: D.C. Heath.

Bizzell, P., & Herzberg, B. (1986). Writing across the curriculum: A bibliographic essay. In D. A. McQuade (Ed.), *The territory of language: Linguistics, stylistics, and the teaching of composition* (pp. 340–354). Carbondale: Southern Illinois University Press.

Blair, C. P. (1988). Opinion. Only one of the voices: Dialogic writing across the curriculum. *College English, 50*(4), 383–389.

Blicq, R. S. (1986). *Technically-write: Communicating in a technological era.* Englewood Cliffs, NJ: Prentice Hall.

Bond, L. A., & Magistrale, A. S. (1987). *Writer's guide: Psychology.* Lexington, MA: D.C. Heath.

Bouton, C., & Garth, R. Y. (Eds.). (1983), *Learning in groups.* San Francisco: Jossey-Bass.

Boyer, E. L. (1987). *College: The undergraduate experience in America.* New York: Harper & Row.

Braine, G. (1990). *Writing across the curriculum: A case study of faculty practices at a research university* (Report No. CS21-2-534). Mobile: University of Alabama, Department of English. (ERIC Document Reproduction Service No. ED 324 680)

Britton, J. N. (1972). *Language and learning.* New York: Penguin Books.

Britton, J. (1983). Language and learning across the curriculum. In P. L. Stock (Ed.), *Forum: Essays on theory and practice in the teaching of writing* (pp. 221–223). New York: Boynton/Cook.

Britton, J. N. (1984). Introduction. In C. H. Klaus & N. Jones (Eds.), *Courses for change in writing* (pp. v–ix). Upper Montclair, NJ: Boynton/Cook.

Britton, J. N. (1992). Theories of the disciplines and a learning theory. In A. Herrington & C. Moran (Eds.), *Writing, teaching, and learning in the disciplines* (pp. 47–60). New York: Modern Language Association.

Britton, J. N., Burgess, T., Martin, N., McLeod, A., & Rosen, H. (1975). *The development of writing abilities (11–18).* London: Macmillan.

Brodkey, L. (1987). *Academic writing as social practice.* Philadelphia: Temple University Press.

Bruffee, K. A. (1973). Collaborative learning: Some practical models. *College English, 34*(5), 634–643.

Bruffee, K. A. (1982). Liberal education and social justification of belief. *Liberal Education, 68*(2), 95–114.

Bruffee, K. A. (1983). Writing and reading as collaborative or social acts. In J. N. Hays, P. A. Roth, J. R. Ramsey, & R. D. Foulke (Eds.), *The writer's mind: Writing as a mode of thinking* (pp. 159–170). Urbana, IL: National Council of Teachers of English.

Bruffee, K. A. (1984a). Collaborative learning and the "conversation of mankind." *College English, 46*(7), 635–652.

Bruffee, K. A. (1984b). *A short course in writing* (3rd ed.). Boston: Little, Brown.

Bruffee, K. A. (1985). Liberal education, scholarly community, and the authority of knowledge. *Liberal Education, 71*(3), 231–239.

Bruffee, K. (1986). Getting started. In D. A. McQuade (Ed.), *The territory of language: Linguistics, stylistics, and the teaching of composition* (pp. 103–113). Carbondale: Southern Illinois University Press.

Bruffee, K. A. (1987). The art of collaborative learning. *Change, 19,* 42–47.

Bruffee, K. A. (1989). Thinking and writing as social acts. In E. P. Maimon, B. F. Nodine, & F. W. O'Connor (Eds.), *Thinking, reasoning, and writing* (pp. 213–222). New York: Longman.

Bruner, J. S. (1960). *The process of education.* New York: Vintage Books.

Bruner, J. S. (1962). *On knowing: Essays for the left hand.* Cambridge, MA: Harvard University Press.

Bruner, J. S. (1966). *Toward a theory of instruction.* Cambridge, MA: Harvard University Press.

Chatmen, S., & Levin, S. R. (Eds.). (1967). *Essays on the language of literature.* Boston: Houghton Mifflin.

Cooper, M. M., & Holzman, M. (1989). *Writing as social action.* Portsmouth, NH: Boynton/Cook.

Corbett, E.P.J. (1986). Teaching style. In D. A. McQuade (Ed.), *The territory of language: Linguistics, stylistics, and the teaching of composition* (pp. 23–33). Carbondale: Southern Illinois University Press.

Cox, M. (1990, April). Paulo Freire: Interview. *Omni,* pp. 74–76, 79, 93, 94.

D'Angelo, F. J. (1983). Imitation and the teaching of style. In P. L. Stock (Ed.), *Fforum: Essays on theory and practice in the teaching of writing* (pp. 173–187). New York: Boynton/Cook.

D'Angelo, F. J. (1986). Topoi and form in composition. In D. A. McQuade (Ed.), *The territory of language: Linguistics, stylistics, and the teaching of composition* (pp. 114–122). Carbondale: Southern Illinois University Press.

D'Angelo, F. J. (1987). Aims, modes, and forms of discourse. In G. Tate (Ed.), *Teaching composition: Twelve bibliographical essays* (pp. 131–154). Fort Worth: Texas Christian University.

D'Angelo, F. J. (1988). Imitation and style. In G. Tate & E.P.J. Corbett (Eds.), *The writing teacher's sourcebook* (pp. 199–207). New York: Oxford University Press.

Davidson, P. (1984). Writing across the disciplines: A memo to colleagues. In C. H. Klaus & N. Jones (Eds.), *Courses for change in writing* (pp. 241–259). Upper Montclair, NJ: Boynton/Cook.

Davis, D. J. (1987). Eight faculty members talk about student writing. *College Teaching, 35*(1), 31–35.

Dewey, J. (1938). *Experience and education.* London: Collier Books.

Donovan, T. R., & McClelland, B. W. (Eds.). (1980). *Eight approaches to teaching composition.* Urbana, IL: National Council of Teachers of English.

Eblen, C. (1983). Writing across the curriculum: A survey of a university faculty's views and classroom practices. *Research in the Teaching of English, 17*(4), 343–348.

Elbow, P. (1983). Teaching writing by not paying attention to writing. In P. L. Stock (Ed.), *Fforum: Essays on theory and practice in the teaching of writing* (pp. 234–239). New York: Boynton/Cook.

Elbow, P. (1988). Embracing contraries in the teaching process. In G. Tate & E.P.J. Corbett (Eds.), *The writing teacher's sourcebook* (pp. 219–231). New York: Oxford University Press.

Emig, J. (1983a). Literature and freedom. In D. Goswami & M. Butler (Eds.), *The web of meaning* (pp. 171–178). Upper Montclair, NJ: Boynton/Cook.

Emig, J. (1983b). Non-magical thinking. In D. Goswami & M. Butler (Eds.), *The web of meaning* (pp. 132–145). Upper Montclair, NJ: Boynton/Cook.

Emig, J. (1983c). Writing as a mode of learning. In D. Goswami & M. Butler (Eds.), *The web of meaning* (pp. 123–131). Upper Montclair, NJ: Boynton/Cook.

Eschholz, P. A. (1980). The prose models approach: Using products in the process. In T. R. Donovan & B. W. McClelland (Eds.), *Eight approaches to teaching composition* (pp. 21–36). Urbana, IL: National Council of Teachers of English.

Faigley, L. (1986). The problem of topic in texts. In D. A. McQuade (Ed.), *The territory of language: Linguistics, stylistics, and the teaching of composition* (pp. 123–141). Carbondale: Southern Illinois University Press.

Faigley, L., & Hanson, K. (1985). Learning to write in the social sciences. *College Composition and Communication, 36*(2), 140–149.

Faigley, L., & Miller, T. P. (1982). What we learn from writing on the job. *College English, 44*(6), 557–569.

Farris, C. (1992). Writing in the academic disciplines, 1970–1990: A curricular history [Review of *Writing in the academic disciplines*]. *ACADEME, 78*(5), 57.

Fish, S. (1980). *Is there a text in this class?: The authority of interpretive communities.* Cambridge, MA: Harvard University Press.

Fish, S. (1988). Being interdisciplinary is so very hard to do. *Profession, 89,* 15–22.

Fister, B. (1992). The research processes of undergraduate students. *Journal of Academic Librarianship, 18*(3), 163–169.

Fister, B. (1993). Teaching the rhetorical dimensions of research. *Research Strategies, 11*(4), 211–219.

Flower, L. (1979). Writer-based prose: A cognitive basis for problems in writing. *College English, 41*(1), 19–37.

Flower, L., & Hayes, J. R. (1981, December). A cognitive process theory of writing. *College Composition and Communication, 32,* 365–387.

Flower, L., & Hayes, J. R. (1988). The cognition of discovery: Defining a rhetorical problem. In G. Tate & E.P.J. Corbett (Eds.), *The writing teacher's sourcebook* (pp. 92–102). New York: Oxford University Press.

Flower, L., Stein, V., Ackerman, J., Kantz, M. J., McCormick, K., & Peck, W. C. (1990). *Reading-to-write: Exploring a cognitive and social process.* New York: Oxford University Press.

Foster, D. (1992). *A primer for writing teachers: Theories, theorists, issues, problems* (2nd ed.). Portsmouth, NH: Boynton/Cook.

Freire, P. (1982). *Pedagogy of the oppressed.* New York: Continuum.

Freire, P. (1987). *Literacy: Reading the word and the world.* South Hadley, MA: Bergin and Garvey.

Freire, P. (1989). *Learning to question: A pedagogy for liberation.* New York: Continuum.

Freisinger, R. (1982). Cross-disciplinary writing programs: Beginnings. In T. Fulwiler & A. Young (Eds.), *Language connections: Writing and reading across the curriculum* (pp. 3–14). Urbana, IL: National Council of Teachers of English.

Fulwiler, T. (1982a). The personal connection: Journal writing across the curriculum. In T. Fulwiler & A. Young (Eds.), *Language connections: Writing and reading across the curriculum* (pp. 15–32). Urbana, IL: National Council of Teachers of English.

Fulwiler, T. (1982b). Writing: An act of cognition. In C. W. Griffin (Ed.), *Teaching writing in all disciplines* (pp. 15–26). San Francisco: Jossey-Bass.

Fulwiler, T. (1983). Why we teach writing in the first place. In P. L. Stock (Ed.), *Fforum: Essays on the theory and practice in the teaching of writing* (pp. 273–286). Upper Montclair, NJ: Boynton/Cook.

Fulwiler, T. (1984). How well does writing across the curriculum work? *College English, 46*(2), 113–125.

Fulwiler, T. (Ed.). (1987). *The journal book.* Portsmouth, NH: Heinemann.

Fulwiler, T. (1988a). Evaluating writing across the curriculum programs. In S. H. McLeod (Ed.), *Strengthening programs for writing across the curriculum* (pp. 61–76). San Francisco: Jossey-Bass.

Fulwiler, T. (1988b). How well does writing across the curriculum work? In G. Tate & E.P.J. Corbett (Eds.), *The writing teacher's sourcebook* (pp. 248–259). New York: Oxford University Press.

Fulwiler, T. (1990). *The friends and enemies of writing across the curriculum* (Report No. CS21-2-289). Chicago, IL: The University of Vermont. (ERIC Document Reproduction Service No. ED 318 006)

Fulwiler, T., & Biddle, A. W. (Eds.). (1992). *A community of voices: Reading and writing in the disciplines.* New York: Macmillan.

Fulwiler, T., & Jones, R. (1982). Assigning and evaluating transactional writing. In T. Fulwiler & A. Young (Eds.), *Language connections: Writing and reading across the curriculum* (pp. 45–56). Urbana, IL: National Council of Teachers of English.

Fulwiler, T., & Young, A. (Eds.). (1990). *Programs that work.* Portsmouth, NH: Boynton/Cook.

Gebhard, A. O. (1983). Teaching writing in reading and the context areas. *Journal of Reading, 27*(3), 207–211.

Gere, A. R. (Ed.). (1985). *Roots in the sawdust: Writing to learn across the disciplines.* Urbana, IL: National Council of Teachers of English.

Gere, A. R. (1987). *Writing groups: History, theory, and implications.* Carbondale: Southern Illinois University Press.

Golub, J. (1988). *Focus on collaborative learning.* Urbana, IL: National Council of Teachers of English.

Graves, D. H. (1983). Break the welfare cycle: Let writers choose their topics. In P. L. Stock (Ed.), *Fforum: Essays on theory and practice in the teaching of writing* (pp. 98–100). Upper Montclair, NJ: Boynton/Cook.

Graves, R. L. (1976). CEHAE: Five steps for teaching writing. In R. L. Graves (Ed.), *Rhetoric and composition: A sourcebook for teachers* (pp. 239–245). Rochelle Park, NJ: Hayden Book Company.

Gray, D. J. (1988). Writing across the college curriculum. *Phi Delta Kappan, 69*(10), 729–733.

Gregg, L. W., & Steinberg, E. R. (1980). *Cognitive processes in writing.* Hillsdale, NJ: Lawrence Erlbaum Associates.

Griffin, C. W. (Ed.). (1982). *Teaching writing in all disciplines.* San Francisco: Jossey-Bass.

Griffin, C. W. (1983). Using writing to teach many disciplines. *Improving College and University Teaching, 31*(3), 121–128.

Griffin, C. W. (1985). Programs for writing across the curriculum: A report. *College Composition and Communication, 36*(4), 398–403.

Hall, D. (1973). *Writing well.* Boston: Little, Brown.

Hamilton, D. (1980). Interdisciplinary writing. *College English, 41*(7), 780–796.

Haring-Smith, T. (Ed.). (1985). *A guide to writing programs: Writing centers, peer tutoring programs, and writing-across-the-curriculum.* Glenview, IL: Scott, Foresman.

Harris, J., & Hult, C. (1985). Using a survey of writing assignments to make informed curricular decisions. *Writing Program Administration, 8*(3), 7–14.

Harris, M. (1986). *Teaching one-to-one: The writing conference.* Urbana, IL: National Council of Teachers of English.

Harvard, R. M., Hess, D., & Darby, M. F. (1989). A comment on only one of the voices and why English departments should house writing across the curriculum. *College English, 51*(4), 433–437.

Hays, J. N., Roth, P. A., Ramsey, J. R., & Foulke, R. D. (Eds.). (1983). *A writer's mind: Writing as a mode of thinking.* Urbana, IL: National Council of Teachers of English.

Hedley, J., & Parker, J. E. (1991). Writing across the curriculum: The vantage of the liberal arts. *ADE Bulletin, 98,* 22–28.

Herrington, A., & Moran, C. (1992). Writing in the disciplines: A prospect. In A. Herrington & C. Moran (Eds.), *Writing, teaching, and learning in the disciplines* (pp. 231–244). New York: Modern Language Association.

Hillocks, G., Jr. (1986). *Research on written composition.* New York: National Institute of Education.

Hobbuch, S. M. (1987). *Writing research papers across the curriculum.* New York: Holt, Rinehart and Winston.

Hoff, K. T. (1992). *WAC policies: Winning friends and influencing people* (Report No. CS21-3-303). Cincinnati, OH: Conference on College Composition and Communication. (ERIC Document Reproduction Service No. ED 344 234)

Jensen, G. H. (1991). *From texts to text: Mastering academic discourse.* New York: HarperCollins.

Joliffe, D. A. (Ed.). (1987). *Advances in writing research, Vol. 2: Writing in academic disciplines.* Norwood, NJ: Ablex.

Kelly, G. (1963). *A theory of personality: The psychology of personal constructs.* New York: W. W. Norton.

Kelly, K. A. (1985). *Writing across the curriculum: What the literature tells us* (Report No. CS21-0-045). Wellesley, MA: Babson College. (ERIC Document Reproduction Service No. ED 274 975)

Kinneavy, J. L. (1983). Writing across the curriculum. *ADE Bulletin, 76,* 14–21.

Kinneavy, J. L. (1986). The relation of the whole to the part in interpretation theory and in the composing process. In D. A. McQuade (Ed.), *The territory of language: Linguistics, stylistics, and the teaching of composition* (pp. 292–312). Carbondale: Southern Illinois University Press.

Kinneavy, J. L. (1987). Writing across the curriculum. In G. Tate (Ed.), *Teaching composition: Twelve bibliographical essays* (pp. 253–377). Fort Worth: Texas Christian University.

Kirsch, G., Finkel, D. C., & France, M. F. (1989). Three comments on only one of the voices: Dialogic writing across the curriculum. *College English, 51*(1), 99–106.

Klaus, C. H., & Jones, N. (Eds.). (1984). *Courses for change in writing.* Upper Montclair, NJ: Boynton/Cook.

Knoblach, C. H. (1983). Rhetoric and the teaching of writing. In P. L. Stock (Ed.), *Fforum: Essays on theory and practice in the teaching of writing* (pp. 295–299). Upper Montclair, NJ: Boynton/Cook.

Knoblach, C. H., & Brannon, L. (1983). Writing as learning through the curriculum. *College English, 45*(5), 465–474.

LaBaugh, R. T. (1992). BI vignettes: BI is a proper noun. *Research Strategies, 10,* 34–39.

Langer, J. A. (1992). Speaking of knowing: Concepts of understanding in academic disciplines. In A. Herrington & C. Moran (Eds.), *Writing, teaching, and learning in the disciplines* (pp. 69–85). New York: Modern Language Association.

Larson, R. (1982). The research paper in the writing course: A non-form of writing. *College English, 44*(8), 811–816.

Larson, R. (1983). The writer's mind: Recent research and unanswered questions. In J. N. Hays, P. A. Roth, J. R. Ramsey, & R. D. Foulke (Eds.), *The writer's mind: Writing as a mode of thinking* (pp. 239–252). Urbana, IL: National Council of Teachers of English.

Larson, R. L. (1986). Language studies and composing processes. In D. A. McQuade (Ed.), *The territory of language: Linguistics, stylistics, and the teaching of composition* (pp. 213–226). Carbondale: Southern Illinois University Press.

Larson, R. L. (1988). The research paper in the writing course: A non-form of writing. In G. Tate & E.P.J. Corbett (Eds.), *The writing teacher's sourcebook* (pp. 361–365). New York: Oxford University Press.

Lehr, F. (1980). Writing as learning in the content areas. *College English, 69,* 23–25.

Limerick, P. N. (1993, October 31). Dancing with professors: The trouble with academic prose. *The New York Times Book Review,* pp. 3, 23–24.

Luria, A. R. (1976). *Cognitive development: Its cultural and social foundations.* Cambridge: Harvard University Press.

Lutzker, M. (1988). *Research projects for college students: What to write across the curriculum.* Westport, CT: Greenwood.

Magee, R. M. (1988). *The project at Emory University: The importance of being eclectic* (Report No. CS21-1-273). St. Louis, MO: Emory University. (ERIC Document Reproduction Service No. ED 295 179)

Magistrale, T. (1985). Writing across the curriculum: From theory to implementation. *Journal of Teaching Writing, 5*(1), 151–157.

Maimon, E. P. (1979). Talking to strangers. *College Composition and Communication, 30,* 364–369.

Maimon, E. P. (1982). Writing across the curriculum: Past, present, and future. In C. W. Griffin (Ed.), *Teaching writing in all disciplines* (pp. 67–74). San Francisco: Jossey-Bass.

Maimon, E. P. (1986a). Collaborative learning and writing across the curriculum. *Writing Program Administration, 9*(3), 9–15.

Maimon, E. P. (1986b). Knowledge, acknowledgment, and writing across the curriculum: Toward an educated community. In D. A. McQuade (Ed.), *The territory of language: Linguistics, stylistics, and the teaching of composition* (pp. 89–102). Carbondale: Southern Illinois University Press.

Maimon, E. P. (1988). Cultivating the prose garden. *Phi Delta Kappan, 69*(10), 734–739.

Maimon, E. P. (1990, January). Remarks made at *Writing and Thinking Across the Curriculum.* Conference held at Rhode Island College, Providence, RI.

Maimon, E. P. (1991). *Errors and expectations in writing across the curriculum: Diversity, equity, and the ideology of writing across the curriculum* (Report No. CS21-2-8-9). Paper presented at the Conference on College Composition and Communication (CCCC), March 21, Boston, MA. (ERIC Document Reproduction Service No. ED 331 092)

Maimon, E. P., Belcher, G. L., Hearn, G. W., Nodine, B. F., & O'Connor, F. W. (1981). *Writing in the arts and sciences.* Cambridge, MA: Winthrop Publishers.

Maimon, E. P., Nodine, B. F., & O'Connor, F. W. (Eds.). (1989). *Thinking, reasoning, and writing.* New York: Longman.

McCarthy, L. P. (1987). A stranger in strange lands: A college student writing across the curriculum. *Research in the Teaching of English, 21*(3), 233–265.

McCrimmon, J. M. (1976). Writing as a way of knowing. In R. L. Graves (Ed.), *Rhetoric and composition: A sourcebook for teachers* (pp. 3–12). Rochelle Park, NJ: Hayden Book Company.

McLeod, S. H. (1988). Translating enthusiasm into curricular change. In S. H. McLeod (Ed.), *Strengthening programs for writing across the curriculum* (pp. 5–12). San Francisco: Jossey-Bass.

McLeod, S. H., & Soven, M. (Eds.). (1992). *Writing across the curriculum: A guide to developing programs.* London: Sage Publications.

Moffett, J. (1968). *Teaching the universe of discourse.* Boston: Houghton Mifflin.

Moffett, J. (1983). On essaying. In P. L. Stock (Ed.), *Fforum: Essays on theory and practice in the teaching of writing* (pp. 170–172). Upper Montclair, NJ: Boynton/Cook.

Moore, L. E., & Peterson, L. H. (1986). Convention as connection: Linking the composition course to the English and college curriculum. *College Composition and Communication, 37*(4), 466–477.

Moss, A., & Holder, C. (1982). *Improving student writing: A guidebook for faculty in all disciplines.* Pomona, CA: California State Polytechnic University.

Murray, D. M. (1976). Teach writing as process not product. In R. L. Graves (Ed.), *Rhetoric and composition: A sourcebook for teachers* (pp. 79–85). Rochelle Park, NJ: Hayden Book Company.

Murray, D. M. (1979). The listening eye: Reflections on the writing conference. *College English, 41*(1), 13–18.

Murray, D. M. (1980). Writing as process: How writing finds its own meaning. In T. R. Donovan & B. W. McClelland (Eds.), *Eight approaches to teaching composition* (pp. 3–20). Urbana, IL: National Council of Teachers of English.

Murray, D. M. (1983). First silence, then paper. In P. L. Stock (Ed.), *Fforum: Essays on theory and practice in the teaching of writing* (pp. 227–233). New York: Boynton/Cook.

Murray, D. M. (1985). *A writer teaches writing* (2nd ed.). Boston: Hougton Mifflin.

Murray, D. M. (1988). The listening eye: Reflections on the writing conference. In G. Tate & E.P.J. Corbett (Eds.), *The writing teacher's sourcebook* (pp. 232–237). New York: Oxford University Press.

Oberman, C., & Strauch, K. (Eds.). (1982). *Theories of bibliographic education: Designs for teaching.* New York: R. R. Bowker.

Odell, L. (1973). Piaget, problem-solving, and freshman composition. *College Composition and Communication, 24*(1), 36–42.

Odell, L. (1983a). How English teachers can help their colleagues teach writing. In P. L. Stock (Ed.), *Fforum: Essays on theory and practice in the teaching of writing* (pp. 269–272). New York: Boynton/Cook.

Odell, L. (1983b). Written products and the writing process. In J. N. Hays, P. A. Roth, J. R. Ramsey, & R. D. Foulke (Eds.), *The writer's mind: Writing as a mode of thinking* (pp. 53–66). Urbana, IL: National Council of Teachers of English.

Odell, L. (1988). The process of writing and the process of learning. In G. Tate & E.P.J. Corbett (Eds.), *The writing teacher's sourcebook* (pp. 103–109). New York: Oxford University Press.

Odell, L. (1992). Context specific ways of knowing and the evaluation of writing. In A. Herrington & C. Moran (Eds.), *Writing, teaching, and learning in the disciplines* (pp. 86–100). New York: Modern Language Association.

Peroni, P. A. (1981). *The second kind of knowledge: The role of library instruction in writing across the curriculum* (Report No. CS21-7-050). Bernside, PA: Beaver College, National Endowment for the Humanities Summer Institute in the Teaching of Writing. (ERIC Document Reproduction Service No. ED 217 487)

Polanyi, M. (1964). *Personal knowledge: Towards a post-critical philosophy.* New York: Harper and Row.

Rackham, J., & Bertagnolli, O. (1986). *From sight to insight: Stages in the writing process.* New York: Holt, Reinhart and Winston.

Raimes, A. (1980). Writing and learning across the curriculum: The experience of a faculty seminar. *College English, 41*(7), 797–801.

Reichel, M., & Ramey, M. A. (Eds.). (1987). *Conceptual frameworks for bibliographic education: Theory into practice.* Littleton, CO: Libraries Unlimited.

Reither, J. A. (1988). Writing and knowing: Toward redefining the writing process. In G. Tate & E.P.J. Corbett (Eds.), *The writing teacher's sourcebook* (pp. 140–147). New York: Oxford University Press.

Russell, D. R. (1986). Writing across the curriculum in 1913: James Fleming Hosic on co-operation. *English Journal, 75*(5), 34–37.

Russell, D. R. (1990). Writing across the curriculum in historical perspective: Toward a social interpretation. *College English, 52*(1), 52–73.

Russell, D. R. (1991). *Writing in the academic disciplines, 1870–1990: A curricular history.* Carbondale: Southern Illinois University Press.

Russell, D. R. (1992). American origins of the writing-across-the-curriculum movement. In A. Herrington & C. Moran (Eds.), *Writing, teaching, and learning in the disciplines* (pp. 22–44). New York: Modern Language Association.

Schwegler, R. A., & Shamoon, L. K. (1982). The aims and process of the research paper. *College English, 44*(8), 817–824.

Shaughnessy, M. P. (1977). *Errors and expectations: A guide for the teacher of basic writing.* New York: Oxford University Press.

Shaughnessy, M. P. (1987). Basic writing. In G. Tate (Ed.), *Teaching composition: Twelve bibliographical essays* (pp. 177–206). Fort Worth: Texas Christian University.

Shaughnessy, M. P. (1988). Diving in: An introduction to basic writing. In G. Tate & E.P.J. Corbett (Eds.), *The writing teacher's sourcebook* (pp. 297–302). New York: Oxford University Press.

Sheridan, J. (1986). Andragogy: A new concept for academic librarians. *Research Strategies, 4,* 156–167.

Sheridan, J. (1989). Collaborative learning: Some notes from the field. *College Teaching,* *37*(2), 49–53.

Sheridan, J. (1990). The reflective librarian: Some observations on bibliographic instruction in the academic library. *Journal of Academic Librarianship, 16*(1), 22–26.

Sheridan, J. (1992). WAC and libraries: A look at the literature. *Journal of Academic Librarianship, 18*(2), 90–94.

Shor, I. (Ed.). (1987). *Freire for the classroom.* Portsmouth, NH: Boynton/Cook.

Sills, C. K. (1991). Paired composition courses: Everything relates. *College Teaching,* *39*(2), 61–64.

Sipple, J. M. (1989). A planning process for building writing across the curriculum programs to last. *Journal of Higher Education, 60*(4), 444–457.

Smit, D. W. (1991, September). *Improving student writing (Idea paper no. 25).* Manhattan: Kansas State University, Center for Faculty Evaluation and Development.

Smith, D. J. (1989). An examination of higher education: A view from the college library. *The Journal of Academic Librarianship, 15*(3), 140–146.

Smith, L. Z. (1988). Opinion: Why English departments should house writing across the curriculum. *College English, 50*(4), 390–395.

Sommer, R. F. (1989). *Teaching writing to adults: Strategies and concepts for improving learner performance.* San Francisco: Jossey-Bass.

Steffens, H. J. (1990, January). Talk given at *Writing and Thinking Across the Curriculum.* Conference conducted at Rhode Island College, Providence, RI.

Steffens, H. J., & Dickerson, M. J. (1987). *Writer's guide: History.* Lexington, MA: D. C. Heath.

Stevenson, J. W. (1984). Writing as a liberal art. *Liberal Education, 70*(1), 57–62.

Stock, P. L. (1983a). A comprehensive literacy program: The English composition board. In P. L. Stock (Ed.), *Fforum: Essays on theory and practice in the teaching of writing* (pp. 85–90). Upper Montclair, NJ: Boynton/Cook.

Stock, P. L., & Wixson, K. K. (1983b). Reading and writing–together. In P. L. Stock (Ed.), *Fforum: Essays on theory and practice in the teaching of writing* (pp. 201–219). New York: Boynton/Cook.

Stout, B. R., & Magnotto, J. (1988). Writing across the curriculum at community colleges. In S. H. McLeod (Ed.), *Strengthening programs for writing across the curriculum* (pp. 21–30). San Francisco: Jossey-Bass.

Streepy, J., Totten, N., Carr, G., & Reynolds, T. (1987). *Writing and research across the curriculum: A proposal for a new course* (Report No. CS-211-537). New Albany: Indiana University, Southeast. (ERIC Document Reproduction Service No. ED 300 807)

Strenski, E. (1988). Writing across the curriculum at research universities. In S. H. McLeod (Ed.), *Strengthening programs for writing across the curriculum* (pp. 31–42). San Francisco: Jossey-Bass.

Tchudi, S. N. (1986). *Teaching writing in the content areas: College level.* Washington, DC: National Education Association of the United States.

Thaiss, C. (1982). The Virginia consortium of faculty writing programs: A variety of practices. In C. W. Griffin (Ed.), *Teaching writing in all disciplines* (pp. 45–52). San Francisco: Jossey-Bass.

Thaiss, C. (Ed.). (1983). *Writing to learn: Essays and reflections on writing across the curriculum.* Dubuque, IA: Kendall/Hunt.

Thaiss, C. (1988). The future of writing across the curriculum. In S. H. McLeod (Ed.), *Strengthening programs for writing across the curriculum* (pp. 91–102). San Francisco: Jossey-Bass.

Ulisse, P. (1988). *Writing across the curriculum* (Report No. JC89-0-436). Stratford, CT: Housatonic Community College. (ERIC Document Reproduction Service No. ED 310 828)

Vygotsky, L. S. (1962). *Thought and language.* Cambridge, MA: M.I.T. Press.

Walker, A. (1988). Writing across the curriculum: The second decade. *English Quarterly, 21*(2), 93–103.

Walvoord, B. E. (1986). *Helping students write well* (2nd ed.). New York: Modern Language Association.

Walvoord, B. E., & McCarthy, L. P. (1990). *Thinking and writing in college: A naturalistic study of students in four disciplines.* Urbana, IL: National Council of Teachers of English.

Ward, J. A. (1991). *WAC reconsidered: Issues for the '90's* (Report No. CS21-2-900). Boston, MA: Thiel College, Department of English. (ERIC Document Reproduction Service No. ED 333 456)

Weiss, R. H. (1980). Writing in the total curriculum: A program for cross-disciplinary cooperation. In T. R. Donovan & B. W. McClelland (Eds.) *Eight approaches to teaching composition* (pp. 133–149). Urbana, IL: National Council of Teachers of English.

"Why Johnny Can't Write." (1975, December 8). *Newsweek,* pp. 58–62, 64.

Williams, J. M. (1994). *Style: Ten lessons in clarity and grace* (4th ed.). New York: HarperCollins.

Williamson, M. M. (1988). A model for investigating the functions of written language in different disciplines. In D. A. Jolliffe (Ed.), *Advances in writing research, Vol. 2: Writing in the academic disciplines* (pp. 89–132). Norwood, NJ: Ablex.

Winterowd, W. R. (1986). Brain, rhetoric, and style. In D. A. McQuade (Ed.), *The territory of language: Linguistics, stylistics, and the teaching of composition* (pp. 34–64). Carbondale: Southern Illinois University Press.

Winterowd, W. R. (1987). Literacy, linguistics, and rhetoric. In G. Tate (Ed.), *Teaching composition: Twelve bibliographic essays* (pp. 265–290). Fort Worth: Texas Christian University.

Winterowd, W. R. (1988). The grammar of coherence. In G. Tate & E.P.J. Corbett (Eds.), *The writing teacher's sourcebook* (pp. 208–214). New York: Oxford University Press.

Young, A. (1983). Value and purpose in writing. In P. L. Stock (Ed.), *Fforum: Essays on theory and practice in the teaching of writing* (pp. 240–244). New York: Boynton/Cook.

Young, A., & Fulwiler, T. (Eds.). (1986). *Writing across the disciplines: Research into practice.* Upper Montclair, NJ: Boynton/Cook.

Zinsser, W. (1986, April 13). A bolder way to teach writing. *New York Times,* p. 58–63.

Index

About the Editor and Contributors

JEAN SHERIDAN is Associate Professor at the University of Rhode Island/ Kingston, and is Reference Bibliographer in the Social Sciences with responsibility for Business and Economics. She has published in the fields of adult education and bibliographic instruction.

BARBARA FISTER is Bibliographic Instruction Librarian at Gustavus Adolphus College. Her research interests lie in composition theory, Third World literature, and the sociology of knowledge, with a particular interest in research and the composing of knowledge.

CRAIG GIBSON is currently Head of Library User Education, Washington State University Libraries. His research interests include critical thinking and its role in bibliographic instruction, and search methodologies for the Internet.

THOMAS G. KIRK, JR. serves as College Librarian at Earlham College, Richmond, Indiana. He has contributed many essays and chapters of books in the field of bibliographic instruction, college librarianship, networking, and collection development, and he is the author of *Library Research Guide to Biology* (1978) and the editor of *Increasing the Teaching Role of Academic Libraries* (1989).

ROSS LaBAUGH is Coordinator of Library Information Services at the University of Massachusetts at Dartmouth. In addition to his work as a librarian, he teaches basic composition, technical writing, and library research courses.

MARILYN LUTZKER is Professor and Chief Librarian at John Jay College of Criminal Justice, City University of New York. Her previous publications include *Multiculturalism in the College Curriculum: A Handbook of Strategies and Resources for Faculty* (1995), *Research Projects for College Students: What to Write Across the Curriculum* (1988), and *Criminal Justice Research in Libraries* (with Eleanor Ferrall, 1986), all published by Greenwood Press. She has conducted seminars for numerous groups of librarians and teaching faculty about creative approaches to student research projects.

ELAINE P. MAIMON is Dean of Experimental Programs and Professor of English at Queens College/CUNY, where she also is responsible for making connections between the community and the curriculum. Her publications *Writing in the Arts and Sciences* (1981), *Readings in the Arts and Sciences* (1984), and *Thinking, Reasoning, and Writing* (1989) focus on the teaching of writing, reading, and thinking.

ISBN 0-313-29134-9

90000>

EAN

9 780313 291340

HARDCOVER BAR CODE